TEST YOUR CULTURAL LITERACY

Diane Zahler
Kathy A. Zahler

Prentice Hall
New York • London • Toronto • Sydney • Tokyo • Singapore

Poem on page 185 from MORE CRICKET SONGS Japanese haiku translated by Harry Behn. Copyright © 1971 by Harry Behn. All rights reserved. Reprinted by permission of Marian Reiner.

The Authors gratefully acknowledge the contributions made by Dr. E. D. Hirsch Jr. in popularizing the concept and the phrase *Cultural Literacy*. Neither Dr. Hirsch nor the Cultural Literacy Foundation, however, authorizes or endorses this publication.

Second Edition

 Prentice Hall General Reference
15 Columbus Circle
New York, NY 10023

An Arco Book

Arco, Prentice Hall, and colophons are
registered trademarks of Simon & Schuster, Inc.

Library of Congress Cataloging-in-Publication Data

Zahler, Diane.
    Test your cultural literacy / Diane Zahler, Kathy A. Zahler.
        p.   cm
    Includes bibliographical references (p. 307).
    ISBN 0-671-84716-3
        1. United States—Civilization—Examinations, questions, etc.
2. Culture—Examinations, questions, etc. I. Zahler, Kathy A. II. Title.
E169.1.Z33   1993   92-35387
973'.076—dc20   CIP

Manufactured in the United States of America

1 2 3 4 5 6 7 8 9 10

Contents

Acknowledgments / v

Introduction / vii

Scoring Key / xv

Test 1   Conceived in Liberty: American History / 1

Test 2   What's Past Is Prologue: World History / 19

Test 3   We the People: Civics / 39

Test 4   Spaceship Earth: Geography / 57

Test 5   Worth a Thousand Words: Art and Architecture / 73

Test 6   The Food of Love: Music / 105

Test 7   All's Right with the World: Myth and Religion / 123

Test 8   A Well-Turned Phrase: Quotes, Phrases, and Aphorisms / 141

Test 9   Of Thee I Sing: American Literature / 157

Test 10   Mightier Than the Sword: World Literature / 177

Test 11   The Birds and the Bees: Life Science / 199

Test 12   A Swiftly Tilting Planet: Physical Science / 219

Test 13   The Wave of the Future: Technology / 239

Test 14   The Queen of the Sciences and the Dismal Science: Mathematics and Economics / 257

Test 15   Here and Now: Current Events / 279

Bibliography / 307

Acknowledgments

Our thanks to PZ, YY, ML, PS, JG, JZ, and SAZ for their expertise, suggestions, and/or support; special thanks to PS and PZ, who answered every question, many of them correctly.

Introduction

There you are, sitting back in your favorite chair, scanning your favorite magazine, when you come across this paragraph:

> Here is a man who seemed to have the Midas touch, a man who had been welcomed after the years of the junta as a conquering hero, the new Fidel. Within one year of his coming to power, even his family acts as if a giant cockroach had been deposited in their midst. His refusal to take orders from either the Kremlin or Washington worries his followers. His speech in Brasilia before leaders of five nations invoked Emerson and Rousseau as well as Thomas Paine and Mao. As the internal disharmony builds to a crescendo, CIA operatives migrate toward the border and wait, anticipating the chain reaction that usually follows a speech like the one last Friday.

The author has made certain assumptions about you, the reader. Her words are not difficult to decode and understand, but to comprehend the deep structure of the paragraph you must have a passing knowledge of a dozen subject areas. The author assumes that you know what the *Midas touch* is and that she need not define *crescendo*, locate *Brasilia*, or identify *Fidel*. She trusts that her reference to a *cockroach* will not mystify you and that you will not link *Emerson* to Lake and Palmer or *Rousseau* to primitive paintings of fantastic creatures. On an even deeper level, she assumes that she can use *Kremlin* and *Washington* as parallel concepts and have you understand the parallelism, and she expects you to understand the ramifications of a *migration* of CIA operatives and the violence implied by her choice of the words *chain reaction*.

That is a lot to expect, but it is no more than is expected of every active reader every day. Reading is a complex connection between a writer and a reader, with everything the writer knows applied to the writing and everything the reader knows applied to the reading. They will never know exactly the same things, but the reader will always make assumptions about the writer's meaning, and the writer will always make assumptions about the reader's understanding. Where these assumptions intersect is an amorphous area of shared memories that forms the basis of cultural literacy.

What Is Cultural Literacy?

E. D. Hirsch defines cultural literacy as "the network of information that all competent readers possess."[1] Ira Shor defines it as "the ability to speak, write, read and make references within the elite idiom."[2] In fact, it is both. Literacy, the ability to read and write, was once the prerogative of the ruling class. In some ways it still is. The language of a nation's elite is the language that nation uses to instruct,

[1] E. D. Hirsch, *Cultural Literacy: What Every American Needs to Know* (Boston: Houghton Mifflin, 1987), p. 2.

[2] Ira Shor, *Culture Wars: School and Society in the Conservative Restoration 1969–1984* (Boston: Routledge & Kegan Paul, 1986), p. 190.

record, and inform. Historically, it has been in people's best interest to comprehend the language of their nation's power structure, even if it sometimes meant being biliterate. Schools, politicians, and mass media use a particular language and have particular expectations about the people they address. To be a "competent," successful reader or listener, you must understand that language and meet those expectations.

It has long been clear to reading researchers that competent reading depends on background knowledge as well as ability to decode print. Jeanne Chall's recent work delineates five levels of literacy, from initial reading and decoding through "a world view." Each stage entails a level of background or world knowledge. Beginning readers relate words on a page to known objects. The most advanced readers construct a personal philosophy by synthesizing information and accepting or rejecting points of view.[3]

The notion that a common background knowledge exists is the rationale behind the development of any school curriculum. Controversy has always surrounded the building of core curricula, since few people can agree on what that common knowledge should be. The 1980s have seen a backlash against decisions made in the 1960s to integrate new concepts into curricula at the expense of old ideas. The problem, of course, is that world knowledge is not stable; it expands at one end faster than it contracts at the other. We simply have more things to learn than our ancestors did. We must learn the alphabet and study the ancient Greeks as they did, but we must also become computer literate and read about Watergate. The War of 1812 does not drop out of our background knowledge to make way for Vietnam.

Because they have not found a way to accommodate new concepts, many educators today call for a return to the "basics," by which they mean any number of things. Mortimer Adler's *Paideia Proposal* of 1982 urged "the same course of study for all," a course of study that emphasized

---

[3] Jeanne S. Chall, *Stages of Reading Development* (New York: McGraw-Hill, 1983), pp. 15–25.

"the acquisition of organized knowledge" and rejected the notion of specialization.[4] More recently, in *The Closing of the American Mind*, Allan Bloom argued against departmentalization and called for a return to "a liberal education," based on the contentious idea that there exists a universal truth and that it can be approached through careful analysis of the classics.[5] Numerous studies, from the 1983 report of the National Commission on Excellence in Education, *A Nation at Risk*, to *What Do Our 17-Year-Olds Know?* by Diane Ravitch and Chester Finn, Jr., lament our children's failure to achieve background knowledge necessary for "competent" reading.[6]

The "elite idiom" changes very slowly. Eventually, it must expand to make room for new information, and such expansion inevitably results in controversy—"*Webster's Third* is too slangy"; "The reforms called for by the California State Board of Education are impossibly drastic"; "I refuse to listen to any politician who hints that the U.S. is no longer a world power"; and so on. Change does come, but until it does, it is in your best interest to learn the idiom at hand. It is the one used by government, school, church, and media; and as such, like it or not, it names much of your world.

The Tests

Just as few educators agree on what constitutes "the basics," no two people would come up with the same fifty items for any area we have chosen to test. Heated discussions and

[4] Mortimer Adler, *The Paideia Proposal: An Educational Manifesto* (New York: Macmillan, 1982), p. 24.

[5] Allan Bloom, *The Closing of the American Mind* (New York: Simon & Schuster, 1987), pp. 336–347.

[6] National Commission on Excellence in Education, *A Nation at Risk: The Imperative for Educational Reform*, April, 1983; and Diane Ravitch and Chester E. Finn, Jr., *What Do Our 17-Year-Olds Know? A Report on The First National Assessment of History and Literature* (New York: Harper & Row, 1987).

compromises marked our development of these items, and any choice we made is bound to be controversial. Because we have used existing textbooks and conventional sources to create our items, our tests are biased significantly toward Western history and culture. A case can certainly be made for the notion that Middle Eastern history is more relevant to an American today than is the Hundred Years' War. However, that involves a change in the idiom, and that is not our present enterprise. A case might also be made that television, film, and weekly magazines are more of a cultural link for people in the late twentieth century than are books or paintings. We have opted for a more conservative definition of cultural literacy.

This book contains fifteen tests of fifty questions each. The areas tested are American history; world history; civics; geography; art and architecture; music; myth and religion; quotes, phrases, and aphorisms; American literature; world literature; life science; physical science; technology; mathematics and economics; and current events.

The items are multiple-choice, and four possibilities are listed for each:

26. Washington Irving created which of the following characters?

   a. Diedrich Knickerbocker and Rip Van Winkle

   b. Meg, Beth, Amy, and Jo

   c. Little Eva and Topsy

   d. Billy Budd and Queequeg

In many cases, either you will know the answer or you won't. In other cases, the ability to eliminate choices through informed decision-making is as valuable as instant recall.

How Did You Do?

When you complete a test, use the Explanatory Answers that follow the test to check your responses. The answers should give enough information for you to determine *why* your response was correct or incorrect.

26. **(a)** Washington Irving (1783–1859) grew up as a wealthy member of New York society, which he satirized in *History of New York*, a burlesque that he claimed was by the historian Diedrich Knickerbocker. The word *knickerbocker* is now used to name any resident of New York State, particularly one descended from the early Dutch settlers. Rip Van Winkle is the hero of one tale in *Sketch Book of Geoffrey Crayon, Gent.*, usually considered to be the first collection of short stories in America. Rip falls asleep for twenty years. When he wakes, an old man, he finds his wife dead and the British colonies replaced by the United States. The other characters listed are from works by Louisa May Alcott, Harriet Beecher Stowe, and Herman Melville.

Use the Scoring Key that follows the introduction to grade yourself.

What Should You Do Now?

In theory, you should be equally informed in all areas tested, since all areas tested are part of your cultural legacy. It is far more likely, however, that your score will be high in some areas and low in others. Perhaps you are quite literate in the social sciences: American history, world history, civics, geography, and economics. You are strong, too, in literature: American literature; world literature; myth and religion; and quotes, phrases, and aphorisms. Your score drops in the arts: art and architecture and music. It falls even farther in the sciences: life science, physical science, and technology. Your friend, on the other hand, scores well in the sciences and terribly in literature. What does this mean?

It probably means that you have different life experiences. It almost certainly implies that you avoid certain kinds of reading, and your friend avoids other kinds. You avoid them either because you lack interest or because you lack the background knowledge necessary to read them with understanding. If the latter is the case, the cure is up to you. You can begin with our suggestions in the Bibliography. These suggestions are general works in the fields we have tested. They, in turn, will lead you to other works, and so on.

Perhaps you have scored magnificently on all fourteen tests. Is your education complete? Unfortunately for you, learning is not a quantum process, with facts in discrete bundles orbiting your brain. "To be literate is not to have arrived at some predetermined destination, but to utilize reading, writing, and speaking skills so that our understanding of the world is progressively enlarged."[7] If you read our explanatory answers carefully, you will find many places where facts overlap; where one concept explains or defines another, or where two concepts in tandem assist your understanding of a third. Knowing the facts is only the beginning. Being able to link them together, to discard one in favor of another, to synthesize them into a personal philosophy—that is the ultimate measure of literacy.

---

[7] Robert Mackie (ed.), *Literacy and Revolution: The Pedagogy of Paulo Freire* (New York: Continuum, 1981), p. 1; cited in Keith Walters, et al., "Formal and Functional Approaches to Literacy," *Language Arts,* Vol. 64, No. 8, December 1987, p. 865.

SCORING KEY

Give yourself two points for each correct answer.

90–100	*Excellent.* You are on your way to true cultural literacy.
80–89	*Good.* You have more than a passing knowledge of this subject.
70–79	*Fair.* You have a competent grasp of many aspects of this subject.
60–69	*Poor.* You could use some improvement in this area.
Below 60	*Time for literacy training.* See the bibliography in the back of this book.

Conceived in Liberty: American History

A people without history is like the wind on the buffalo grass.

—SIOUX SAYING

1. Which three states were among those that seceded from the Union to form the Confederacy?
   a. Kentucky, Mississippi, and West Virginia
   b. South Carolina, Florida, and Ohio
   c. Alabama, Tennessee, and Georgia
   d. Virginia, Maryland, and Delaware

2. What happened at Pearl Harbor on December 7, 1941?
   a. Japanese forces bombed a U.S. naval base.
   b. The Atlantic Charter was signed by Winston S. Churchill and Franklin D. Roosevelt.
   c. The first atomic bomb was completed.
   d. The U.S. fleet set sail to recapture the Philippines from the Japanese.

3. The precursor of the U.S. Constitution was
   a. the Declaration of Independence
   b. the Emancipation Proclamation
   c. the Mayflower Compact
   d. the Articles of Confederation

4. The Missouri Compromise determined that Missouri could become a state if

    a. slavery was prohibited throughout the rest of the Louisiana Purchase north of Missouri

    b. slavery was outlawed within the state

    c. the Indians of Missouri signed a peace treaty with the government

    d. the inhabitants renounced their alliance with France

5. The Open Door policy required that

    a. all nations must welcome immigrants from China

    b. no nation could claim exclusive trading rights in China

    c. reporters must be allowed to observe the effects of the Chinese Cultural Revolution

    d. the United States and the Soviet Union must conduct cultural exchanges

6. The Bay of Pigs episode took place when

    a. Cuban exiles from Florida landed in Cuba in an attempt to overthrow Fidel Castro

    b. U.S. troops invaded Mexico in pursuit of Pancho Villa

    c. UN forces undertook an amphibious landing behind enemy lines in Korea

    d. U.S. marines were sent by President Lyndon Johnson to the Dominican Republic

7. The first Thanksgiving was celebrated to give thanks for

    a. the rescue of Captain John Smith by Pocahontas

    b. the establishment of the colony at Jamestown

    c. the survival of the Plymouth Pilgrims through their first year

    d. the unification of the thirteen American colonies

8. U.S. forces fought in Europe in World War I during the years
  a. 1914–1918
  b. 1914–1921
  c. 1917–1918
  d. 1917–1921

9. The term "Seward's Folly" refers to
  a. the purchase of Alaska negotiated by Secretary of State William Seward
  b. the impeachment of Andrew Johnson urged by Secretary of State William Seward
  c. the cornering of gold by financier George Seward, which led to the stock market crash of 1869
  d. the Great Fire of Chicago, which started in Seward's Tavern

10. What happened on July 4, 1776?
  a. The first shots of the American Revolution were fired.
  b. The treaty ending the American Revolution was signed.
  c. The Continental Congress adopted the Declaration of Independence.
  d. The Continental Congress adopted the Constitution.

11. The Korean War was a conflict between
  a. North Korea, supported by the United States, and South Korea, supported by China
  b. South Korea, supported by the United States, and North Korea, supported by China and the Soviet Union
  c. Korea, supported by the United States, and China
  d. South Korea, supported by the United States, and North Korea, supported by the Chinese Nationalists

12. In the Dred Scott case, the Supreme Court ruled that
  a. an escaped slave could be forcibly returned to his master

    b. segregated facilities in public places were legal

    c. no slave could claim U.S. citizenship

    d. public schools must be desegregated

13. Why is the year 1492 important in American history?

    a. In 1492 Henry Hudson sailed up the Hudson River to New York.

    b. In 1492 the first English colony was established at Jamestown.

    c. In 1492 the Spanish settled St. Augustine, the first colony in America.

    d. In 1492 Christopher Columbus landed in the New World.

14. The "Great Awakening" of the 1740s concerned

    a. a rise in anti-British feeling among the American colonists

    b. a series of discoveries by colonial American scientists

    c. the beginnings of the Industrial Revolution in the American colonies

    d. a widespread religious revival among the American colonists

15. What was the final result of the political rivalry between Alexander Hamilton and Aaron Burr?

    a. a duel in which Alexander Hamilton was shot and killed

    b. an election in which Aaron Burr became vice president

    c. a duel in which both men were wounded

    d. a feud that forced Alexander Hamilton to flee to Canada

16. What was the initial purpose of the League of Nations?

    a. It was intended to reduce Germany's power after World War II.

    b. It was intended to found a Jewish homeland after World War II.

c. It was intended to combat the growing threat of Germany and Italy before World War I

d. It was intended to preserve peace after World War I.

17. The United States acquired California, Nevada, Utah, and parts of Texas, Arizona, Colorado, New Mexico, and Wyoming as a result of

a. the Gadsden Purchase of 1853

b. the Mexican War of the 1840s

c. the Land Grant Act of 1862

d. the Louisiana Purchase of 1803

18. What happened at My Lai, Vietnam, in 1968?

a. Communist troops attacked the town, resulting in the Tet offensive.

b. Peace talks began among the Viet Cong, the South Vietnamese, the North Vietnamese, and the Americans.

c. Ngo Dinh Diem, president of South Vietnam, was assassinated.

d. Lieutenant William Calley, Jr. led an attack that resulted in the massacre of twenty-two South Vietnamese.

19. For what is Senator Joseph McCarthy best known?

a. running unsuccessfully for President in 1972

b. playing a leading part in the settling of the Oregon Territory

c. leading investigations of numerous people suspected of being Communists in the 1950s

d. opposing American involvement in the Vietnam War in the 1960s

20. The French and Indian War was a conflict between

a. France and India over control of the spice trade

b. French Canadians and the Iroquois Nation

    c. England and France in the worldwide struggle for empire

    d. French settlers and their Carib slaves

21. Four presidents of the United States have been assassinated while in office. Who were they?

    a. Abraham Lincoln, William McKinley, James Garfield, and John F. Kennedy

    b. William McKinley, Andrew Johnson, John F. Kennedy, and Franklin Roosevelt

    c. Abraham Lincoln, John F. Kennedy, James Madison, and Millard Fillmore

    d. William Henry Harrison, Abraham Lincoln, Martin Van Buren, and James Buchanan

22. The "energy crisis" of the 1970s was primarily caused by

    a. the embargo of Arab oil shipments to the United States

    b. the failure of the Alaska pipeline

    c. the explosion of the Three Mile Island nuclear power plant

    d. the massive increase in the number of automobiles owned by Americans

23. What was the League of the Iroquois?

    a. an Indian congress formed to oppose the resettlement of Indians on reservations

    b. a group of Plains Indians who united to oppose white settlement

    c. a group of five eastern Indian tribes that shared a common language

    d. a community of pueblo-dwelling Indians who lived by farming

24. What was Custer's Last Stand?

    a. a steel mill strike at Homestead, Pennsylvania, in which eighteen people were killed

    b. the battle of Little Big Horn, in which 264 soldiers were killed

    c. the siege of the Alamo by Mexicans under Santa Ana

    d. the attack on Harper's Ferry by abolitionists

25. Theodore Roosevelt's "trustbusting" efforts were directed against

    a. political opponents who tried to destroy the public's trust in elected officials

    b. stock market speculators who made investments without security to back them up

    c. huge corporations that prevented competition in business

    d. political machines that controlled power in major American cities

26. One of the most famous residents of Jamestown, Virginia, was

    a. William Penn

    b. Pocahontas

    c. Lord Baltimore

    d. James I

27. In U.S. history, *Prohibition* meant

    a. the closing of U.S. borders to new immigrants

    b. the outlawing of slavery

    c. laws forbidding the manufacture and sale of alcoholic beverages

    d. state regulations against collective bargaining

28. The War of 1812 was primarily caused by

    a. Britain's interference with American commerce

    b. Napoleon's sale of the Louisiana Territory

    c. Jefferson's refusal to serve a third term

    d. the colonists' desire to be free of British rule

29. The New Deal was the name given to

    a. Theodore Roosevelt's foreign policy

    b. Harry S. Truman's domestic programs

    c. Franklin D. Roosevelt's social and economic reforms

    d. Lyndon B. Johnson's social programs

30. In his Emancipation Proclamation, Abraham Lincoln

    a. declared that the slaves in the Confederate States would henceforth be considered free

    b. announced the withdrawal of Union troops from the South

    c. dedicated a cemetery in Pennsylvania

    d. declared war on the Confederacy

31. An immigrant arriving at Ellis Island in 1900 was most likely to be from

    a. England or Ireland

    b. Scandinavia

    c. Latin America

    d. eastern Europe

32. Which of the following statements is *not* true of the Spanish-American War?

    a. The United States asked Spain to withdraw from Cuba.

    b. Theodore Roosevelt was involved in the fighting.

    c. Guam and Puerto Rico became U.S. territories.

    d. Germany aided the Nationalists.

33. The pony express was no longer needed after

    a. coast-to-coast telegraph lines were completed

    b. cattle rustling became a federal offense

    c. wagon trains began to head west

    d. Texas was admitted to the Union

34. The town of Salem, Massachussetts, is perhaps best known for

    a. Paul Revere's ride in 1775

    b. the St. Valentine's Day Massacre of 1929

    c. witchcraft trials in 1692

    d. the Triangle Shirtwaist Company fire of 1911

35. U.S. military involvement in Vietnam followed

    a. the defeat of the French and partition of the country in 1954

    b. the Tet Offensive in 1968

    c. the death of Ho Chi Minh in 1969

    d. the invasion of Cambodia by Vietnamese forces in 1978

36. Valley Forge was the site of an encampment by

    a. Union troops under Grant during the winter of 1863

    b. federal troops under Lee preceding the Harpers Ferry raid

    c. British forces under Cornwallis in 1783

    d. the Continental army under Washington in 1777–1778

37. The Monroe Doctrine and its "Roosevelt corollary" were used to

    a. lower tariffs and make trade with Europe easier

    b. provide incentives for farmers to switch to ranching

    c. support policies of European exclusion and American domination in the Western Hemisphere

    d. allow the United States to abandon isolationism and form alliances

38. An oil reserve called Teapot Dome gave its name to

    a. a scandal involving bribery during the Harding administration

    b. a corrupt group of New York City Democrats under Boss Tweed

    c. an energy commission set up by Jimmy Carter

    d. an act of rebellion by Boston colonists

39. The Watergate scandal began when

    a. Richard Nixon resigned the presidency under pressure from Congress

b. five men were arrested for breaking into an office

c. a U.S. pilot was caught running guns to Nicaragua

d. the House Un-American Activities Committee discovered Communist sympathizers in the Senate

40. Aided by an Indian woman named Sacajawea, Meriwether Lewis and William Clark

  a. led a party of explorers to the fountain of youth

  b. defeated Chief Sitting Bull at Little Bighorn

  c. charted a route from Missouri to the Pacific

  d. searched for the headwaters of the Hudson River

41. Carpetbaggers, scalawags, and the Ku Klux Klan were groups that flourished during the Reconstruction period

  a. between the World Wars

  b. after the Civil War

  c. in the post-Depression years

  d. following the American Revolution

42. During the Boston Tea Party,

  a. John Brown led an uprising in support of abolitionism

  b. thousands protested the execution of Sacco and Vanzetti

  c. colonists protested taxation by the British

  d. Minutemen celebrated their siege of Boston

43. Which of the following was *not* a result of the Homestead Act?

  a. The Middle West experienced a great increase in population.

  b. Steelworkers achieved the right to organize unions.

  c. U.S. agricultural production increased dramatically.

  d. People with little money were able to own land.

44. What important event took place in Seneca Falls, New York, in 1848?

    a. Women met to call for their rights as citizens.

    b. The Johnstown Flood killed over two thousand people.

    c. A revelation led Joseph Smith to create the Book of Mormon.

    d. The Erie Canal was completed.

45. Which country has the United States occupied militarily?

    a. Haiti

    b. Grenada

    c. Nicaragua

    d. all of the above

46. The gold rush of 1848

    a. justified the purchase of Alaska

    b. ensured the conversion of paper money to gold

    c. brought 100,000 settlers into a new territory

    d. made millionaires of Andrew Carnegie and John D. Rockefeller

47. Which of the following was *not* an episode in the civil rights movement of the 1950s and 1960s?

    a. the enactment of the Jim Crow laws

    b. the March on Washington

    c. the passage of the Voting Rights Act

    d. the "freedom rides"

48. Harriet Tubman is primarily known for

    a. founding the first college for black students

    b. spying for Confederate forces during the Civil War

    c. leading slaves north on the Underground Railroad

    d. her work with the suffragist movement

49. Through the Marshall Plan, the United States
   a. aided European economies after World War II
   b. supplied arms to developing nations in the 1970s
   c. allied with France and Great Britain in 1917
   d. developed plans for the League of Nations

50. The term *isolationism* describes
   a. American foreign policy during the 1970s and 1980s
   b. a military theory best paraphrased as "divide and conquer"
   c. an ideal economic balance between nations
   d. a policy of nonintervention in other countries' affairs

TEST 1: Explanatory Answers

1. (c) The states that seceded from the Union in 1860–1861 to form the Confederacy were Mississippi, Florida, Alabama, Georgia, Louisiana, Texas, Virginia, Arkansas, Tennessee, North Carolina, and South Carolina. Parts of Kentucky and Missouri also seceded; their representatives were seated in the Confederate Congress.

2. (a) On December 7, 1941, Japanese bombers attacked the American base at Pearl Harbor, Hawaii, sinking or damaging nineteen ships and killing twenty-three hundred soldiers and civilians. On December 8, the United States declared war on Japan.

3. (d) By the Articles of Confederation, adopted at the second Continental Congress in 1777, the states united in a "firm league of friendship." A one-house congress was created in which each state had one vote; however, no provision was made for a president or a federal court system.

4. (a) When Missouri sought to become a state in 1820, the Union was equally divided between slave states and free states. To maintain the balance, legislators worked out a compromise by which Missouri slave owners could keep their slaves but slavery was outlawed throughout the rest of the Louisiana Purchase north of Missouri.

5. (b) In 1899 the United States, concerned about being excluded by the European powers from trading with China, proposed the Open Door policy, under which all nations interested in trading with China would have equal trading rights. The policy was rarely honored by any of the nations involved.

6. (a) In 1961, U.S. President John F. Kennedy approved a plan prepared under the Eisenhower administration to land American-trained Cuban exiles in Cuba in an attempt to overthrow the government of Fidel Castro. The landing, at the Bay of Pigs, was a failure, and many of the invaders were killed or captured. Many Cuban exiles later blamed their loss on a lack of U.S. military air support.

7. (c) After their first year at Plymouth in 1620–1621, during which half of the colonists died, the Pilgrims celebrated in the fall with a feast from the crops the local Indians helped them grow.

8. (c) Although World War I began in Europe in 1914, the United States remained neutral until April 1917, when German submarine attacks at last led President Woodrow Wilson to seek a declaration of war. The fighting in Europe continued until November 11, 1918.

9. (a) In 1867 William Seward negotiated the purchase of Alaska from Russia for $7.2 million; this was called "Seward's Folly" because, until the discovery of gold and oil in Alaska, Americans could not see any use for the distant, frozen territory.

10. (c) The Declaration of Independence, which declared the American colonies' independence from Great Britain, was adopted on July 4, 1776, a date that is now a national holiday, the Fourth of July or Independence Day.

11. (b) After World War II, the Soviet Union occupied northern Korea, and the United States occupied southern Korea. Separate North Korean and South Korean states were established. In June 1950 the North Korean army invaded South Korea; UN and U.S. troops fought back. China later entered the war on the side of North Korea; the fighting continued until a cease-fire was reached in 1953.

12. (c) Dred Scott, a slave from Missouri, sued for his freedom in 1847 after having been taken to live in a free state. The case eventually went to the Supreme Court, which, in 1857, ruled that Scott and all other slaves were merely property and had no claim to the rights of citizenship. This decision encouraged Southern slaveholders. However, it infuriated many Northerners, who believed that slaves were not property but "persons held to service by state laws." These Northerners contended that, in the case of slaves, the government's duty was not to defend property but to protect liberty.

13. **(d)** In October 1492, three small ships commanded by Christopher Columbus reached the Bahamas, making Europe's first documented contact with the Americas.

14. **(d)** The "Great Awakening" of the 1740s was a widespread Protestant religious revival that swept throughout the British American colonies. The best-known figure in this movement was the great New England preacher Jonathan Edwards.

15. **(a)** In 1804 Alexander Hamilton, a liberal who advocated a strong federal government, and Aaron Burr, who believed in states' rights, fought a duel in Weehawken, New Jersey, that ended in Hamilton's death. The duel took place because Burr blamed his loss of an election campaign on Hamilton's criticism of his character.

16. **(d)** President Woodrow Wilson proposed the creation of the League of Nations to preserve the hard-won post-World War I peace. Ironically, however, the United States never became a member because the U.S. Senate refused to ratify the Versailles Peace Treaty, which established the League.

17. **(b)** In 1845 the United States annexed most of what is now Texas; disputes over the remainder soon led to war, and in 1848 Mexico ceded claim to much of what is now the American West and Southwest.

18. **(d)** In March 1968 Lieutenant Calley led an attack on the village of My Lai that led to the murder of twenty-two Vietnamese civilians. Calley was convicted of premeditated murder in 1971 and sentenced to life in prison, a sentence that was later reduced to twenty years. The incident galvanized antiwar sentiment in the United States.

19. **(c)** During the mid-1950s, Senator Joseph R. McCarthy, a Wisconsin Republican, leveled charges of Communist sympathy or conspiracy against numerous officials, writers, journalists, teachers, and others. In 1953–1954 he headed the House Committee on Un-American Activities, which investigated many suspected Communists. McCarthy's accusations

were frequently unsubstantiated, but many Americans lost their jobs or went to jail as a result of "McCarthyism."

20. **(c)** The French and Indian War (1754–1763) was a North American extension of a conflict that was then taking place in Europe between France and England, a conflict called the Seven Years' War. The French allied with local Indians and sought control of the Ohio Valley. However, the British were eventually victorious, and France lost its territory both in the Ohio Valley and in Canada.

21. **(a)** On April 14, 1865, Abraham Lincoln was shot in Washington, D.C.; he died on April 15. On July 2, 1881, James A. Garfield was shot in Washington, D.C.; he died on September 12. On September 6, 1901, William McKinley was shot in Buffalo, New York; he died on September 14. On November 22, 1963, John F. Kennedy was shot and killed in Dallas, Texas.

22. **(a)** After the Arab-Israeli War of 1973, Arab nations refused for a time to ship oil to the United States, which had supported Israel. This embargo sparked a shortage that raised prices sharply and caused an economic recession.

23. **(c)** The League of the Iroquois, which lasted for hundreds of years, included the Cayugas, the Mohawks, the Oneidas, the Onondagas, and the Senecas and was established to bring an end to destructive warfare among these tribes of the eastern seaboard.

24. **(b)** In June 1876 General George Custer and his Seventh Cavalry were killed to the last man in this Dakota Territory battle against the Sioux Indians.

25. **(c)** The formation of the U.S. Steel Corporation and of the Northern Securities Company in 1901 alerted President Roosevelt to the fact that through great monopolies, or "trusts," control of the nation's economy was passing into the hands of just a few individuals. Roosevelt's efforts against trusts later led to the Clayton Antitrust Act of 1914.

26. **(b)** Jamestown, founded in Virginia in 1607, was the first British settlement in the New World. The daughter of the Indian chief Powhatan, Pocahontas married colonist John Rolfe after supposedly saving Captain John Smith from death at the hands of her tribe. The marriage briefly helped stabilize relations between the Indians and colonists.

27. (c) Temperance movements gained strength in the early 1900s, culminating after World War I in the Eighteenth Amendment and the Volstead Act. The Amendment stated that "the manufacture, sale, or transportation of intoxicating liquors . . . is hereby prohibited." In 1933 the Twenty-first Amendment repealed Prohibition.

28. (a) The United States asked for neutral shipping rights during hostilities between France and Great Britain, but the British confiscated U.S. ships and generally interfered with trade. In 1812 Congress declared war on Great Britain. The war was unpopular and costly for both sides. A peace treaty was signed in December 1814, but the real end of the war came with Andrew Jackson's defeat of British troops at the Battle of New Orleans in January 1815.

29. (c) The "New Deal" was designed in the early 1930s by the Roosevelt administration to enable the United States to recover from the Great Depression. It consisted of regulatory policies, emergency organizations, public work projects, and social and economic legislation.

30. (a) The Emancipation Proclamation in fact freed no one; it proclaimed the freeing of slaves in areas no longer loyal to the Union. Nevertheless, it guided the actions of the Union army, which liberated the slaves in each new territory that came under its control.

31. (d) Whereas the majority of earlier immigrants had arrived from northern and western Europe, ports of entry now saw a dramatic increase in peoples from eastern Europe, southern Europe, and Asia. These immigrants were considered undesirable by nativist groups, and lobbying by these groups led to strict quotas on immigrants in the 1920s.

32. (d) Nazi Germany aided the Nationalists in the Spanish Civil War (1936–1939), a war that involved volunteers from many countries. The Spanish-American War (1898) pitted the United States against Spain over Spain's harsh treatment of Cuban rebels. The sinking of the U.S.S. *Maine* in the harbor of Havana set the stage for war. Theodore Roosevelt and his Rough Riders fought a major battle on San Juan Hill in Cuba in July. Eventual U.S. victory led to U.S. control of Cuba, Puerto Rico, Guam, and the Philippines.

33. (a) A horse-and-rider system of mail delivery sped mail from Missouri to the West Coast in a little over a week. After transcontinental telegraph service began in 1861, the pony express was phased out.

34. (c) In 1692 three girls in Salem claimed to be possessed by Satan. Their accusations of neighbors led to the execution of nineteen people for witchcraft.

35. (a) After French colonial forces in Indochina were defeated by Nationalists and Communists, France withdrew and the country was divided into South Vietnam and Communist-led North Vietnam. President Eisenhower sent American advisers to train the South Vietnamese army, thus initiating twenty years of American involvement in the region.

36. (d) Following a disastrous campaign in Philadelphia and Germantown, George Washington's troops wintered at Valley Forge, Pennsylvania, in 1777–1778.

37. (c) Under the Monroe Doctrine (1823), the United States regarded any European intervention or attempt at colonization of the Americas as an act of aggression. In 1904, President Theodore Roosevelt proclaimed a "corollary" asserting the right of the United States to act as an "international police power" in the Americas and to intervene militarily anywhere in the region whenever circumstances required it.

38. (a) The assignment of oil field leases to the highest briber by Secretary of the Interior Albert Fall led to one of the greatest scandals in American politics. Fall was convicted in 1929.

39. (b) On June 17, 1972, five men were found breaking into Democratic party headquarters in the Watergate apartment complex in Washington, D.C. Accusations of involvement of high officials in the Nixon administration led to Nixon's resignation in 1974.

40. (c) Meriwether Lewis and William Clark were commissioned by the U.S. government to map the lands between St. Louis and the Pacific. Their trip took two years (1804–1806). Sacajawea, a Shoshone, served as a guide and interpreter for much of the journey.

41. (b) After the end of the Civil War, economic and political power in the war-ravaged Southern states was wielded by Northern businessmen (carpetbaggers) who sought financial gain amid the ruined economy, and Southern white Republicans (scalawags), who supported the federal government. Other Southern whites organized the Ku Klux Klan, a racist terrorist group that aimed to prevent Southern blacks from voting.

42. **(c)** The Boston Tea Party of 1773 was a protest by colonists against Britain's high tax on tea. Protestors stole aboard British ships in Boston harbor, seized their cargoes of tea, and threw the tea overboard. The British government's retaliatory measures led to the convening of the First Continental Congress.

43. **(b)** The Homestead Act of 1862 granted 160 acres of land to any settler who would spend five years on the land. To take advantage of this offer, great numbers of people—many of them propertyless immigrants—moved into the Middle West in the 1860s and 1870s. The new farms they established resulted in a huge increase in agricultural production.

44. **(a)** The Seneca Falls Convention was organized by the great women's rights advocate Elizabeth Cady Stanton. The convention produced a declaration of women's rights drafted by Stanton, Lucretia Mott, and other suffragists.

45. **(d)** Haiti was occupied from 1915 to 1934 by U.S. Marines. U.S. troops invaded Grenada in 1983. Nicaragua was occupied by U.S. forces from 1855 to 1857, and the United States maintained a military presence there from 1912 to 1933, with increased forces added in 1926.

46. **(c)** The newly formed territory of California was invaded by thousands of prospectors after gold was discovered at Sutter's Mill in 1848. Although few found gold, the new population was enough to force the issue of statehood for the new territory.

47. **(a)** The Jim Crow laws were passed by Southern states during the Reconstruction era. They were designed to segregate blacks from whites in public facilities. Civil rights activists worked to eliminate these laws in the 1950s and 1960s.

48. **(c)** Harriet Tubman, herself an escaped slave, led more than three hundred slaves to freedom on the Underground Railroad before working as a spy for Union forces during the Civil War.

49. **(a)** The Marshall Plan, also known as the European Recovery Program, was a program supported by Secretary of State George Marshall and designed to promote the economic recovery of Europe following World War II. More than $12 billion in economic aid was distributed between 1948 and 1952.

50. **(d)** Isolationism was the keystone of U.S. foreign policy in much of the nineteenth century and during the years immediately following World War I.

TEST 2

What's Past Is Prologue: World History

History is the witness that testifies to the passing of time; it illumines reality, vitalizes memory, provides guidance in daily life, and brings us tidings of antiquity.

—*MARCUS TULLIUS CICERO*

1. Simón Bolívar was a hero of the
   a. American Revolution
   b. Spanish civil war
   c. South American wars of independence
   d. era of exploration during the Spanish Golden Age

2. The major result of the Peloponnesian Wars was
   a. Athens' loss of supremacy
   b. Julius Caesar's fall from power
   c. the rise of Islam in the Middle East and North Africa
   d. the establishment of the Ottoman Empire

3. Which of the following was *not* a result of South Africa's policy of apartheid?
   a. South Africa left the British Commonwealth.

   b. Black Africans in South Africa were forbidden to own businesses.

   c. Black Africans in South Africa were resettled in "homelands."

   d. Asians and black Africans in South Africa were forced to live in separate areas.

4. The revolutions of 1848 took place in

   a. France, Germany, Austria, and Italy

   b. England and Ireland

   c. Venezuela, Brazil, and Ecuador

   d. Lithuania and Latvia

5. The World War II coalition known as the Axis consisted of

   a. the United States, Great Britain, and France

   b. the Soviet Union and Germany

   c. the neutral nations

   d. Germany, Italy, and Japan

6. Niccolò Machiavelli is best known for

   a. his writings on the uses of political power

   b. economic theories that led to the decline of federalism

   c. fighting alongside Garibaldi in the wars for Italian unification

   d. founding the Italian Communist party

7. An important event during the reign of Henry VIII was

   a. the English civil war

   b. the signing of Magna Carta

   c. the Wars of the Roses

   d. the creation of the Church of England

8. Which of the following was *not* a result of the Russian Revolution of 1917?

   a. The Bolsheviks came to power under Lenin.

   b. Czar Nicholas and his family were executed.

   c. Karl Marx became head of the First International.

   d. Russia signed a peace treaty with Germany and withdrew from World War I.

9. The term *Third World* is applied to

   a. any area found after the discovery of the New World

   b. a cartel of Commonwealth nations and NATO nations

   c. any country in Africa or South America

   d. nations that are economically underdeveloped

10. Mohandas (Mahatma) Gandhi is famous for

   a. resisting British rule in India

   b. leading India at the turn of the century

   c. supervising the creation of Pakistan

   d. instructing American civil rights activists in "passive resistance"

11. Charlemagne ruled a large part of western and central Europe in the years

   a. 30 B.C.–20 A.D.

   b. 800–814

   c. 1050–1070

   d. 1400–1410

12. In 1949 Mao Zedong

   a. became chairman of the People's Republic of China

   b. led the Chinese Cultural Revolution

   c. overthrew the Ch'ing dynasty

   d. fled to Taiwan to establish a nationalist republic

13. The countries most involved in world exploration during the fifteenth, sixteenth, and seventeenth centuries were

   a. Belgium, France, Austria, and Germany

   b. Spain, France, England, Portugal, and the Netherlands

   c. England, Scotland, Norway, Denmark, and Spain

   d. Germany, France, Spain, and Italy

14. The Soviet Union under Joseph Stalin witnessed all of the following *except*

   a. collectivization of farms and increased industrialization

   b. the siege of Leningrad during World War II

   c. political repression and executions

   d. the Hungarian revolt and the invasion of Czechoslovakia

15. The year 1066 is the date of

   a. the invasion of England by the Norman king William

   b. the beginning of the English Reformation

   c. the Children's Crusade

   d. Caesar's triumph in the Gallic Wars

16. The term *chivalry* refers to

   a. a code of laws developed by Hammurabi

   b. a blend of Christian and military ideals

   c. a technique of mounted warfare

   d. the Eastern influence on Western thought

17. The first Opium War was a conflict between

   a. samurai warriors and the emperor of Japan

   b. China and Japan over control of poppy fields in Korea

   c. Great Britain and China over trade and the import of opium

   d. Russia and Great Britain over control of Afghanistan

18. The French term *détente* was used to describe

   a. efforts to relax tension between the Soviet Union and the United States

   b. the first of several nuclear test-ban treaties

   c. the crisis that followed the French student and worker strikes of 1968

   d. an informal alliance between France and Britain in the years before World War I

19. NATO was formed

    a. in 1919 to maintain security in Europe against revived German military power

    b. in 1948 to promote cooperation between Latin America and the United States

    c. in 1949 by the United States and Western Europe to counter the Soviet threat

    d. in 1960 to overthrow the South Vietnamese government

20. What was the Reign of Terror?

    a. the imprisonment and execution of opponents of the French Revolution

    b. the elimination of the political opposition under Stalin

    c. the expulsion of Jews from Spain

    d. the rise of the Medicis to power in Florence

21. The Victorian Age, the height of the British Empire, covered the years

    a. 1640–1688

    b. 1790–1820

    c. 1837–1901

    d. 1930–1948

22. The Hundred Years' War between France and England led to all of the following *except*

    a. the decimation of the French nobility

    b. the consolidation of the power of the French king

    c. the expulsion of England from all but a tiny area of continental Europe

    d. the end of the monarchy in England

23. Who was Benito Mussolini?

    a. an Italian dictator and head of the Fascist Party

    b. the leader of the Italian Communist Party in the 1930s

    c. the leader of the first government of Italy following World War II

    d. a leading figure in the art world of Renaissance Venice

24. Oliver Cromwell was responsible for

    a. acting as chief counselor to Henry VIII

    b. defeating the English monarchy and establishing a republican regime

    c. establishing the Bank of England

    d. all of the above

25. What were the Crusades?

    a. exploratory expeditions by Europeans through Africa and the Far East

    b. campaigns by government forces against Protestants in Germany and France

    c. attempts by Europeans to wrest the Holy Land from the Muslims

    d. trials and executions of so-called infidels in Spain

26. The European powers fought each other in World War I during the years

    a. 1914–1918

    b. 1917–1918

    c. 1917–1921

    d. 1914–1921

27. Who was Genghis Khan?

    a. the leader of the Huns who terrified Europe in the 300s

    b. the leader of the Visigoths who sacked Rome in 410

    c. the leader of the Mongols who conquered Persia and much of China in the 1200s

    d. the leader of the Chinese who led the Long March in the 1930s

28. The Boer War was a conflict between
   a. blacks and Dutch settlers in southern Africa
   b. Belgians and the indigenous peoples of the Belgian Congo
   c. the British government in India and the Indians
   d. Dutch-settler republics in southern Africa and the British

29. The empire of Alexander the Great included
   a. Russia, Italy, Greece, and Palestine
   b. Asia Minor, Syria, Egypt, and Greece
   c. Britain, Gaul, Iberia, and Asia Minor
   d. Arabia, Egypt, Gaul, and Asia Minor

30. The area that became Israel in 1948 had formerly been known as
   a. Palestine
   b. Jordan
   c. Syria
   d. Arabia

31. The guilds of the Middle Ages were
   a. fairs held in large towns to increase trade
   b. military expeditions to the Middle East to reclaim Jerusalem for Christendom
   c. organizations of merchants and skilled workers
   d. workers bound to the land and their lord

32. The French Revolution was *not* a result of
   a. inequality among the classes of society
   b. rising taxes and prices of food and clothing
   c. the influx of immigrants from eastern Europe
   d. the weak monarchies of Louis XV and Louis XVI

33. The Thirty Years' War broke out because of
   a. religious differences between Protestants and Catholics in seventeenth-century central Europe

   b. clashes between Yorkists and Lancastrians in fifteenth-century England

   c. the death of Czar Peter the Great in the eighteenth century

   d. the feud between Pope Boniface VIII and Philip IV of Spain in the thirteenth century

34. In a historical context the term *Holocaust* refers to

   a. the pogroms that took place in Russia under the nineteenth-century czars

   b. the Great Fire of 1871 that destroyed much of Chicago

   c. the explosions of the atomic bombs of Hiroshima and Nagasaki

   d. the systematic murder of 6 million Jews by the Nazis

35. The Vikings were

   a. traders from Denmark

   b. explorers from Britain

   c. troubadours from Gaul

   d. warriors from Scandinavia

36. Napoleon Bonaparte is *not* known for

   a. codifying French law

   b. freeing the serfs

   c. becoming emperor of France

   d. losing a vital battle at Waterloo

37. The Spanish Armada was defeated by the

   a. Americans under Theodore Roosevelt

   b. Germans under Adolf Hitler

   c. English under Elizabeth I

   d. French under Napoleon

38. The Humanists of Renaissance Europe believed that

   a. religion was a useless and dangerous thing

   b. human beings were in danger of damnation unless they became more spiritual

   c. a classical education led to individual achievement and the ability to lead a moral life

   d. the teachings of Martin Luther were the answer to a corrupt church

39. Which of these did *not* contribute to the Cold War?

   a. the division of Germany into two separate states

   b. the German-Soviet Nonagression Pact

   c. the Soviet Union's development of the atomic bomb

   d. the suppression of the revolt in Hungary

40. Who was Joan of Arc?

   a. a French peasant who was burned at the stake for witchcraft

   b. the mistress of King Louis XIV

   c. the mother of King Richard Lionheart and King John

   d. the queen of France responsible for the St. Bartholemew's Day massacre

41. The Berlin Wall was built to

   a. keep the Mongol invaders out of Germany

   b. halt the advance of Russian troops

   c. protect Berlin against the peasant uprisings in Germany

   d. stop the flow of refugees from East Germany to the West

42. What was the Weimar Republic?

   a. the wartime German government under Adolf Hitler

   b. the post-World War I German government

   c. the Austrian government after the fall of the Hapsburgs

   d. the government established in East Germany after World War II

43. The Holy Roman Empire existed from

    a. 31 B.C. to the 400s

    b. 800 to the early 1800s

    c. 527 A.D. to 1453

    d. 1 A.D. to the 1500s

44. What did Adolf Hitler and British Prime Minister Neville Chamberlain agree on at Munich in 1938?

    a. to permit Germany to occupy parts of Czechoslovakia

    b. to release Germany from its responsibility to pay reparations for World War I

    c. to permit Germany to annex Austria

    d. to form a German-British alliance against the Soviet Union

45. For which of the following is Julius Caesar *not* known?

    a. invading Britain

    b. being assassinated while attending a session of the Roman Senate

    c. persecuting Christians

    d. establishing the 365-day calendar

46. The Industrial Revolution is generally considered to have begun

    a. in the United States at the start of the nineteenth century

    b. in Germany in the middle of the nineteenth century

    c. in France following the French Revolution

    d. in Great Britain at the end of the eighteenth century

47. Which of the following was *not* a feature of the Byzantine Empire?

    a. the widespread use of mosaics in art

    b. intense devotion to the Eastern Orthodox church

    c. the worship of Buddha in Zen monasteries

    d. codification of the laws in Justinian's Code

48. The Sino-Japanese War was fought
 a. between Japan and England over control of the opium trade
 b. between Japan and China over control of Korea
 c. between Japan and the United States over control of the Philippines
 d. between Japan and Siam over control of trade in the South China Sea

49. Why was the Magna Carta written?
 a. to bring an end to the Hundred Years' War
 b. to declare America's independence from Great Britain
 c. to limit the power of King John of England
 d. to prevent Julius Caesar from becoming emperor

50. The Easter Rebellion of 1916 took place
 a. in St. Petersburg, Russia, in an attempt to overthrow the czar
 b. in Dublin, in an effort to gain independence from Great Britain for Ireland
 c. in Berlin, in protest against the rising toll of World War I
 d. in Beijing, in an attempt by Chinese republicans to overthrow the child emperor Pu-Yi

TEST 2: Explanatory Answers

1. (c) Simón Bolívar made his name during the Venezuelan revolution of 1810. For the next fifteen years he helped lead resistance to Spanish rule in Ecuador, Peru, and Upper Peru (later renamed Bolivia). In 1819 he became president of a country that is now divided into Colombia, Ecuador, and Venezuela.

2. (a) Athens fought the Peloponnesian League, a band of city-states loyal to Sparta, from 460 to 445 B.C. and again from 431 to 404 B.C. The Spartans then dominated Greece until the onset of Theban rule in 370 B.C.

3. **(b)** Apartheid aimed at the complete separation of all racial groups in South Africa: whites, blacks, and people of Indian descent. To this end, many black Africans were resettled in "homelands"—often areas of little economic value—and forced to travel long distances to jobs in predominantly white areas. Black Africans were not, however, forbidden to own businesses. See Test 15, question 9, for up-to-date information on the breakdown of apartheid in South Africa.

4. **(a)** The February Revolution in France overthrew King Louis Philippe and marked the beginning of a period of nationalistic uprisings throughout Europe. Hapsburg Austria was faced with revolutions in Hungary, Bohemia, and Italy.

5. **(d)** In 1936 Germany signed treaties with Italy and with Japan. These led to the Berlin Pact of 1940. Opposition to and defeat of the Axis powers came from the Allies, led by Great Britain, the United States, France, the Soviet Union, and China.

6. **(a)** Machiavelli (1496–1527) probably based his most famous work, *The Prince*, on the exploits of Cesare Borgia, the cruel and opportunistic son of Pope Alexander I.

7. **(d)** In his desire to divorce Catherine of Aragon and marry Anne Boleyn, Henry VIII defied the authority of the Roman Catholic Church. His resulting excommunication led him to create a separate Church of England, of which, by the Act of Supremacy in 1534, he became the head.

8. **(c)** The writings of the German political economist Karl Marx (1818–1883) profoundly influenced Lenin's Communist movement in the Soviet Union. Besides writing the *Communist Manifesto* and *Das Kapital*, Marx headed the First International, a Socialist labor federation founded in London in 1864.

9. **(d)** The term *Third World* was coined to label economically underdeveloped nations in Asia, Africa, and Latin America, usually nations that desired to remain unaligned either to the First World (capitalist) nations or to the Second World (socialist) nations. *Fourth World* is a recent appellation given to countries with an annual per capita income under $300.

10. **(a)** Gandhi (1869–1948) led the movement against British rule in India, using a systematic program of nonviolent protest and refusal to support British policies. His techniques of passive resistance were later utilized by civil rights protestors in the United States and in other countries. In 1947 India

was granted independence and divided into West and East
Pakistan and India. Gandhi was assassinated in 1948 by a
Hindu fanatic who opposed his desire to reconcile Hindus and
Muslims.

11. **(b)** Charlemagne, king of the Franks, conquered vast portions
    of western and central Europe in the years 773–798. In 800
    at Rome he was crowned emperor of the western Roman
    Empire by Pope Leo III.

12. **(a)** As chairman of the Chinese Communist party and leader
    of the struggle against the Nationalist Kuomintang, Mao led
    his Red Army on the Long March in 1934–1935 and established
    Communist control in the northwestern provinces. Not until
    after World War II did the Communists gain control of the
    Chinese government, forcing Chiang Kai-shek and the Na-
    tionalists to flee to Taiwan.

13. **(b)** Spain, France, England, Portugal, and the Netherlands all
    established vast colonial empires during the Age of Explora-
    tion. Motivated by desire for wealth and power, the govern-
    ments of these countries sponsored colonialization in Asia,
    the Americas, and Africa.

14. **(d)** Joseph Stalin led the Soviet Union from the death of Lenin
    in 1924 until his own death in 1953. His five-year plans called
    for stepped-up industrial production and collectivized agri-
    culture. Stalin's paranoia about opposition led to a series of
    purge trials and executions. Both the Hungarian revolt (1956)
    and the invasion of Czechoslovakia (1968) took place after his
    death.

15. **(a)** The Norman Conquest of England, led by William the
    Conqueror, resulted in the end of Anglo-Saxon rule.

16. **(b)** Chivalry flourished during the time of the Crusades. The
    key ideals of a chivalrous knight were love of God, loyalty to
    his lord, courtesy, courage, and chastity.

17. **(c)** China was primarily isolationist, but it opened Canton to
    limited trade in 1834. After China declared the import of
    opium illegal and destroyed British-owned opium in Canton,
    Great Britain used the incident to attack China, winning trade
    concessions and sovereignty over Hong Kong with the war's
    termination in 1842.

18. **(a)** *Détente* (literally "relaxation") was a term used in the
    1960s and 1970s to describe attempts to lessen the tensions

of the Cold War. Strategic Arms Limitation Talks (SALT) were part of this effort.

19. **(c)** The North Atlantic Treaty Organization is an alliance formed to defend against possible aggression by the Soviet Union and its allies. The original members included the United States, Canada, France, Great Britain, Iceland, Italy, Denmark, Norway, Portugal, Belgium, Luxembourg, and the Netherlands. Greece, Turkey, and West Germany joined later.

20. **(a)** In 1793 a dictatorship was established in France under the auspices of the Committee of Public Safety, led by Maximilien Robespierre. The government was centralized, the military was strengthened, and thousands of suspected counter-revolutionaries were executed. The overthrow of Robespierre in 1794 ended the Terror.

21. **(c)** Victoria reigned through most of the nineteenth century, a period that saw British industrial supremacy and the extension of British rule to one-quarter of the world's land area.

22. **(d)** The war, which lasted from 1337 to 1453, devastated the population of France as it destroyed British power on the Continent. War, famine, and the plague decimated the nobility in France, creating an opportunity for the consolidation of royal power.

23. **(a)** Mussolini (1883–1945) founded the National Fascist party in Italy in 1921. In 1922 he was asked to form a government by King Victor Emmanuel III. By 1928 he had established himself as dictator. In the 1930s he sent Italian troops to invade Ethiopia and Albania; during World War II he was an ally of Hitler.

24. **(b)** Cromwell, a Puritan, led the armies of Parliament against Charles I during the English Civil War (1642–1648). After the defeat and execution of the King, a republican regime was established, and in 1653 Cromwell was made Lord Protector. After Cromwell's death in 1658, the monarchy was restored.

25. **(c)** A particularly brutal series of military campaigns, the Crusades were holy wars that pitted European Christians against Muslims between the years 1096 and 1291. Besides draining the treasuries of European countries, the Crusades saw areas of the Middle East change hands numerous times between Crusaders and Muslim Turks and Egyptians.

26. **(a)** Following the assassination of Austrian archduke Franz Ferdinand at Sarajevo in 1914, Europe was plunged into a

four-year war that pitted Germany, Austria, Hungary, Bulgaria, and the Ottoman Empire against Great Britain, France, Russia, and, eventually, twenty nine other countries. The war in Europe ended officially on Armistice Day, November 11, 1918.

27. **(c)** Led by Genghis Khan, the Mongol army, known for its fierceness and love of warfare, fought on horseback with bows and arrows. The Mongols captured Beijing, most of Persia, and Russian Turkestan in the 1200s.

28. **(d)** When gold was discovered in southern Africa in the 1880s, Britain tried to annex the Dutch (Boer) republic of the Transvaal. In 1899 war broke out between Britain and the Transvaal and another Boer republic, the Orange Free State. By 1902 both republics were subjugated; they later became part of the British-ruled Union of South Africa (today's Republic of South Africa).

29. **(b)** In 336 B.C., Alexander, educated by Aristotle, became ruler of Greece and Macedonia. He conquered Asia Minor, then moved on to the Middle East and Africa. When he died in 323 B.C. at the age of thirty-three, he had conquered most of the Mediterranean region.

30. **(a)** In 1947 the United Nations voted to divide Palestine into separate Jewish and Arab states. Displaced Palestinians won Arab support, and Israel was attacked by several Arab nations in 1948. Although outnumbered, the Israelis won the war; the Arab section of Palestine was then absorbed by Jordan. Palestinians, still without a homeland, continue to protest—sometimes violently—the loss of their country.

31. **(c)** Guilds began as associations of merchants established for the purpose of regulating the rules of commerce. Eventually, skilled craftsmen also formed guilds, which regulated working hours, fixed wages, and looked after the ill and families of deceased members.

32. **(c)** Economic conditions in France for the artisanal and peasant classes grew steadily worse under Louis XV and Louis XVI. Meanwhile, the noble classes increased their power at the expense of the weak monarchy, frustrating the aspirations of a rising merchant class. Finally in 1789 the monarchy found itself bankrupt and was obliged to call a gathering of notables, the States General, to remedy the situation. When this group met, the representatives of the merchant class, called the Third Estate, reconstituted themselves as a National

Assembly and set about drafting a constitution. Meanwhile in Paris, a crowd of shopkeepers and laborers stormed the Bastille Prison, inaugurating a full-scale revolution.

33. **(a)** The Thirty Years' War began in 1620 as a Protestant revolt against the Holy Roman Emperor. Protestants of Germany, Denmark, and Sweden entered the war, and later France, though mostly Catholic, came in on the side of the Protestants. The war ended in 1648 with the Peace of Westphalia, which changed boundaries throughout central Europe and opened the way for the rise of Prussia.

34. **(d)** Adolf Hitler's master plan required the elimination of "racially inferior" peoples, focusing on Jews but including Slavs, gypsies, and others. The Nazis' "Final Solution" was the annihilation of all Jews in Europe. By the end of World War II, at least 6 million Jews had died, most in Nazi concentration camps.

35. **(d)** The Vikings, or Norsemen, were Scandinavians known for their fearlessness and brutality in warfare. They were seafarers, and in the ninth and tenth centuries they terrorized the coasts of Britain, Russia, and France.

36. **(b)** In 1799 Napoleon assumed supreme power in the French government. As head of state his most important work was the revision and codification of French law called the Napoleonic Code. After proclaiming himself emperor in 1804, he began wars with Austria, Great Britain, Russia, and Prussia. In 1814 he was defeated and forced to abdicate, but in 1815 he returned from exile for a last campaign that ended in a final defeat by the British and Prussians at Waterloo.

37. **(c)** The "sea dogs" of England—captains such as Francis Drake and Walter Raleigh—challenged the Spanish monopoly of trade with the Americas. Angered by this and by the execution of the Catholic Mary Queen of Scots by the English Protestants under Elizabeth I, Philip of Spain sent his Armada in 1588 to conquer England. The English fleet, smaller but swifter than the Spanish, was victorious.

38. **(c)** The Humanist movement began in Italy in the 1300s, when scholars rediscovered the study of the humanities through Greek and Roman texts. The movement developed into a philosophy that placed great emphasis on education and practical action and stressed the idea that life on earth as well as the afterlife could be joyous. This belief contributed to

antagonism between the Roman Catholic Church and the Humanists, the most famous of whom was Petrarch.

39. (b) After World War II, Soviet-style governments were set up in the countries occupied by Soviet troops, including the eastern portion of Germany. Increasing antagonism between this Soviet bloc and the West soon led to the formation of opposing military alliances: the Warsaw Pact in the East and NATO in the West. Tensions mounted further when the Soviet Union exploded its own atomic bomb—breaking NATO's monopoly on atomic weapons—and when it forcibly suppressed a revolt in Hungary in 1956. (The German-Soviet Nonaggression Pact, signed in 1939, signaled the start of World War II.)

40. (a) Joan of Arc, a fifteenth-century French peasant girl, claimed she spoke to angels who told her to lead the French armies against the English in the Hundred Years' War. She won the confidence of the heir to the French throne, and in 1429 she led the French forces that defeated the English at Orléans. Soon afterward, however, Joan was captured by the English, convicted of witchcraft, and burned at the stake.

41. (d) After Germany was divided into separate Communist and non-Communist states, refugees from the East poured into West Berlin. To stop this flow of people, in 1961 the East German government built a wall around the western portion of the city. See Test 15, question 28, for information about the fall of the Berlin Wall.

42. (b) Following the collapse of the German monarchy at the end of World War I in 1918, a German national assembly met in Weimar to draft a constitution. The resulting so-called Weimar Republic was unpopular; it signed the Versailles Treaty and allowed runaway inflation. Adolf Hitler, the Republic's last chancellor, abolished it in 1934.

43. (b) The coronation in 800 of Charlemagne as Emperor of the West by Pope Leo III established the Holy Roman Empire. After the death of Charlemagne's son, the empire broke up, to be reestablished in 962 by Otto the Great as a confederation of German and northern Italian territories. The empire existed in various forms, ruled by emperors from almost every European country, until Napoleon abolished it in the early 1800s.

44. (a) At Munich, Chamberlain, believing that Hitler's territorial ambitions could thus be satisfied, agreed to permit German occupation of the Czech border zones. This policy of "appeasement" was a failure; less than a year later World War II began when Germany invaded Poland.

45. **(c)** Julius Caesar (101–44 B.C.) was a Roman general and consul who led the conquest of Gaul (France) and an invasion of Britain. After defeating his rival, Pompey, he gained supreme power in Rome, being appointed dictator for life in 45 B.C. His accomplishments included reform of the Senate, expansion of the empire, and establishment of the Julian calendar, which is almost the same calendar that we use today. His power so threatened the conservative families of Rome that in 44 B.C. he was assassinated in the precincts of the Senate by a group of his own friends and subordinates, to whom his grandiose ambitions had become intolerable.

46. **(d)** Beginning in Great Britain at the end of the eighteenth century, the Industrial Revolution changed the world. Mechanization of production, the growth of a class of factory workers, improvements in living standards, the development of new forms of transportation, and the rise of labor unions are among the results of the economic changes that started taking place in the late 1700s.

47. **(c)** In 330 the Roman emperor Constantine transferred the seat of power to Constantinople, a new city built on the site of Byzantium on the Bosporus. In 395 the empire was divided into western and eastern halves, and after the extinction of the western empire, the eastern (Byzantine) empire continued on until it was conquered by the Ottoman Turks in 1453. The empire is generally thought to have reached its zenith under Justinian (527–565), who drafted a famous code of laws. Byzantine culture was characterized by intense devotion to the Eastern Orthodox Church and by distinctive styles in architecture and art, particularly the widespread use of mosaics.

48. **(b)** In the late 1800s Japan and China each wanted to rule Korea and periodically intervened in the country. In 1894 a rebellion broke out, and when China and Japan both sent in troops, the situation grew into a war. The Chinese were defeated; by the Treaty of Shimonoseki, Korea achieved nominal independence. Japan was given compensation in money and territory, including Formosa (Taiwan).

49. (c) As king, John was a failure: during his reign many of England's continental possessions were lost, and crushing taxes were levied on the nobles. In 1215 the nobles forced John to sign the Magna Carta ("Great Charter"), which limited his power to tax, required jury trials, and forbade the seizure of property without compensation.

50. (b) In Dublin on April 24–29, 1916, the Irish Republican Brotherhood led the so-called Easter Rebellion against British rule. Hoped-for German aid never materialized, and the revolt was suppressed. Not until 1922 did the southern portion of Ireland gain its independence; Northern Ireland, where a majority of the population is Protestant, remains associated with Britain as part of the United Kingdom.

We the People: Civics

> The people's government, made for
> the people, made by the people,
> and answerable to the people . . .
>
> —*DANIEL WEBSTER*

1. The War Powers Act prevents the president from
   a. declaring war on Third World nations
   b. sending armed forces into hostilities for longer than a specified period without the approval of Congress
   c. shipping arms to be used in a foreign war
   d. acting as head of state in times of war

2. How is the number of representatives from each state in the House of Representatives determined?
   a. by the area of the state
   b. by the wealth of the state
   c. by the population of the state
   d. by the amount of exports the state produces

3. What is a junta?
   a. a group of Communists who meet regularly for political discussion
   b. a council controlling the government after a revolutionary seizure of power

c. an organization that campaigns for a particular presidential candidate

d. the Spanish parliament

4. The National Organization for Women (NOW) works to
   a. pay tuition for disadvantaged women in college
   b. strengthen laws against drunk driving
   c. establish equal rights for women under the law
   d. abolish abortion in the United States

5. The role of a presidential primary is to
   a. select the president of the United States
   b. nominate a party candidate
   c. elect the vice-president of the United States
   d. elect delegates to a party's national convention and express candidate preference

6. One function of the FBI is to
   a. investigate threats to the security of the United States that take place within U.S. borders
   b. stop the spread of communism in Central and South America
   c. protect the president and vice-president
   d. coordinate intelligence operations

7. The Selective Service System is responsible for
   a. selecting the candidates for president
   b. choosing the members of the city council
   c. drafting and induction into the armed forces
   d. selecting workers in private industry for promotion to government jobs

8. What was the Stamp Act?
   a. a law passed by Congress in 1980 raising the price of stamps to 22 cents
   b. a law passed by the British Parliament in 1765 requiring special stamps on various paper products
   c. a law passed by Congress in 1941 requiring everyone to carry a stamped identification card

    d. a law passed by Congress in 1804 requiring that mail bear stamps

9. Which president of the United States has been impeached?

    a. Richard Nixon

    b. Ulysses S. Grant

    c. Andrew Johnson

    d. Lyndon Baines Johnson

10. What is the function of a jury?

    a. to decide on the guilt or innocence of a person accused of a crime

    b. to choose the judge who will preside over a trial

    c. to protect the life of a person accused of a crime

    d. to find evidence to prove a person guilty or innocent of a crime

11. Which group are all members of the president's cabinet?

    a. secretary of defense, minority whip, Speaker of the House

    b. vice-president, secretary of state, chief justice

    c. secretary of state, attorney general, secretary of labor

    d. secretary of transportation, national security advisor, vice-president

12. What happens in a presidential veto?

    a. The president votes in a national election.

    b. The senators vote to impeach the president.

    c. The people vote to choose their president.

    d. The president refuses to sign a bill into law.

13. The governments of Great Britain, Sweden, and Belgium are examples of

    a. republics

    b. aristocracies

    c. constitutional monarchies

    d. absolute monarchies

14. In the case of *Brown* v. *Board of Education of Topeka, Kansas*, the Supreme Court ruled that

   a. public schools must be desegregated

   b. official school prayers were illegal

   c. the publication of controversial or "obscene" articles by minors in school newspapers can be suppressed by school authorities

   d. children could not work in factories

15. What is the job of the secretary of state?

   a. to oversee the defense of the United States

   b. to oversee the judicial systems of the fifty states

   c. to take notes in meetings of state

   d. to handle government affairs involving foreign countries

16. In order, who becomes acting president if the president of the United States dies in office?

   a. secretary of state, vice-president, national security advisor

   b. Speaker of the House, vice-president, attorney general

   c. vice-president, Speaker of the House, president pro tempore of the Senate

   d. vice-president, secretary of state, Speaker of the House

17. Which agency has its offices in the Pentagon?

   a. the CIA

   b. the Department of Defense

   c. the presidential cabinet

   d. the Department of State

18. The electoral college is

   a. a school for politicians in Washington, D.C.

   b. the group representing a presidential candidate at a national convention

    c. the group of electors who actually choose the president

    d. the name for the votes of citizens in a presidential election before they are tallied

19. What does the Nineteenth Amendment to the U.S. Constitution state?

    a. The right to vote shall not be denied because of sex.

    b. The sale of alcohol is prohibited.

    c. The government can collect income taxes.

    d. Slavery shall be abolished.

20. What are the terms in office of these officials: president, senator, representative?

    a. eight years, four years, four years

    b. four years, six years, two years

    c. two years, two years, one year

    d. four years, two years, two years

21. When you cast your ballot, you

    a. nominate a candidate for your party

    b. refrain from voting due to religious beliefs

    c. choose a political party to which you will belong

    d. vote in secret using a machine or a printed form

22. Alexander Hamilton and other Federalists believed that

    a. Canada should become part of the Union

    b. slavery should be abolished

    c. the United States should be ruled by a constitutional monarchy

    d. the United States should have a strong central government

23. The NAACP seeks to

    a. uphold the rights of blacks in the United States

    b. protect consumers against fraud

    c. make sure medicines are safe and effective

    d. ensure world peace

24. When the Senate ratifies a treaty, it

    a. votes it down

    b. approves it by a two-thirds vote

    c. allows the President to veto it

    d. changes its wording

25. What is a naturalized citizen?

    a. someone who was born in the United States

    b. someone whose parents were born in the United States

    c. an immigrant who applies for citizenship and passes a test

    d. an immigrant who has lived in the United States for at least five years

26. The landmark Supreme Court case *Plessy* v. *Ferguson*

    a. gave blacks equal rights under the law

    b. required "separate but equal" treatment for whites and blacks

    c. freed slaves in Southern states

    d. established quotas for hiring minorities in federal positions

27. The Voting Rights Act of 1965

    a. eliminated literacy tests for voters

    b. required literacy tests for voters

    c. gave eighteen-year-olds the vote

    d. gave blacks the vote

28. The right of parties in a case to appeal a decision means

    a. the trial must begin again with brand-new evidence

    b. the jury may reconsider their decision for thirty days

    c. the decision may be reversed or upheld by a higher court

    d. the decision was unwarranted and did not stand up to scrutiny

29. What is the Bill of Rights?

    a. the first ten amendments to the Constitution

    b. the first paragraph of the Declaration of Independence

    c. the code of laws of the thirteen colonies

    d. any constitution created by a state government

30. The historic separation of church and state in the United States

    a. makes it possible for schools to teach creationism

    b. enables the Senate to begin each day with a prayer

    c. forbids the support with public funds of religious groups

    d. means that Christmas is not a federal holiday

31. The system of checks and balances was designed to

    a. make it easier for Congress to pay for federal programs

    b. keep one branch of government from overpowering another

    c. assign the enforcement of laws to the judicial branch

    d. allow the chief executive to select a cabinet

32. To be a democracy, a country *must*

    a. have a constitution and elected representatives

    b. provide economic equality and equal opportunity

    c. allow each citizen one vote on each issue

    d. none of the above

33. You may sue someone for libel if that person

    a. publishes something that is incorrect

    b. publishes a lie that injures you personally or professionally

    c. uses your name without your consent

    d. publishes your writing without your consent

34. Which statement best expresses the primary tenet of socialism and communism?

    a. Economic equality is preferable to private control of resources.

    b. The people belong to the state.

    c. Commerce should be free of governmental interference.

    d. The acquisition of empire is the lifeblood of the system.

35. What is a prime minister?

    a. the head of state in Great Britain

    b. a high-ranking member of the aristocracy

    c. the leader of the Anglican Church

    d. the head of a parliamentary government

36. If you oppose capital punishment, you do not want

    a. convicted criminals to face the death penalty

    b. physical punishment of students by teachers

    c. heads of state to face impeachment

    d. unreasonable search and seizure

37. A nation with a bicameral legislature

    a. is run by a premier and cabinet

    b. is run by the direct vote of the people

    c. has two legislative houses

    d. has two political parties

38. According to the decision in the 1973 Supreme Court case *Roe* v. *Wade,*

    a. segregation in public schools violates equal protection

    b. a wife may charge her husband with rape and assault

c. the Constitution protects the rights of the unborn

d. states may not forbid abortion in the first two trimesters

39. The Iowa caucuses are held in order to

   a. select a candidate for president
   b. send delegates to party conventions
   c. determine which party has more support
   d. allow voters to indicate issues of concern

40. The Alien and Sedition Acts of 1798 did all of the following *except*

   a. prohibit criticism of the government
   b. require fourteen years' residency for naturalization
   c. allow the president to deport or arrest "dangerous" immigrants
   d. restrict the immigration of non-Europeans

41. Strictly defined, liberalism versus conservatism means

   a. change versus preservation of the status quo
   b. government control versus individual freedom
   c. secular humanism versus religious fundamentalism
   d. equal opportunity versus individualism

42. Which of the following is *not* an example of civil disobedience?

   a. boycotting
   b. passive resistance
   c. hijacking
   d. nonpayment of taxes

43. A writ of habeas corpus is intended

   a. to allow a prisoner to hire a lawyer at the public's expense
   b. to suspend civil liberties in times of war
   c. to prevent arbitrary imprisonment and ensure judicial review

    d. to prevent defendants from having to incriminate themselves

44. Which of these is always true of the U.S. Congress?

    a. The majority party in the Senate also leads the House.

    b. The House and Senate may be led by different parties.

    c. If one party leads the House, another leads the Senate.

    d. No one party may dominate either house.

45. If defendants in a case invoke the Fifth Amendment, or "plead the Fifth," they

    a. are asking for extra time to prepare a case

    b. are invoking the right not to testify against themselves

    c. are refusing to answer all questions posed by the judge

    d. can be retried later for the same offense

46. Which of the following is *not* true of bills in the U.S. Congress?

    a. Bills become laws if they are approved by Congress and the president.

    b. Only the House can initiate a bill asking for higher taxes.

    c. If a bill is not passed in one session of Congress, it dies.

    d. The Senate may not add to or change a bill from the House.

47. What is a nomination?

    a. an executive's selection of an appointee

    b. a party's selection of a candidate for office

    c. a or b

    d. neither a nor b

48. The case of *Miranda* v. *Arizona* gave suspects in a crime

   a. the ability to plead guilty to a lesser charge

   b. the right to due process and judicial review

   c. the right to be informed of their rights

   d. money to hire an attorney to represent them

49. The U.S. attorney general has all of these duties *except*

   a. running the Department of Justice

   b. advising the president in legal matters

   c. nominating Supreme Court justices

   d. overseeing cases that involve the government

50. A defense attorney represents the accused, and a prosecuting attorney represents

   a. the victim

   b. the state

   c. the convicted

   d. the court

TEST 3: Explanatory Answers

1. **(b)** In 1973, during the Vietnam War, Congress passed the War Powers Act over President Richard Nixon's veto. The Act stated that the president must consult with Congress before sending U.S. armed forces into hostilities for longer than a specified period of time.

2. **(c)** Whereas each state has two senators, the number of representatives per state depends on the population of the state. However, the Reapportionment Act of 1929 set the permanent number of House members at 435.

3. **(b)** *Junta* is a Spanish word meaning "joined." A junta is a committee or council that controls the government after a revolution. Often a junta is run by the military. Some historic examples of juntas include those formed in Spain in 1808 and in 1930, in Egypt in 1952, and in Nicaragua and El Salvador in 1979.

4. **(c)** NOW, founded in 1966, seeks to end discrimination against women in all sectors of society. It favors liberalization of abortion laws, engages in litigation, and works actively in politics.

5. **(d)** Presidential primaries, both more numerous and more important now than in the past, are used to select delegates, either pledged or unpledged, to go to a party's national convention, where the presidential candidates are nominated.

6. **(a)** Both the Federal Bureau of Investigation (FBI) and the Central Intelligence Agency (CIA) are charged with protecting the security of the United States. However, the difference is that the FBI is limited to investigating security threats that take place within U.S. borders. Another function of the FBI is to investigate criminal cases in which suspects have crossed state lines.

7. **(c)** From 1940 to 1973 the Selective Service System oversaw the drafting and induction of men into the armed forces. In 1973 the armed forces became all-volunteer, and the system was placed on standby. However, in 1980 registration for the draft was reinstated.

8. **(b)** In 1765 the British Parliament passed the Stamp Act, requiring colonists in America to use special stamps, highly taxed, on items such as calendars, newspapers, and contracts. The Act was repealed in 1766 because of strong opposition by the colonists.

9. **(c)** Impeachment, or charging a public official with a crime in a trial before a competent tribunal, has been a possibility for only two U.S. presidents: Andrew Johnson in 1868 and Richard Nixon in 1974. Johnson was impeached, but was acquitted in a trial before the Senate. Nixon resigned before he could be impeached.

10. **(a)** A jury, usually twelve people chosen for their impartiality, has the job of deciding whether a person accused of a crime is guilty or innocent. A *grand jury*, which consists of thirteen to twenty-three people, decides if a person held for a crime should go to trial.

11. **(c)** There are now thirteen members of the cabinet: secretary of state, secretary of the treasury, secretary of defense, attorney general, secretary of the interior, secretary of agriculture, secretary of commerce, secretary of labor, secretary of health

and human services, secretary of housing and urban development, secretary of transportation, secretary of energy, and secretary of education.

12. **(d)** When a president vetoes a bill—refuses to sign it into law—he returns it to the House or Senate and explains why he vetoed it. The bill can be passed over the veto if two-thirds of the Congress vote to do so.

13. **(c)** A constitutional monarchy is a government headed by a king or queen whose power is limited by a constitution.

14. **(a)** *Brown* v. *Board of Education* was a suit brought by the Brown family of Topeka, Kansas, whose children were forced to go to segregated schools. In 1955 the Supreme Court ruled segregation unconstitutional and charged local schools with the responsibility for integrating.

15. **(d)** The Department of State is older than the U.S. Constitution. The secretary of state is the highest ranking executive officer after the president and is responsible for developing foreign policy and handling foreign affairs.

16. **(c)** If the president dies in office, first the vice-president, then the Speaker of the House, then the president pro tempore of the Senate, then the secretary of state become acting president.

17. **(b)** The Department of Defense is housed in the Pentagon, a five-sided building in Arlington, Virginia.

18. **(c)** Electors, the total of whom make up the electoral college, are usually chosen at state party conventions. The number of electors in each state is equal to its total of U.S. senators and representatives. When citizens vote in a presidential election, they are voting for a group of electors representing their candidate. Whichever party wins a majority of votes in a state sends its electors to Washington, where on the first Monday after the second Wednesday in December, they cast their ballots to choose the president. Because of this process it is possible to elect a president who has a minority of popular votes, as happened in 1876 with Rutherford B. Hayes and in 1888 with Benjamin Harrison.

19. **(a)** The Nineteenth Amendment gave women the vote by stating that voting rights could not be denied because of gender.

20. **(b)** A president's term in office is four years, a senator's, six years, and a representative's, two years. Senators and repre-

sentatives can be reelected indefinitely; a president can serve only two terms.

21. **(d)** There are two kinds of ballots in the United States: one on which candidates are listed by the office for which they are running and one on which candidates are listed by political party. When you cast your ballot, you vote in secret for one or more people listed on the ballot.

22. **(d)** Federalists, who believed in a strong federal government, opposed states' rights advocates, who wanted power to remain with the states. During the writing of the U.S. Constitution, this conflict came to a boil; a compromise was reached by which the House of Representatives represents the people, and the Senate represents the states.

23. **(a)** The NAACP, or National Association for the Advancement of Colored People, was formed in 1909 by black rights activists led by W. E. B. DuBois. It works to achieve equality for blacks.

24. **(b)** A treaty is ratified if it is approved by a two-thirds majority in the Senate. A constitutional amendment, however, can be ratified in two ways: by a positive vote by legislators in three-quarters of the states or by a positive vote in conventions in three-quarters of the states.

25. **(c)** To become a naturalized citizen, an immigrant must live in the United States for at least five years and then file an application for citizenship. An applicant is tested on U.S. history, government, and the Constitution before becoming a citizen.

26. **(b)** *Plessy* v. *Ferguson* (1896) upheld a Louisiana law that called for "separate but equal" accommodations for whites and blacks on passenger trains.

27. **(a)** In addition to ending the literacy and character test requirement in states where less than half of the voting-age population was registered, the Voting Rights Act allowed the attorney general to determine when federal registration of voters was needed to comply with the Fifteenth Amendment ("The right of citizens . . . to vote shall not be denied or abridged . . . on account of race, color, or previous condition of servitude").

28. **(c)** The right to an appeal means that the decision of a lower court may be challenged, and the case may be heard again by a higher court, up to and including the Supreme Court.

29. **(a)** The absence of certain guaranteed rights in the U.S. Constitution as originally written led to ten amendments in 1791. These amendments cover such issues as freedoms of speech and religion, right to bear arms, and right to a speedy trial.

30. **(c)** Based on the First Amendment's guarantee of freedom of religion, the separation of church and state implies that public support of any religious organization is unconstitutional. This policy means that prayer in schools is unacceptable, and there can be no national religion. Varying interpretations of the First Amendment have kept the issue alive into our own time.

31. **(b)** The Constitution prescribes a separation of powers among the three branches of government—executive, legislative, and judicial. Few actions may be taken by any branch without the approval of one of the other branches.

32. **(d)** *Democracy* means "rule by the people." In a direct democracy, such as the one in ancient Athens, each citizen (free males in the case of Athens) votes directly on issues. In a representative democracy, government is run by representatives elected by the people. In a social democracy, individuals have equal access to public resources without discrimination. In an economic democracy, individuals have equal opportunity and often share the resources. Historically, the concepts of liberty and equality have been keys to the democratic ideal, but differing emphases on one concept or the other have led to different applications of that ideal.

33. **(b)** To be libelous, a publication must be unjust and must expose the subject to public contempt or cause the subject professional harm.

34. **(a)** Communism and socialism have in common the belief that economic laws can be made that benefit the people as a whole rather than individuals. Substituting communal ownership for private property is believed to ensure equal opportunity.

35. **(d)** The chief executive of a parliament or cabinet is called a prime minister. The prime minister is often head of the majority party. (The head of state in Great Britain is the king or queen.)

36. **(a)** The term *capital punishment* refers to the imposition of the death penalty for particular crimes. Many countries and some states have eliminated the death penalty, and controversy remains over whether or not execution constitutes "cruel and unusual punishment."

37. **(c)** *Bicameral* means "two chambers," and it refers to those legislatures that are made up of two houses. The British Parliament, for example, is composed of the House of Lords and the House of Commons; the U.S. Congress is divided into the House of Representatives and the Senate.

38. **(d)** The 1973 ruling legalized abortions during the first six months of pregnancy. However, in 1977 Congress eliminated abortion from those medical operations covered by Medicaid.

39. **(b)** A caucus is a form of primary. In Iowa delegates to local party conventions are picked in political meetings open to the voting public. Those delegates are expected, but not required, to vote for a particular candidate at the party's national convention.

40. **(d)** Passed to limit the power of the Jeffersonian Republicans who supported France's position in Franco-American disputes, the acts increased the federal government's power. They enabled the executive to expel any objectionable aliens, lengthened requirements for naturalization, and declared written or spoken criticism of the government to be treasonous. Jefferson's reply, written with James Madison, was "The Kentucky and Virginia Resolutions" of 1798 and was to become the foundation of the states' rights movement.

41. **(a)** Modern conservatism arose in response to the changes brought about by the French Revolution and industrialism in Europe. It emphasized the preservation of the old order. Liberalism was intended to favor free development of the individual through progressive reform and limited government. Both terms have undergone significant redefinition. Conservatism now implies freedom from government intervention (or maintenance of the economic status quo), whereas liberalism has come to imply government protection (or social and economic change through legislation).

42. **(c)** The essay "Civil Disobedience" (1849) by Henry David Thoreau calls on citizens to withdraw from cooperation with their governments when those governments undertake acts with which those citizens disagree. Other famous proponents of this idea were Mahatma Gandhi in India and Martin Luther King, Jr. in the United States.

43. (c) Anyone detaining a prisoner is required to bring that prisoner to court and state the reason for his or her arrest. If the judge considers the cause sufficient, the prisoner may or may not be released on bail. If the cause is insufficient, the prisoner must be freed at once.

44. (b) The Senate majority leader is in charge of allocating time and determining the priorities in business conducted in the Senate. The House majority leader leads party debate in the House and assists the Speaker. House and Senate are often controlled by the same party, and that party may be the same as the chief executive's party. However, the legislature may be split, or both houses may be controlled by a party other than the one in control of the White House.

45. (b) The Fifth Amendment holds that no one may be tried for a capital crime unless indicted by a grand jury; that "double jeopardy," or standing trial twice for the same offense, is prohibited; that life, liberty, or property may not be taken without due process of law; and that no one need be "a witness against himself."

46. (d) Although only the House of Representatives may initiate a bill involving raising money, the Senate may amend that bill before approving it. If a bill is approved by the House in one form and by the Senate in another, a joint committee with members from both houses must hammer out the differences before the final bill goes to the president.

47. (c) In the United States, primaries and caucuses enable a party to nominate a single candidate for office. The executive also has the power to nominate people for positions in the judiciary and cabinet.

48. (c) *Escobedo* v. *Illinois* (1964) held that an accused man was denied due process when police refused his request to call a lawyer and his confession was later used as evidence. This case paved the way for *Miranda* v. *Arizona* (1966), which stated that before questioning may take place, suspects must be informed of their rights to remain silent and contact an attorney.

49. (c) The U.S. attorney general is the head of the Department of Justice and a member of the cabinet. Although an attorney general may advise the president on potential nominees, the president alone may appoint federal and Supreme Court justices.

50. **(b)** A prosecuting attorney, who may be a district attorney or a state's attorney, represents the state in criminal cases involving state law. In federal cases the prosecutor is a U.S. attorney, who represents the federal government.

TEST 4

Spaceship Earth: Geography

I have always read that the world, both land and water, was spherical.

—CHRISTOPHER COLUMBUS

Questions 1-3 refer to the following map.

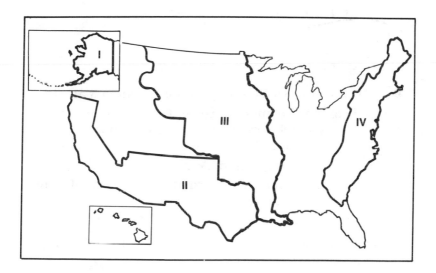

1. On page 57, the Louisiana Purchase is the section of the map labeled
   a. I   **b.** II   **c.** III   **d.** IV

2. The original thirteen colonies are the section of the map labeled
   a. I   **b.** II   **c.** III   **d.** IV

3. The forty-ninth state is in the section of the map labeled
   a. I   **b.** II   **c.** III   **d.** IV

4. What is the capital of New York State?
   a. New York City
   b. Buffalo
   c. Albany
   d. none of the above

5. In which city is the Kremlin located?
   a. St. Petersburg
   b. Moscow
   c. Warsaw
   d. Berlin

6. Which countries all belong to the Common Market?
   a. Belgium, Denmark, France, Great Britain, Ireland, Italy, Luxembourg, the Netherlands, Germany, Greece, Portugal, Spain
   b. Great Britain, Ireland, Australia
   c. Bulgaria, Ukraine, Germany, Hungary, Poland, Rumania, Russia
   d. Denmark, France, Norway, Portugal, Spain, Sweden

7. The equator is to latitude as which of the following is to longitude?
   a. Tropic of Cancer
   b. Tropic of Capricorn
   c. international date line
   d. prime meridian

8. Which of the following is *not* true of the Nile River?

    a. It is the longest river in the world.

    b. It empties into the Mediterranean Sea.

    (**c.**) It is the main source of water for Senegal.

    d. The Aswan Dam is built across it.

9. The Pacific Northwest is made up of which states?

    a. Washington, Oregon, and part of Idaho

    (**b.**) Oregon and California

    c. Idaho, Montana, and part of Washington

    d. California and Arizona

10. Where is Libya?

    a. in the Middle East, bordering Syria and Lebanon

    b. in the Middle East, bordering Saudi Arabia

    (**c.**) in northern Africa, bordering Egypt

    d. in Asia, bordering Brunei

11. What is the capital of Germany?

    a. Bonn

    (**b.**) Berlin

    c. Munich

    d. Vienna

12. What do Guam and Puerto Rico have in common?

    a. They are both islands in the Caribbean.

    b. Their residents are U.S. citizens.

    c. They are both constitutional monarchies.

    (**d.**) They are both south of the equator.

13. The Thirty-eighth Parallel is the line of latitude that marks

    a. the northern tip of the Oregon Territory

    b. the division of Korea after World War II

    c. the location of the Panama Canal

    d. the line of German defenses in World War I

14. Which of the following is *not* true of the Mississippi River?

    a. It divides Kansas from Oklahoma.

    b. It flows from north to south.

    c. It ends in Louisiana at the Gulf of Mexico.

    d. It forms the western border of Illinois.

Questions 15–17 refer to the above map.

15. The line running from north to south represents

    a. the Great Divide

    b. the Mason-Dixon line

    c. the San Andreas fault

    d. the Oregon Trail

16. The capital of this state is
   a. Sacramento
   b. Los Angeles
   c. San Francisco
   d. San Diego

17. The southernmost city on this map is
   a. Sacramento
   b. Los Angeles
   c. San Francisco
   d. San Diego

18. Which country is *not* an island chain?
   a. Fiji
   b. Philippines
   c. Indonesia
   d. Myanmar

19. Which of the following countries does *not* border Israel?
   a. Iran   **c.** Jordan
   b. Lebanon   **d.** Egypt

20. What are the Himalayas?
   a. the mountains that link western and eastern Europe
   b. a mountain range in Tanzania containing Mount Kilimanjaro
   c. the highest mountains in the world, located in Asia
   d. the often impassable mountains of Afghanistan

21. Spanish is the primary language of all of these countries *except*
   a. Cuba and the Dominican Republic
   b. Venezuela and Guatemala
   c. Colombia and Argentina
   d. Haiti and Brazil

22. Which of the following states does *not* border Iowa?

a. Nebraska   c. Wisconsin

b. North Dakota   d. Missouri

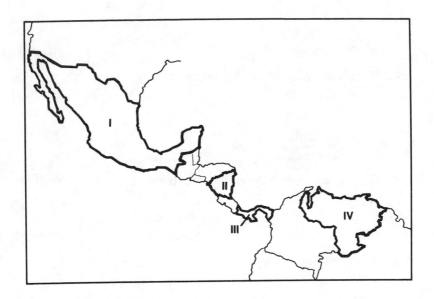

23. Mexico is the section of the map labeled

    a. I   b. II   c. III   d. IV

24. Venezuela is the section of the map labeled

    a. I   b. II   c. III   d. IV

25. Panama is the section of the map labeled

    a. I   b. II   c. III   d. IV

26. Scandinavia is the section of the map labeled

    a. I   **b.** II   **c.** III   **d.** IV

27. Great Britain is the section of the map labeled

    a. I   **b.** II   **c.** III   **d.** IV

28. Iberia is the section of the map labeled

    a. I   **b.** II   **c.** III   **d.** IV

29. The country once known as ancient Mesopotamia is now
   a. India and Pakistan
   b. Egypt and parts of Sudan and Ethiopia
   c. Iraq and parts of Iran, Syria, and Turkey
   d. Israel

30. Suez, Erie, and Panama are names of
   a. socialist republics   **c.** mountain ranges
   b. rivers   **d.** canals

31. The Alps run through the countries of
   a. France, Austria, Switzerland, and Italy
   b. Spain, France, Belgium, and Switzerland
   c. Germany, Austria, Holland, and Denmark
   d. Switzerland, Italy, Hungary, and Poland

32. Which countries do *not* border Brazil?
   a. Guyana and Venezuela
   b. Ecuador and Chile
   c. Bolivia and Paraguay
   d. Peru and Argentina

33. What country was once known as Persia?
   a. Syria   **c.** Afghanistan
   b. Egypt   **d.** Iran

34. What is the capital of Ethiopia?
   a. Addis Ababa   **c.** Nairobi
   b. Harar   **d.** Pretoria

35. Where is the headquarters of the United Nations?
   a. Washington, D.C.   **c.** New York, N.Y.
   b. Paris, France   **d.** Brussels, Belgium

36. Japan is the section of the map labeled

    a. I   **b.** II   **c.** III   **d.** IV

37. China is the section of the map labeled

    a. I   **b.** II   **c.** III   **d.** IV

38. Vietnam is the section of the map labeled

    a. I   **b.** II   **c.** III   **d.** IV

39. What is the capital of Texas?
   a. Houston
   b. Austin
   c. Dallas
   d. Texas City

40. What is the capital of Canada?
   a. Toronto
   b. Ontario
   c. Ottawa
   d. Quebec

41. Erie, Superior, Huron, Michigan, and Ontario are names of
   a. the Finger Lakes
   b. the Great Lakes
   c. the bodies of water in the British Lake District
   d. the lakes of the Ozarks

42. What is Vatican City?
   a. a free state within Rome where the pope lives
   b. the capital of Italy
   c. a city now known as Istanbul, where the Eastern patriarch lives
   d. the capital of the Netherlands

43. Which countries belong to the British Commonwealth of Nations?
   a. Greenland, Singapore, India, and Taiwan
   b. Trinidad and Tobago, Tonga, Canada, and New Zealand
   c. Jamaica, Ireland, Zaire, and Rumania
   d. Australia, Iceland, Barbados, and Terra del Fuego

44. What is the largest state in the United States?
   a. Hawaii
   b. Texas
   c. Alaska
   d. California

45. Which city is *not* in the Northern Hemisphere?
   a. Mexico City
   b. New York City
   c. Calcutta, India
   d. Sydney, Australia

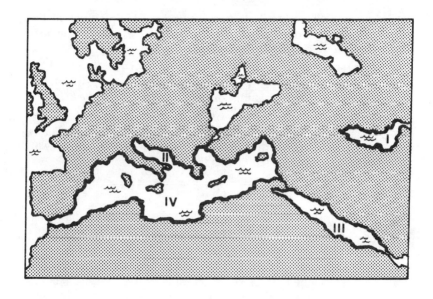

46. The Mediterranean Sea is the section of the map labeled
   a. I   **b.** II   **c.** III   **d.** IV

47. The Persian Gulf is the section of the map labeled
   a. I   **b.** II   **c.** III   **d.** IV

48. The Red Sea is the section of the map labeled
   a. I   **b.** II   **c.** III   **d.** IV

49. What is the capital of Brazil?
   a. Rio de Janeiro   **c.** São Paulo
   b. Brasilia   **d.** Caracas

50. Which of the following is *not* true of the Amazon River?
   a. It was named for a tribe of warrior women.
   b. It runs through Peru and Brazil.
   c. It is the longest river in the world.
   d. It carries more water than any other river.

TEST 4: *Explanatory Answers*

1. **(c)** In 1803 the United States purchased land west of the Mississippi from France for around $27 million. The new territory was over 800,000 square miles in area.

2. **(d)** These British colonies revolted against England and became the United States. They included New Hampshire, Massachusetts, Rhode Island, Connecticut, New York, New Jersey, Pennsylvania, Maryland, Delaware, North Carolina, South Carolina, Virginia, and Georgia.

3. **(a)** Alaska became the forty-ninth state in 1959, and Hawaii became the fiftieth state later that year.

4. **(c)** Albany, a city on the Hudson River, has been the capital of New York State since 1797.

5. **(b)** From 1918 to 1989 the Kremlin housed the administration of the Soviet Union in the capital city, Moscow. A kremlin was a medieval walled city. Moscow's Kremlin dates from 1156.

6. **(a)** The Common Market, or European Economic Community, was established in 1957 to simplify trade among Western European nations. Denmark, Great Britain, and Ireland joined in 1973. In the 1980s, Greece, Portugal, and Spain joined, and applications from Austria, Cyprus, Malta, Sweden, and Turkey are being considered.

7. **(d)** The equator is an imaginary circle around the earth designated 0° latitude. The prime meridian is a similar great circle through the poles designated 0° longitude.

8. **(c)** The Nile runs north from sources in Burundi through Rwanda to Sudan, where its branches, the Blue Nile and the White Nile, converge. The Aswan Dam helps to supply hydroelectric power and irrigation for much of southern Egypt. The river passes through Cairo and forms a huge delta before emptying into the Mediterranean.

9. **(a)** The Pacific Northwest is an area that encompasses Washington, Oregon, and part of Idaho. The area was home to the Nez Percé, Yakima, Chinook, Bannock, Klamath, and Modoc tribes during the first white explorations by James Cook in the 1770s and Lewis and Clark in 1805–1806.

10. **(c)** Libya is bordered by the Mediterranean on the north, Egypt and Sudan on the east, Niger and Chad on the south, and Tunisia and Algeria on the west.

11. **(b)** Before 1990, Bonn was the capital of West Germany. However, when West and East Germany were reunited, Berlin was named the new capital.

12. **(b)** Guam, an island in the West Pacific, and Puerto Rico, an island in the Caribbean, were both ceded to the United States by the Spanish in 1898. Puerto Rico is a self-governing country, but Guam is administered by the U.S. Department of the Interior. Residents of both islands are U.S. citizens, but they are not empowered to vote in U.S. elections.

13. **(b)** Following World War II the United States occupied Korea south of the Thirty-eighth Parallel, and the Soviet Union occupied the region to the north. Both countries withdrew in 1949, but forces from the north invaded the south in 1950, leading to the Korean War.

14. **(a)** The Mississippi flows between Minnesota and Wisconsin, Iowa and Illinois, Missouri and Kentucky, Arkansas and Tennessee, and Louisiana and Mississippi. It enters the Gulf of Mexico south of New Orleans.

15. **(c)** The San Andreas fault marks the edges of two geologic plates that slide along each other and cause earthquakes throughout much of California.

16. **(a)** Sacramento was settled in 1839 and grew rapidly during the California gold rush of 1849. It became the state capital in 1854.

17. **(d)** San Diego is not far from the southern border of the United States. The compass rose on a map indicates north (N), south (S), east (E), and west (W).

18. **(d)** Myanmar (formerly Burma) is bordered by India, China, Thailand, Laos, and the Bay of Bengal.

19. **(a)** Israel's borders are with Syria on the north, Jordan on the east, Egypt on the south, and the Mediterranean on the west.

20. **(c)** The Himalayas run through Pakistan, India, Tibet, Nepal, Sikkim, and Bhutan. Mount Everest, usually considered the highest mountain in the world at 28,208 feet, is found in the southern range.

21. **(d)** French is the official language of Haiti, although Creole is widely spoken. This stems from the influx in the 1600s of French planters, who imported slaves from Africa and went on to make Haiti one of the largest producers of coffee and sugar. When Toussaint L'Ouverture, a former slave, overthrew

the government and abolished slavery, Haiti became only the second independent country in the Americas, the United States being the first. Portugal ruled Brazil for centuries, and at one time Rio de Janeiro was the capital of the Portuguese empire. Brazil became a republic in 1889, and Portuguese remains the official language.

22. **(b)** Iowa is bordered by six states: Minnesota on the north, Wisconsin and Illinois on the east, Missouri on the south, and Nebraska and South Dakota on the west.

23. **(a)** Mexico is the southernmost country in North America. Its northern border is with the United States; it is bordered on the south by Belize and Guatemala.

24. **(d)** Venezuela, a republic in northern South America, shares borders with Colombia on the west, Brazil on the south, and Guyana on the east.

25. **(c)** Because of its location Panama was chosen as the most likely prospect for a canal linking the Caribbean and the Pacific. Its northern neighbor is Costa Rica, and its southern border is with Colombia.

26. **(b)** Scandinavia includes the countries Denmark, Sweden, Norway, and Finland.

27. **(a)** Great Britain includes England, Scotland, Wales, Northern Ireland, the Channel Islands, and the Isle of Man.

28. **(c)** Iberia includes the countries Portugal and Spain.

29. **(c)** Ancient Mesopotamia, the cradle of civilization, where the Tigris and Euphrates rivers flow, extended from the Persian Gulf north to the mountains of Armenia and from the Zagres Mountains west to the Syrian desert. The earliest settlements in Mesopotamia date from about 5000 B.C. Today the region includes portions of Iran, Turkey, Syria, and Iraq.

30. **(d)** The Suez Canal is a waterway connecting the Gulf of Suez with the Mediterranean. The Panama Canal connects the Atlantic Ocean with the Pacific Ocean. The Erie Canal connected the Hudson River with Lake Erie but fell into disuse with the rise of the railroads.

31. **(a)** The Alps are a mountain system that runs through France, Switzerland, northern Italy, Germany, Austria, Slovenia, and Croatia.

32. **(b)** Brazil is bordered by French Guiana, Suriname, Guyana, Venezuela, Colombia, Peru, Bolivia, Paraguay, Argentina, and Uruguay.

33. **(d)** The country that had been called Persia since ancient times was officially renamed Iran in 1935. In 1978 a revolution in Iran overthrew the ruler, or Shah, and the country was led by the Ayatollah Khomeini, a Muslim holy man, until his death in 1989.

34. **(a)** In 1889 the city of Addis Ababa was made the capital of Ethiopia. Ravaged by war and famine, the country remains economically and industrially underdeveloped.

35. **(c)** The UN is based in New York. It was founded in October 1945 and has more than 150 members. Its aims are to maintain peace, to promote equal rights, to develop international co-operation, and to encourage respect for human rights.

36. **(d)** Japan is a string of islands in the Pacific, including the islands of Hokkaido, Honshu, Shikoku, and Kyushu. Its capital is Tokyo.

37. **(b)** The People's Republic of China is bordered by North Korea, Mongolia, Kazahkstan, Russia, Tajikistan, Kyrgyzstan, Vietnam, Laos, Myanmar, Bhutan, Nepal, Pakistan, Afghanistan, Sikkim, and India. Its capital is Beijing.

38. **(c)** Vietnam, an ancient country, was ravaged by war for decades following World War II. Divided for more than twenty years into North Vietnam and South Vietnam, it was reunited in 1976 when troops from the north captured the city of Saigon in the south. Vietnam's capital is Hanoi.

39. **(b)** In 1870, after Texas was admitted to the Union, Austin was named its capital.

40. **(c)** Canada is divided into ten provinces and two territories: Alberta, British Columbia, Manitoba, New Brunswick, Newfoundland, Northwest Territories, Nova Scotia, Ontario, Prince Edward Island, Quebec, Saskatchewan, and Yukon Territory. Ottawa, its capital, was founded in 1827 and became the capital in 1867.

41. **(b)** The Great Lakes of North America comprise the largest body of fresh water in the world. They were formed by glaciers at the end of the Ice Age and were explored by Samuel de Champlain and Robert LaSalle in the seventeenth century.

42. **(a)** Vatican City, the residence of the pope and the headquarters of the Roman Catholic church, is located within the boundaries of the city of Rome. It has been an independent state with its own currency and citizenship since 1929.

43. (b) The Commonwealth of Nations was established in 1931 and consists of more than forty sovereign and associated states, including Great Britain. Most of the member states have their own governments, but a few, such as Nevis–St. Kitts and St. Lucia, are governed by Great Britain. There is no formal constitution for the Commonwealth, but all members acknowledge the British monarch as its head and can consult with one another on common problems.

44. (c) The largest state in the United States is Alaska, with an area of 570,833 square miles. The next largest is Texas, with an area of 262,015 square miles.

45. (d) The Northern Hemisphere is the half of the earth that lies north of the equator. The Southern Hemisphere lies south of the equator. Australia is in the Southern Hemisphere.

46. (d) The Mediterranean Sea, the world's largest inland sea, connects with the Atlantic Ocean, the Black Sea, and the Red Sea. Many ancient civilizations flourished on its shores, including those of the Phoenicians, the Greeks, and the Romans.

47. (a) The Persian Gulf, a six-hundred-mile-long extension of the Arabian Sea, was an important trading route in ancient times and has become important again since oil was discovered along its shores in the early 1900s.

48. (c) The Red Sea lies between Africa and the Arabian peninsula. It was probably named for the red-hued algae in its waters. The Suez Canal was opened between the Red Sea and the Mediterranean in 1869, but today its importance has declined because it is not wide enough to accommodate modern supertankers.

49. (b) The capital of Brazil, Brasilia, is one of the newest cities in the world. It was founded in 1960, when officials decided to move the capital inland to encourage development of the interior of the country.

50. (c) The Amazon, which originates in northern Peru, flows across Brazil before emptying into the Atlantic. It is the second longest river in the world but carries more water than any other river. It was named by explorer Francisco de Orellana, who claimed to have seen female warriors on its banks.

Worth a Thousand Words: Art and Architecture

*. . . Art, admired in general,
is always actually personal.*

—*MARIANNE MOORE*

1. What is the monument on page 73?
   a. Hadrian's Wall
   b. the Great Wall of China
   c. the Iron Curtain
   d. the Berlin Wall

2. Who was Christopher Wren?
   a. an English painter in the nineteenth century
   b. a sixteenth-century Dutch landscape artist
   c. an English architect of the seventeenth century
   d. an eighteenth-century Belgian sculptor

3. This is a sculpture of
   a. David by Michelangelo
   b. King Solomon by Bernini
   c. Moses by Michelangelo
   d. John the Baptist by Rodin

4. Ionic, Doric, and Corinthian are styles of

   a. still lifes   **c.** stained glass

   b. church naves   **d.** columns

5. This picture shows three

   a. Grecian columns

   b. Mayan temple towers

   c. Indian totem poles

   d. Persian ornamental staffs

6. For what is Edgar Degas best known?

   a. his landscapes of the French countryside

   b. his paintings of dancers

   c. his abstract sculptures

   d. his graceful Gothic cathedrals

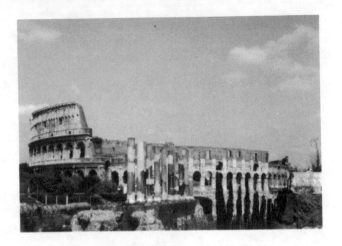

7. What is this edifice?

   a. the Roman forum

   b. the Greek Parthenon

   c. the temple at Delphi

   d. the Colosseum in Rome

8. For what are these artists known: Alfred Eisenstaedt, Margaret Bourke-White, Ansel Adams?

   a. their photography

   b. their portraits

   c. their sculptures

   d. their landscapes

9. What is this statue called?

   a. *Winged Victory*

   b. *Aphrodite*

   c. *Venus de Milo*

   d. *The Rape of the Sabine Women*

10. A pietà is a depiction of

   a. Christ on the cross

   b. the dead Christ held by Mary

   c. an angel announcing the birth of Christ to Mary

   d. the baptism of Christ by John the Baptist

11. This is the church called

   a. St. Peter's

   b. St. Paul's

   c. Westminster Abbey

   d. Ste. Chapelle

12. How is a fresco made?

   a. by carving from marble or stone

   b. by fusing colored glass to a metal ground

   c. by firing colored glass rods together and cutting them in sections

   d. by painting on wet plaster and allowing it to dry

13. This is a typical example of art from
   a. ancient Egypt
   b. sixteenth-century Holland
   c. Renaissance Italy
   d. ancient Greece

14. For what stylistic trait is Rembrandt best known?
   a. the use of pointillism in painting
   b. the subtle use of light and shadow in painting
   c. the development of the baroque in architecture
   d. the development of photorealism in painting

15. This picture shows

  a. a piece of cloisonné enamel

  b. an illuminated manuscript

  c. a mosaic

  d. a tryptich

16. The great museum of Paris is called

  a. the Metropolitan Museum of Art

  b. the National Gallery

  c. the Uffizi

  d. the Louvre

17. What is this picture called?

   a. *Portrait of Diane de Poitiers*

   b. *The Jewish Bride*

   c. *Arrangement in Black and Gray: The Artist's Mother*

   d. *The Seated Woman*

18. Pieter Breughel the Elder is best known for his

   a. portraits of kings and queens

   b. sculptures of children at play

   c. paintings showing seasonal scenes of peasant life

   d. frescoes of the life of St. Francis of Assisi

19. This picture depicts

   a. an Oriental pagoda

   b. a Hindu temple

   c. a Romanesque church

   d. a Moslem mosque

20. What are some of the identifying features of a Gothic cathedral?

   a. rounded arches, small windows, flying buttresses

   b. domed roof, colonnades, elaborate tympanum

   c. thin walls, pointed arches, large windows

   d. simple lines, heavy vaults, mosaic roof

21. This painting is found in

   a. St. Paul's in London

   b. the Louvre in Paris

   c. Notre Dame in Paris

   d. the Sistine Chapel in the Vatican

22. Jacob van Ruisdael, John Constable, and William Turner are best known for their

   a. book illustrations

   b. portraits

   c. still lifes

   d. landscapes

23. This painting is an example of
   a. cubism by Pablo Picasso
   b. pop art by Andy Warhol
   c. fauvism by Henri Matisse
   d. dadaism by Marcel Duchamp

24. The Great Sphinx is
   a. a Greek god to whom a huge temple was built
   b. a Roman emperor of whom a giant statue was built
   c. an Egyptian statue that stands near the Pyramids
   d. the name of the largest Egyptian pyramid

25. The painting above depicts
   a. a pietà
   b. an adoration
   c. an annunciation
   d. a crucifixion

26. For what are these men known: Federico Fellini, Ingmar Bergman, John Huston?
   a. developing the movement called pop art
   b. directing classic films
   c. experimenting with still photography
   d. perfecting the art of portraiture

27. The painting above is a typical

   a. landscape

   b. trompe l'oeil

   c. altarpiece

   d. still life

28. The art of inlaying colored tile and gold in mosaics typifies

   a. Byzantine art of the sixth century

   b. Egyptian art around 4000 B.C.

   c. Flemish art of the 1400s

   d. Nigerian art of the ninth century

29. What is this building?

    a. the Pitti Palace, built in the fifteenth century in Florence

    b. Notre Dame, built in the twelfth–fourteenth centuries in Paris

    c. the Pantheon, built in the first century B.C. in Rome

    d. Hampton Court Palace, built in the sixteenth century near London

30. Which artist helped initiate the era of abstract expressionism?

    a. Paul Gauguin

    b. Jackson Pollock

    c. Georgia O'Keeffe

    d. Henri de Toulouse-Lautrec

31. This photograph shows
   a. the Brooklyn Bridge
   b. London Bridge
   c. the Golden Gate Bridge
   d. the Bridge of Sighs

32. Frank Lloyd Wright is famous for
   a. stressing horizontal lines and "organic" architecture
   b. designing tall columns of steel and glass
   c. introducing energy efficiency to housing
   d. merging Gothic and Romanesque features with modern materials

33. This example of Islamic architecture is known as
   a. the Alhambra
   b. Santa Sophia
   c. the Qutab Minar
   d. the Taj Mahal

34. Like the Egyptian pyramids, the Mayan pyramids
   a. house crypts
   b. are made of stone or mud blocks
   c. contain carvings and paintings
   d. all of the above

35. Name the painter and subject of this portrait.

   a. Vincent van Gogh; George Sand

   b. Pablo Picasso; Gertrude Stein

   c. Andrew Wyeth; Helga

   d. Pierre Renoir; Madame Charpentier

36. The style called rococo was known for its

   a. grand scale and dramatic flair

   b. intricate and delicate decoration

   c. emphasis on line and symmetry

   d. use of themes from Norse and Roman mythology

37. What is this statue?

    a. *The Sleeping Muse* by Brancusi

    b. *Adam* by Lombardo

    c. *Recumbent Figure* by Moore

    d. *The Thinker* by Rodin

38. The Parthenon is

    a. a Doric temple dedicated to Athena in Athens

    b. a temple for worship of all gods in Rome

    c. a bridge connecting the Left Bank to Île de la Cité in Paris

    d. a museum housing European masterpieces in St. Petersburg

39. Who painted this work?

   a. Rembrandt

   b. Holbein

   c. Leonardo da Vinci

   d. Michelangelo

40. The term *bas-relief* refers to

   a. a style of painting

   b. a weaving technique

   c. a kind of sculpture

   d. a ceramic glaze

41. What is the significance of this group of stones?

   a. They were brought to England from Africa by Caesar's army.

   b. The structure was built by hand by Egyptian slaves.

   c. They may be the ruins of an arena designed by Alexander.

   d. Their arrangement indicates a possible astronomical function.

42. Artists painting in the traditional Japanese style are likely to use

   a. tempera on rice paper

   b. ink on paper or silk

   c. watercolor on canvas

   d. acrylics on oiled paper

43. This mask is typical of the traditional art of
  a. Pakistan
  b. West Africa
  c. the Seminole Indians
  d. Persia

44. Which of these painters are known for their portraits?
  a. Reynolds, Stuart, Gainsborough
  b. Turner, Constable, Delacroix
  c. Monet, Renoir, Pissarro
  d. Dürer, Bosch, Correggio

45. Name the painter and the subject of this portrait.
   a. James Whistler; John Ruskin
   b. Vincent van Gogh; Vincent van Gogh
   c. Dante Gabriel Rossetti; Raphael
   d. Mary Cassatt; Paul Cézanne

46. Which of these artists are known for their sculpture?
   a. Smith, Giacometti, Duchamp
   b. Dubuffet, Johns, Klee
   c. Magritte, Dali, Chagall
   d. Rivera, Klimt, Hopper

47. Who painted this work?

    a. Grandma Moses

    b. José Orozco

    c. Dorothea Lange

    d. Grant Wood

48. What is an aqueduct?

    a. a technique of etching that produces a wash effect

    b. a conduit built to carry water

    c. a deep well drilled into water-bearing rock

    d. an ornate shrub often pictured in Greek and Roman art

49. This painting is representative of

   a. the Ashcan school   **c.** the Hudson River school

   b. primitivism   **d.** German expressionism

50. What is this building?

   a. Mount Vernon   **c.** the Capitol

   b. the White House   **d.** Monticello

TEST 5: Explanatory Answers

1. **(b)** The Great Wall of China, fifteen hundred miles long, was built in the third century B.C. by the Ch'in dynasty to protect the country from Central Asian nomads. It averages twenty-five feet in height, and space shuttle astronauts claim it is the only landmark they can see from space.

2. **(c)** Sir Christopher Wren's (1632–1723) prominence was the result of a disaster—the Great Fire of London of 1666, which burned down St. Paul's Cathedral. Commissioned to rebuild the church, Wren designed it in the Roman baroque style, with a dome like that of St. Peter's.

3. **(a)** Michelangelo was a Renaissance sculptor, painter, and designer who believed that an artist's job, like God's, was to "make men." His *David*, completed in 1504, is considered one of the greatest statues of the Renaissance.

4. **(d)** While Doric, Ionic, and Corinthian are actually names of three Greek orders of architecture, their differences are reflected in the columns used in temple building. The Doric column is grooved or fluted and has a simple flaring capital. The Ionic column is also fluted but has a capital with a large scroll. The Corinthian column is smooth, and the capital is decorated with shoots and leaves.

5. **(c)** The picture shows a Haida Indian chieftain's house with three totem poles in front. The poles are carved to show plants, animals, and inanimate objects and depict legends that act both as a history of the tribe and a method of identifying the family.

6. **(b)** Degas, one of the best-known Impressionist painters (though he always denied being an Impressionist), usually painted people. He executed many paintings of dancers, performing or in class, as well as statues of dancers in motion.

7. **(d)** The Colosseum, completed in 80 A.D., is one of the largest single buildings in the world. It held fifty thousand spectators and was used for gladiatorial games.

8. **(a)** Alfred Eisenstaedt (b.1898) is a photographer who completed more than fifteen hundred assignments for *Life* magazine in the 1930s and 1940s. Margaret Bourke-White (1906–1971) also photographed for *Life*. She was the only American

to record the Nazi bombing of Moscow and is known for her photographs of concentration camps. Ansel Adams (1902–1984) was a landscape photographer whose photographs of the Far West show nature on a grand scale.

9. **(c)** The statue is called *Venus de Milo* and was sculpted in the first century B.C. It was found on Melos Island in Greece and is thought to belong to a group of statues that also included a Cupid.

10. **(b)** A *pietà* depicts Christ taken from the cross and held by Mary. One of the most famous pietàs is the statue by Michelangelo, now housed in St. Peter's in Rome.

11. **(a)** Originally built in 326, St. Peter's, erected on the burial site of the apostle Peter in Rome, was rebuilt in the sixteenth and seventeenth centuries. Much of the present-day building was designed by Michelangelo and Bernini. St. Peter's is a basilica, with a domed roof; it is where the pope offers Mass when he is in Rome.

12. **(d)** A fresco is a painting made on wet plaster so that the plaster absorbs the pigment. One of the most famous frescoes is Leonardo da Vinci's *Last Supper*, in Milan. Unfortunately, this fresco has faded and been damaged by pollution, and is no longer on public display.

13. **(a)** The picture shows a statue of the goddess Selket, who balances her emblem, a scorpion, on her head. Her heavily lined eyes, clothing, and stance proclaim her to be Egyptian.

14. **(b)** Rembrandt van Rijn, a Dutch painter of the seventeenth century, is known for the way he used light and shadow in his paintings. Such masterpieces as *The Man with the Golden Helmet* and *The Night Watch* clearly show that he is one of the great geniuses of Dutch art.

15. **(b)** In the Middle Ages, before the invention of the printing press, manuscripts were copied by hand, usually by monks, who were among the few literate groups of the time. Because most manuscripts were religious in nature, the monks painted, or illuminated, them with illustrations, believing that the beauty of their work added to the glory of God.

16. **(d)** Originally a palace, the Louvre was made a museum after the French Revolution. It houses Leonardo da Vinci's *Mona Lisa*, the *Venus de Milo*, Whistler's painting of his mother, and thousands of other great works of art.

17. (c) James McNeill Whistler (1834–1903) was an American who lived in Paris and London. He promoted the idea of art for art's sake, insisting that painting had no mission to fulfill and did not have to tell a story. His best-known painting, often called "Whistler's Mother," is actually titled *Arrangement in Black and Gray: The Artist's Mother.*

18. (c) Pieter Breughel the Elder (1525–1569) painted some of the earliest depictions of peasant life in European art, often concentrating on the ways in which the seasons affected his subjects. His sons Jan and Pieter the Younger were also painters and frequently used a style similar to their father's.

19. (a) Pagodas, found in China, Korea, and Japan, are used as Buddhist shrines, tombs, or memorials. They are usually built of wood or brick. This pagoda in Kyoto, Japan, dates from 951 A.D.

20. (c) Gothic architecture, a style typical of the European Middle Ages, produced a lighter, higher building than did the Romanesque style that preceded it. Pointed arches and vaults helped take the strain from the walls and allowed for larger windows and higher ceilings. High Gothic cathedrals such as the one at Chartres have flying buttresses to reduce the strain further, complex rib valuting, and elaborate decorative carvings.

21. (d) The ceiling of the Sistine Chapel, painted by Michelangelo between 1508 and 1512, depicts scenes from the Creation in the Old Testament. The section pictured shows God giving Adam the spark of life.

22. (d) Jacob van Ruisdael (c. 1629–1682) was a Dutch landscape painter of the seventeenth century. Constable (1776–1837) and Turner (1775–1851) were both British; Constable believed landscape painting should be the result of observation, whereas Turner often linked his landscapes with literary themes or historical events in the Romantic style.

23. (b) The painting, by Andy Warhol, is an example of pop art, a movement of the 1950s and 1960s whose imagery was based on American mass media. Fauvism was a movement of the turn of the century that included heavy outlines, primitive forms, and flat planes of color. Cubism, which developed at the same time, is identified by the angles and facets that make up its forms. Dadaism was an often nihilistic movement whose advocates felt that all values were made meaningless by World War I.

24. **(c)** The Great Sphinx is a statue guarding the Pyramids at Giza. It is in the shape of a lion with a human head, probably that of the pharaoh Chephren, and stands sixty-five feet high.

25. **(c)** *Annunciation,* or "announcement," refers to the moment when the Archangel Gabriel tells the Virgin Mary that she is carrying the Son of God. It is a common motif of European painting, especially painting of the Middle Ages and Renaissance. This example was painted in 1333 for Siena Cathedral by Simone Martini and Lippo Memmi.

26. **(b)** Federico Fellini (b. 1920), an Italian director, is best known for his strange, often surrealistic films, such as *La Dolce Vita, Satyricon,* and, recently, *And the Ship Sailed On.* Bergman (b. 1918), a Swedish director, has among his works *Smiles of a Summer Night, The Seventh Seal, Cries and Whispers,* and *The Magic Flute,* a film version of Mozart's opera. John Huston (1906–1987), an American, directed the films *The Maltese Falcon, The African Queen,* and, just before his death, the film version of James Joyce's "The Dead."

27. **(d)** Since ancient times people had painted inanimate objects, but in the Renaissance such paintings became a genre of their own. Masters of the art over the centuries include the van Eycks, Rubens, Rembrandt, the Peales, and Cézanne, whose *Still Life with Onions* is shown here.

28. **(a)** Mosaics, composed of inlaid colored glass, marble, tile, or gemstone, are used in many cultures. The Romans used them to decorate floors, and pre-Columbian art contains examples of this craft. The construction of Santa Sophia in Constantinople (now Istanbul) marked the pinnacle of the art form. Magnificent gold mosaics may still be seen there today.

29. **(b)** Notre Dame de Paris is an example of early Gothic architecture. It was begun in 1163 but was not completed until the fourteenth century. Its famous gargoyles were added much later.

30. **(b)** Jackson Pollock (1912–1956), influenced by the Surrealists, created a style of abstract art sometimes called "action painting." In rapid, rhythmic motions, he dripped or threw paint onto canvases, creating swirling patterns of color.

31. **(c)** The Golden Gate Bridge was built across San Francisco Bay in the 1930s. At 9,266 feet in length, it is one of the longest suspension bridges in the world.

32. **(a)** The American architect Frank Lloyd Wright (1869–1959) developed a theory of architecture stressing the needs of the people who used it. His unornamented, clean-looking buildings contained functional rooms that allowed interaction both with the rest of the building and with the landscape outside.

33. **(d)** The Taj Mahal in Agra, India, was designed by a Turk and built to house the tomb of Mumtaz Mahal by her husband, Shah Jahan. Construction took from 1630 to 1648. The dome, minarets, and intricate decoration mark it as Islamic in style.

34. **(d)** Egyptian pyramids were built around 2700 B.C.–2200 B.C. to preserve the mummified bodies of rulers. Mayan pyramids of the Yucatan and Central America were constructed some three thousand years later. Like the Egyptian pyramids, they were decorated, and they often contained tombs. Whereas the Egyptian pyramids had steep triangular sides, Mayan pyramids were built of steeply stepped blocks and often rose to ritual chambers at the summit.

35. **(b)** The facial lines in this portrait of Gertrude Stein, painted in 1906, prefigure Picasso's (1881–1973) turn to cubism.

36. **(b)** Fanciful ornamentation, shellwork, and airy asymmetry distinguished rococo art and architecture of the eighteenth century from the heavy baroque style of the seventeenth century.

37. **(d)** Auguste Rodin (1840–1917) was a French sculptor known for his work in bronze and marble. *The Thinker* was intended to be part of a great pair of doors called *The Gates of Hell*, but the doors were never finished.

38. **(a)** Built around 440 B.C., the Parthenon on the Acropolis in Athens housed vast quantities of sculpture depicting scenes from Greek mythology. In 1806 the Earl of Elgin removed many of the ancient friezes and sculptures from the Parthenon to England, where they remain in the British Museum, to the dismay of many Greeks.

39. **(c)** Arguably the most famous painting in the world, *Mona Lisa* (1503) now hangs in the Louvre. Because of his excellence in the areas of painting, sculpture, architecture, engineering, and music, Leonardo is often considered the model of the Renaissance man.

40. (c) Bas-relief is a type of sculpture in which the form projects only slightly from the surrounding surface and is not wholly separated from it.

41. (d) Stonehenge is an ancient monument in the south of England, dating back perhaps four thousand years. The stones are thought to have served a religious purpose, possibly involving the movements of the sun and stars. Although there are many theories, no one is really sure how the ancients moved the stones to this location.

42. (b) Traditional Japanese painting, beginning in the eighth century, was done with Chinese ink or watercolor on silk or paper. The paintings were either horizontal or vertical scrolls.

43. (b) Masks are used in the religious and social rituals of many cultures. This Ibo mask is a style called *opanwa*. Masks of this kind represent young girls but are worn in performances by men.

44. (a) Many painters in the eighteenth and nineteenth centuries made a living painting portraits in order to support their other, less lucrative work. Joshua Reynolds (1723–1792) painted more than two thousand portraits of English notables. Gilbert Stuart (1755–1828), an American, is best known for his paintings of George Washington, including the one reproduced on the $1 bill. Thomas Gainsborough (1727–1788) was known for his portraits but preferred landscape painting. *The Blue Boy* is one of his most famous works.

45. (b) Vincent van Gogh's (1853–1890) *Self-portrait with Palette* shows his characteristic linear brush strokes and heavy application of paint. Most of van Gogh's work was done in the two years before his death in 1890, years during which he went progressively mad.

46. (a) David Smith (1906–1965), an American, worked in steel and wrought iron. Alberto Giacometti (1901–1966) was a Swiss Surrealist who sculpted elongated forms in bronze. Marcel Duchamp (1887–1968), the French painter, was among the first to exhibit "found objects" or "ready-mades" as art.

47. (d) Grant Wood's stylized paintings of midwestern landscapes and people came to national attention through the Federal Arts Project of Franklin D. Roosevelt's administration. *American Gothic* was painted in 1930.

48. (b) An aqueduct is a pipeline or conduit that carries water from a source to where it is needed. The long, arched structures built during the Roman Empire to house conduits may still be seen in many parts of Europe.

49. (c) Romantic paintings of the American landscape were the product of the Hudson River school of the nineteenth century. *The Oxbow* by Thomas Cole, a principal member of the group, was painted in 1836. It contains typical elements of the Hudson River style: grand scale, vast sky, and detailed foreground. The Ashcan school was a group of eight American painters of different styles who banded together in the early 1900s to introduce modern European painters to the American public. Their penchant for painting everyday city scenes led to their title. At around the same time, German Expressionists were using art to express emotion and inner feeling rather than surface or objective reality. Primitivism refers to a simple, naïve style such as that of Grandma Moses (1860–1961).

50. (c) The Capitol is built on a hill in Washington, D.C., on a site selected by George Washington and the architect Pierre L'Enfant. Many architects worked on the building over time, but much of their work was destroyed by fire in the War of 1812. In 1830 the building was finished, although the dome and wings were not added until the 1860s. The Capitol is the seat of the U.S. legislature.

The Food of Love: Music

> *Music is the universal language of mankind.*
>
> —HENRY WADSWORTH LONGFELLOW

1. Which of these instruments is *not* in the woodwind family?

    a. flute   **c.** trombone

    b. bassoon   **d.** oboe

2. Ludwig van Beethoven's work includes

    a. nine symphonies and several piano concertos

    b. nine books of madrigals and three operas

    c. three nocturnes and two choral pieces

    d. four scherzos and dozens of polkas and mazurkas

3. What is a hymn?

    a. a composition for male voices

    b. a special kind of religious song

    c. a tune composed for closed-mouth vocalization

    d. a primitive kind of folk song

4. The development of the chord is part of the history of

    a. cadence   **c.** pitch

    b. harmony   **d.** ligature

5. Which of these are considered origins of jazz?
- **a.** spirituals, Caribbean music, work songs
- **b.** soul, rock and roll, rap
- **c.** folk songs, atonality, program music
- **d.** country dances, baroque music, monody

6. Which list arranges vocal ranges from highest to lowest?
- **a.** contralto, soprano, countertenor, baritone, bass
- **b.** soprano, mezzo-soprano, contralto, tenor, baritone, bass
- **c.** treble, tenor, contralto, baritone, countertenor
- **d.** soprano, contralto, tenor, bass, baritone

7. Handel's *Messiah* is an oratorio, which means that
- **a.** it is performed outdoors
- **b.** it does not use a full orchestra
- **c.** it calls for no staging or costumes
- **d.** it uses soloists in lieu of a chorus

8. Louis Armstrong is known for
- **a.** his clarinet playing and orchestration
- **b.** astonishing fingering feats on piano
- **c.** an improvisatory trumpet and vocal style
- **d.** inventing the form called "be-bop"

9. From the sixteenth century, the word *ballad* has referred to
- **a.** a dance for two partners
- **b.** any simple melody for piano or guitar
- **c.** a very short piece of music
- **d.** a story told in song

10. An octave is
- **a.** a group of eight players
- **b.** the complete work of a composer
- **c.** an interval of eight notes
- **d.** the distance between thumb and little finger on the piano

11. Who was Enrico Caruso?

    a. an Italian operatic tenor

    b. a Spanish cellist

    c. a composer of twelve-tone music

    d. a conductor of the New York Philharmonic

12. W. S. Gilbert and Sir Arthur Sullivan are known for their

    a. operas based on the lives of British heroes

    b. Broadway musical comedies

    c. orchestral arrangements for films

    d. comic operettas

13. What is a waltz?

    a. a dance involving changes of partner

    b. a very slow form of polka

    c. dance music with three beats to the bar

    d. a stately dance in 2/4 time

14. The kind of sonata written by Beethoven or Mozart

    a. has one movement and is performed by an orchestra

    b. has three or four movements and is performed by one or two instruments

    c. is in the same form as a sonata written by Bach or Handel

    d. is a vocal work containing arias and recitatives

15. George Balanchine is primarily known as a

    a. dancer

    b. composer

    c. choreographer

    d. pianist

16. If one line of music is in counterpoint with another,

    a. it harmonizes with the line but has a tune of its own

    b. it parallels the line one octave higher or lower

    c. it repeats each phrase in a minor key

    d. it exactly reverses the melody of the other

17. An overture originally was

    a. the first movement in a symphony

    b. lesser vibrations when a string is plucked

    c. a solo piece for piano or voice

    d. the opening to an oratorio or opera

18. What is the difference between rhythm and tempo?

    a. Rhythm involves speed, and tempo involves loudness.

    b. Rhythm involves pitch, and tempo involves accent.

    c. Rhythm involves beat, and tempo involves speed.

    d. There is no difference; they both involve rate and pitch.

19. Which of these instruments is *not* in the percussion family?

    a. xylophone

    b. castanet

    c. snare drum

    d. banjo

20. Duke Ellington's style of composing was novel in its

    a. emphasis on tightly structured collective improvisation

    b. lack of notation and reliance on impromptu creation

    c. elegant and unemotional arrangements of classic tunes

    d. integration of Eastern harmonics and Western rhythms

21. *Swan Lake* is likely to be part of the repertoire of

    a. a marching band

    b. a ballet company

    c. an opera company

    d. a chamber group

22. Among the compositions of John Philip Sousa is

    a. "The Stars and Stripes Forever"

    b. "Maple Leaf Rag"

    c. "Rule Britannia"

    d. "Honeysuckle Rose"

23. What is a choir?

    a. a symphony for mixed voices

    b. a vocal group that performs only church music

    c. a group of singers or the place in which they sing

    d. a song to celebrate a religious holiday or feast day

24. The word *flamenco* refers to

    a. a particular kind of music from Spain

    b. a folk dance of southern France

    c. a style of Portuguese folk song

    d. a popular Cuban ballroom dance

25. Among the compositions of Giuseppe Verdi are

    a. *The Barber of Seville, Cenerentola,* and *William Tell*

    b. *Aïda, Otello,* and *Il Trovatore*

    c. *Lohengrin, Parsifal,* and *Tristan und Isolde*

    d. *La Bohème, Madame Butterfly,* and *Tosca*

26. Bach, Telemann, and Handel were composers of the

    a. classical period

    b. baroque period

    c. romantic period

    d. rococo period

27. What is a melody?

    a. a logical succession of single musical notes

    b. a structure of chords

    c. a body of singers with several performers for each part

    d. a written symbol used to represent duration and pitch

28. The composer of the *Brandenburg Concertos*, the *Mass in B Minor*, and *The Well-Tempered Clavier* is

    a. Philip Glass

    b. Peter Ilyich Tchaikovsky

    c. Johann Sebastian Bach

    d. Ludwig van Beethoven

29. For what was Billie Holiday best known?

    a. her interpretation of the roles of Aïda and Mimi in *La Bohème*

    b. collaborating with Oscar Hammerstein to write *South Pacific*

    c. interpreting and singing the blues and popular music

    d. winning the Brussels Music Competition at the age of twelve

30. *Afternoon of a Faun*, *Les Sylphides*, and *Parade* are all

    a. ballets

    b. operas

    c. cantatas

    d. none of the above

31. Igor Stravinsky composed

    a. *Der Rosenkavalier*, *Salomé*, and *Don Quixote*

    b. *The Moldau*, *Czech Dances*, and *The Bartered Bride*

    c. *The Firebird*, *The Rites of Spring*, and *Petroushka*

    d. *The Heir Apparent* and *Maharajah*

32. What is a symphony?

   a. a vocal work with instrumental accompaniment

   b. an orchestral work, usually in three or four movements

   c. a dance in slow 3/4 time with syncopated rhythms

   d. a sacred text set to music for chorus, soloists, and orchestra

33. *Das Rheingold, Die Walküre, Siegfried,* and *Die Götterdämmerung* are

   a. a series of ballets by Peter Ilyich Tchaikovsky

   b. a group of cantatas by Johann Sebastian Bach

   c. a cycle of operas by Richard Wagner

   d. a collection of symphonies by Ludwig van Beethoven

34. What is chamber music?

   a. instrumental music limited to a few performers

   b. opera performed in a small room, or chamber

   c. organ music performed in the chamber adjoining a church nave

   d. a work in several movements intended for evening entertainment

35. Which instruments belong to the brass family?

   a. violin, viola, cello, bass

   b. harpsichord, piano, accordion, organ

   c. flute, oboe, bassoon, clarinet

   d. cornet, trombone, tuba, flügelhorn

36. Johannes Brahms was a master of

   a. the symphony

   b. chamber music

   c. the sonata

   d. all of the above

37. What is a concerto?

    a. a work in which a soloist contrasts with other instruments

    b. a small group of performers playing different instruments

    c. a dance in 3/4 time that came into popularity during the eighteenth century

    d. a song for two or three voices to a text about the birth of Christ

38. When a musical piece builds to a crescendo,

    a. a chorus joins in

    b. it gets louder

    c. the wind section joins in

    d. it gets quieter

39. Among Aaron Copland's compositions are

    a. *The Three-Cornered Hat* and *Nights in the Gardens of Spain*

    b. *Krazy Kat*, *Skyscrapers*, and *Adventures in a Perambulator*

    c. *Billy the Kid*, *Rodeo*, and *Appalachian Spring*

    d. *Shaneurs* and *At Dawning*

40. When and where might you have danced the minuet?

    a. England in the sixteenth century

    b. France in the seventeenth century

    c. Germany in the nineteenth century

    d. Italy in the fourteenth century

41. What is harmony?

    a. the bass line in a choral piece

    b. a recurring theme in a musical composition symbolizing an idea or object

    c. the structure and relationships of chords

    d. a change of key

42. *Eugene Onegin, Romeo and Juliet,* and *Sleeping Beauty* are compositions by

  a. Frédéric Chopin

  b. Giacomo Puccini

  c. Richard Strauss

  d. Peter Ilyich Tchaikovsky

43. The string section of an orchestra includes

  a. xylophone, triangle, and cymbals

  b. bassoon, piccolo, oboe, and flute

  c. cello, viola, double bass, and violin

  d. lute, guitar, theorboe, and chitarrone

44. *La Traviata, Carmen,* and *Madame Butterfly* are examples of

  a. operas

  b. ballets

  c. études

  d. symphonies

45. *Don Giovanni, Eine kleine Nachtmusik,* and *The Magic Flute* are works by

  a. Ludwig van Beethoven

  b. Gian-Carlo Menotti

  c. Wolfgang Amadeus Mozart

  d. Henry Purcell

46. What is a synthesizer?

  a. a wind instrument similar to the oboe

  b. an electronic apparatus that can produce musical sounds

  c. a device used by composers to vary the stress on notes

  d. the section of an organ that increases or diminishes the volume of sound

47. Which of these composers wrote during the romantic period?

   a. Haydn, Mozart, and Gluck

   b. Monteverdi, Vivaldi, and Scarlatti

   c. Schubert, Brahms, and Mendelssohn

   d. Bartok, Debussy, and Schoenberg

48. George Gershwin is the composer of

   a. *Orpheus in Hades* and *Tales of Hoffman*

   b. *Porgy and Bess*, *Rhapsody in Blue*, and *An American in Paris*

   c. *Schelomo*, *Baal Shem*, and *Sacred Service*

   d. *The Three-Penny Opera*, *Down in the Valley*, and *Mahagonny*

49. Chopin is best known for

   a. operas and symphonies

   b. ballets and chorales

   c. mazurkas and études

   d. all of the above

50. The sitar, the tabla, and the sarangi are all

   a. dances from Indonesia

   b. musical instruments from India

   c. musical instruments from Japan

   d. Middle Eastern religious chants

TEST 6: *Explanatory Answers*

   1. **(c)** At one time all woodwind instruments were made of wood. Even when made of metal, woodwinds share certain qualities: They are essentially tubular, with holes along the length of the tube. The holes are covered or uncovered to produce notes of different pitches. Oboes, clarinets, flutes, piccolos, saxophones, bagpipes, and recorders are all woodwinds. The trombone, which has a very different mouthpiece from a woodwind, is in the brass family.

2. **(a)** Beethoven (1770–1827) was a pianist in Bonn and Vienna. At the end of the eighteenth century he began to lose his hearing, and from that time he concentrated on composing. His music brought drama and expressiveness to the old classical forms. His nine symphonies, five piano concertos, one violin concerto, and countless chamber pieces still form a major part of the classical repertoire.

3. **(b)** For centuries hymns were written in Latin and sung by priests. Not until the Reformation of the sixteenth century did the idea that ordinary people could sing in praise of God catch on. Chorales and psalms became popular in the reformed churches, and composers began to write specifically for the church.

4. **(b)** A chord is a group of notes played at the same time. At one time, melody was played as a single line or harmonized by octaves so that high C and middle C might be played at the same time, for example. In the eleventh century, lines of melody sometimes moved in parallel fifths so that middle C and G would be sounded together, for example. Chords were a later invention, based on the concept that every note could form the root of a series of harmonic notes. A common chord is a chord including the root (C, for example), the third above it (E), and the fifth above it (G).

5. **(a)** Basic jazz forms use syncopated rhythms, improvisation, and certain select harmonic sequences. The origins of jazz are many, but key among them are work songs, blues, gospel, spirituals, ragtime, and various Latin styles.

6. **(b)** Female voices are divided by pitch into three classes: soprano (the highest), mezzo-soprano, and contralto. The highest adult male voice is the countertenor, followed by tenor, baritone, and bass. The highest boy's voice is treble, followed by alto.

7. **(c)** An oratorio is something like an opera, except that it is usually performed without action or scenery. The chorus plays a large part in any oratorio, linking arias sung by soloists with stretches of choral music. In a true oratorio the theme is religious.

8. **(c)** Louis Armstrong (1900–1971) came from the New Orleans jazz tradition. He played trumpet on riverboats before moving to Chicago and then New York, where he played in Fletcher Henderson's big band. He triumphed as a solo player with his own bands in the 1920s and 1930s and then went on to a career that included scat singing and movie roles.

9. **(d)** A ballad is a song based on a narrative poem. Traditional folk songs such as "Barbara Allen" and "Casey Jones" are ballads.

10. **(c)** *Octo* is a root meaning "eight," and an octave is the eight notes that make up a scale. Acoustically, a note one octave above another has twice its frequency. These intervals of eight notes are a key element of Western music.

11. **(a)** Caruso (1873–1921) had an astonishing range and great power, but his real fame derives from the fact that he was the first great opera star to be recorded and thus was the first to live on after his career ended.

12. **(d)** Sir Arthur Sullivan, an English composer, teamed with lyricist W. S. Gilbert in the 1870s and 1880s to create such popular operettas as *The Mikado, The Pirates of Penzance,* and *H.M.S. Pinafore.* They were so successful that impresario Richard D'Oyly Carte constructed a theater called the Savoy expressly for their work.

13. **(c)** A waltz is a piece of music in 3/4 time, usually meant for dancing. Derived from peasant dances of Austria and Bavaria, it reached the height of its popularity in the mid-1800s.

14. **(b)** The baroque sonata, such as those composed by Handel and Bach, is a work for solo instrument made up of several movements. The classical sonata, such as those composed by Beethoven and Mozart, is written for keyboard or for keyboard and one other instrument. It may have three or four movements. The first movement is in "sonata form," which means that it consists of a musical statement containing several themes, a section that elaborates on the themes, and a section that returns to the original statement.

15. **(c)** Balanchine (1904–1983) was a dancer with Diaghilev and his Ballets Russes before moving to the United States in 1933. He helped to found the School of American Ballet and worked as artistic director and principal choreographer of the New York City Ballet for more than thirty years. His choreography emphasized form over story and featured movement applied over the musical structure of a piece.

16. **(a)** Counterpoint is a form of harmony in which melodies are played in conjunction with one another or interwoven. In the simplest form, a fixed melodic line is written, and a note is

written to harmonize with each note of the fixed line. More elaborate forms use inversions, in which an upper part becomes a lower part and vice versa, and imitations, where the second part repeats the first part while the first part continues.

17. **(d)** *Overture* is from the French word *ouverture*, or "opening." It once referred exclusively to orchestral music that opened an opera or oratorio, but in the nineteenth century the term was applied to short, independent orchestral compositions in sonata form, now called concert overtures.

18. **(c)** Rhythm is the beat of a piece of music and the pattern of notes that make up that beat. *Tempo* means "time" in Italian, and the word is used to describe the pace at which a piece is to be played.

19. **(d)** Percussion instruments are those instruments whose sound derives from a tap or blow from the player. Percussion was not in use in orchestras except in special effects until the late nineteenth century. Percussion instruments include drums, bells, triangles, cymbals, pianos, xylophones, and rattles. The banjo is a member of the string family.

20. **(a)** Considered one of the foremost composers of the twentieth century, Ellington (1899–1975) perfected a form of jazz that combined intricately structured written work with improvisation. Working with many of the best artists in the jazz world, Ellington created compositions around the talents of his band members, allowing their creativity to merge with his structure in a process of collaborative composition that many artists today try to emulate. Pieces such as "Mood Indigo" and "Take the A Train" were immensely popular, and Ellington's musicianship and composing ability helped make jazz a recognized art form.

21. **(b)** Tchaikovsky's three ballets, *Swan Lake*, *Sleeping Beauty*, and *The Nutcracker*, choreographed by Lev Ivanov and Marius Petipa, are among the most famous and popular of all ballets in the classical repertoire.

22. **(a)** Sousa led the U.S. Marine Corps band for twelve years in the late 1800s and then went on to lead his own band. He is famous for composing dozens of marches, of which "The Stars and Stripes Forever" is perhaps the best known.

23. **(c)** A choir is simply a group of singers, and the word may also refer to the part of a cathedral between the sanctuary and the nave used by singers in a church choir.

24. **(a)** A mournful song from Andalusia, Spain, is the basis for flamenco. The rhythm and melody derive from Arabic music of Spain's Moorish conquerors. The dance that accompanies this music is highly dramatic and energetic.

25. **(b)** All of the works listed are operas, but only these three are by Giuseppe Verdi (1813–1901), one of the greatest opera composers of all time. Other operas by Verdi include *Rigoletto, La Traviata, Don Carlo, Macbeth,* and *Falstaff.* The other operas listed are by Rossini, Wagner, and Puccini.

26. **(b)** Baroque music was, like the architecture of the time, both lavish and precise. Johann Sebastian Bach (1685–1760), George Frederick Handel (1685–1759), and Georg Telemann (1748–1831) were three of the best-known composers of the period. Opera, oratorio, cantata, suite, sonata, and fugue originated during this time.

27. **(a)** A melody is usually a simple strand of music that is developed in a musical composition against a harmonic background.

28. **(c)** Johann Sebastian Bach (1685–1750), a German composer of the eighteenth century, incorporated the forms of German music, the Italian concerto, and French dance music into his compositions. He brought the forms of fugue, suite, and canon to their greatest expression. More than one thousand of his compositions survive.

29. **(c)** Billie Holiday (1915–1959), also known as Lady Day, had a unique singing style and method of interpreting the blues. One of her best-known songs, "Strange Fruit," is the story of a lynching; she invests the song with a vibrant power that brings out the truth in the words. Critics often compare her singing voice to a horn, but in phrasing and in feeling, she moves far beyond the range of any instrument. She died at forty-four, a victim of drug addiction.

30. **(a)** *Prélude à l'après-midi d'un faune* (1890) by Debussy, *Les Sylphides* (1909) from music by Chopin, and *Parade* (1917) by Eric Satie are ballets, or dances in which performers dance to music to tell a story or set a mood. All three ballets were commissioned by Sergei Diaghilev of the Ballets Russes; *Afternoon of a Faun* was choreographed as a vehicle for the great dancer Nijinsky.

31. **(c)** Igor Stravinsky (1882–1971) was a composer whose ballets, such as *The Firebird, The Rites of Spring,* and *Pe-*

troushka, commissioned by Diaghilev, earned him his fame. He used dissonance, polytonality, and asymmetrical rhythm to produce a distinctive sound.

32. **(b)** Symphonies evolved from the Italian operatic overture of the seventeenth century, which had three movements. After the mid-eighteenth century, a fourth movement was often added. Mozart, Beethoven, and Brahms were masters of the symphonic form.

33. **(c)** *Der Ring des Nibelungen* is a series of four operas by Richard Wagner that took twenty-eight years to produce. The operas tell of a ring made by dwarves that gives its owner mastery of the world, of the love of Siegfried and Brünnhilde, and of the way in which the curse of the ring kills Siegfried and drives Brünnhilde to her own death.

34. **(a)** Chamber music was originally intended to be played in a room in a house, rather than a church or hall. Now it usually refers to music written for a few performers, each playing a different part; it emphasizes clarity and balance.

35. **(d)** Brass instruments are wind instruments that transmit a tone by the vibration of the player's lips. They include trumpet, French horn, trombone, tuba, cornet, flügelhorn, saxhorn, and sousaphone. They are usually made of brass today, though in the past they were made of wood, horn, and glass.

36. **(d)** Johannes Brahms (1833–1897) was a German composer, a contemporary of Liszt and Schumann. He was a conductor and music director for the Prince of Lippe-Detmold. His compositions include four symphonies, concerti, sonatas, character pieces, and chorales.

37. **(a)** *Concerto* is a term that has gone through several meanings. Until the early eighteenth century it was a vocal work with instrumental accompaniment. Bach's *Third Brandenburg* was a concerto for several instruments. A *concerto grosso* provides instrumental solos, and the solo concerto, now the best-known type, has a solo instrument against an orchestra. The one point that all concertos have in common is that they provide a musical contrast: between voice and orchestra, instrument and orchestra, or instrument and instrument.

38. **(b)** *Crescendo* is an Italian term that means "increasing." Music that builds to a crescendo gets louder. The term does not specify a degree of loudness.

39. (c) Born in 1900, Aaron Copland is one of America's greatest composers. He has written three symphonies, chamber music, ballets, an opera, piano music, and music for films. The other pieces mentioned are by Manuel de Falla, John Carpenter, and Percy Atherton.

40. (b) The minuet is a French dance in 3/4 time, introduced around 1650. It was used often in ballets and instrumental pieces until Beethoven quickened its tempo and it became the scherzo.

41. (c) Harmony, once a term that meant music, now means the relationship of chords, their structure and function. Traditional harmonic theory began in the baroque era and lasted until the late nineteenth century, when composers began to find alternatives to traditional harmony.

42. (d) Tchaikovsky (1840–1893) was a Russian composer known for his romantic compositions. He wrote eleven operas, seven symphonies, four suites, more than one hundred songs, and some of today's best-loved ballets.

43. (c) The string section of the orchestra is made up of instruments on which gut or metal wire is bowed, plucked, struck, or rubbed, producing a sound. These instruments include, in order of size, violin, viola, cello, and double bass.

44. (a) *La Traviata* (1853) by Guiseppe Verdi, *Carmen* (1875) by Georges Bizet, and *Madame Butterfly* (1904) by Giacomo Puccini are all operas, stage works that are completely or mostly sung. Opera began in Italy, where a group of composers, using the idea of Greek drama with its cadences and chorus, began setting words to music. *Euridice* (1600) by Jacopo Peri is considered the first opera. Some of the best-known composers of opera are Verdi, Wagner, Mozart, and Puccini.

45. (c) Mozart (1756–1791) was an Austrian whom many consider to be the greatest composer of all time. He began composing at the age of five and wrote his first symphony at nine. He was influenced by Bach, Handel, and Haydn. In all he wrote more than six hundred works, and his mastery of all classical forms makes his work the epitome of classical music.

46. (b) The synthesizer, invented by Robert Moog in 1965, produced a revolution in electronic composition. The system, usually with a keyboard, can memorize, change, and play musical sounds.

47. (c) The romantic period is said to have lasted from about 1820 to 1910. National styles of composition grew popular, and the role of the orchestra became more important. Romantic composers were concerned with the musical past and used influences from the past to write lyrical compositions. As Romantics in philosophy and literature changed their emphases from the universal to the individual, so too in music romanticism focused on the composer as creator and the performer as interpreter, a trend that continues today.

48. (b) George Gershwin (1898–1937) was an American composer whose concert works join the sounds of jazz with those of traditional orchestration. His opera *Porgy and Bess* is a love story set among a group of black workers in South Carolina; it was considered the first successful American opera. The other works listed are by Jacques Offenbach, Ernest Bloch, and Kurt Weill.

49. (c) Frédéric Chopin (1810–1849), a composer of the Romantic school, wrote mostly for the piano. He composed fifty-one mazurkas, twelve polonaises, seventeen waltzes, and twenty-seven études, as well as nocturnes, sonatas, and ballads.

50. (b) Indian music is based on a system of melodic modes called ragas and rhythms called talas. Each raga is performed at a certain time of day or of the year. Indian instruments include the sitar (a large lute), the sarod (a short-necked lute), the sarangi (a stringed instrument), the tabla (a set of drums), and the tamboura (a droning lute).

All's Right with the World: Myth and Religion

Religion in its humility restores man to his only dignity, the courage to live by grace.

—GEORGE SANTAYANA

1. What is Original Sin?
   a. the first sin that a person commits in his or her life
   b. any sin resulting from disobedience of the Ten Commandments
   c. sin resulting from Adam's and Eve's eating of the forbidden fruit
   d. any one of the Seven Deadly Sins

2. What is Mecca?
   a. the holy city of Islam
   b. a directional point on the compass to which religious believers bow when praying
   c. the Egyptian goddess of the River Nile
   d. the Buddhist heaven

3. Isis, Re, and Osiris are all
   a. Hindu prophets
   b. Mayan gods

    c. Scandinavian warrior-gods

    d. Egyptian gods

4. Who was John the Baptist?

    a. the author of the Gospel according to St. John

    b. the man who baptized Christ

    c. one of the twelve apostles of Christ

    d. all of the above

5. Mount Olympus and Asgard are

    a. locations of temples to Apollo

    b. sites of religious pilgrimages

    c. legendary homes of the gods

    d. two of the great pyramids

6. Why was Job considered to be so patient?

    a. He withstood Satan's testing and kept his faith in God.

    b. He followed Christ despite the mockery of his family.

    c. He waited for Moses when Moses went to speak with God.

    d. He did not protest when God refused to accept his sacrifice.

7. What is the Koran?

    a. the ark in which the Jewish holy book is kept

    b. the church built over Christ's tomb in Jerusalem

    c. the name for Moses' Ten Commandments

    d. the holy book of Islam

8. Aphrodite (Venus) was the goddess of

    a. erotic love and marriage

    b. war

    c. the hunt and wild animals

    d. the hearth

9. Methodist, Presbyterian, and Unitarian are names of

    a. the Gospels

    b. Protestant sects

    c. levels in the Catholic hierarchy

    d. Anglican sects

10. What was Charon's job?

    a. He held the world on his shoulders.

    b. He had to find and bring back the Golden Fleece.

    c. He was responsible for answering the Sphinx's riddle.

    d. He ferried the dead across the River Styx to Elysium.

11. The story of Noah involves

    a. the journey out of slavery in Egypt to Israel

    b. the denial of Christ before his crucifixion

    c. an ark built to escape a flood inflicted by God

    d. a wrestling match with an angel

12. Who was Thor?

    a. the Roman god of healing

    b. the Greek god of eloquence and good fortune

    c. the Norse god of thunder

    d. the war god of the Assyrians

13. What is the Torah?

    a. a valley near Jerusalem where the dead are buried

    b. the first five books of the Old Testament

    c. a feast that celebrates the harvest season

    d. the candle that burns between Easter and Ascension Day

14. Athena (Minerva) was the goddess of

    a. war, wisdom, and crafts

    b. the waters and the rainbow

    c. the harvest

    d. fertility and wine

15. Matthew, Mark, Luke, and John were

    a. saints of the Middle Ages who were killed by Muslims

    b. the first kings in the Middle East to convert to Christianity

    c. evangelists who wrote gospels on Jesus' life

    d. apostles who followed Jesus

16. For what is Lazarus known?

    a. writing the book of the Apocalypse

    b. being raised from the dead by Jesus

    c. returning home as the prodigal son

    d. aiding a man who was robbed by thieves

17. What is a phoenix?

    a. a bird that rises from its own ashes

    b. a bird that feeds on elephant calves and possesses a huge egg

    c. a sea monster that makes dangerous whirlpools when surfacing

    d. a monster that is part lion, part goat, and part serpent

18. What was the result of the building of the Tower of Babel?

    a. God flooded the earth for forty days and nights.

    b. God demanded that Abraham sacrifice his son.

    c. God appeared as a burning bush to express his anger.

    d. God confounded the speech of men so that they could not understand each other.

19. A Dionysian celebration, or Bacchanalia, is

    a. a solemn feast during which a goat is slaughtered to worship the gods

    b. a dance at which young virgins are picked as wives by warriors

    c. a revel in which wine and sex are the foremost entertainments

d. a religious rite honoring Dionysus in which candles, signifying eternal life, are burned

20. The Good Samaritan was

a. the man who gave Jesus wine as he hung on the cross

b. a man who helped the victim of a brutal robbery

c. another name for John, who comforted Mary after the Crucifixion

d. a man who gave away all of his riches to follow Jesus

21. In Greek and Roman mythology, the supreme god was known as

a. Apollo

b. Hades or Pluto

c. Mars or Ares

d. Zeus or Jupiter

22. On Yom Kippur, worshippers

a. celebrate the freeing of Jews from slavery in Egypt

b. commemorate the victory of the Maccabees over the Assyrians

c. celebrate the new year

d. fast to atone for their sins

23. In the Book of Revelation, Armageddon is

a. the place where the last battle between good and evil will take place

b. the horseman of the Apocalypse representing Death

c. another name for the Antichrist

d. the mountain on which Jesus stood when Satan tempted him

24. The nine goddesses of the arts were called

a. the Graces

b. the Harpies

    c. the Muses

    d. the Sirens

25. What did the thirty pieces of silver buy?

    a. Jesus' robe as he hung on the cross

    b. Judas's betrayal of Christ

    c. the food for the Last Supper

    d. Joseph's freedom from Potiphar

26. In the Bible, what is the significance of the god Baal?

    a. He is denounced as a false god.

    b. He takes over the kingdom of heaven.

    c. He represents greed and love of money.

    d. He causes a great flood.

27. Our word *narcissism* derives from a myth about

    a. a young woman who cared more for objects than for love

    b. a man who fell in love with his own reflection

    c. a couple torn apart by Zeus and Aphrodite

    d. the goddess of spring

28. What was the Holy Grail?

    a. the shroud covering the dead Christ

    b. a sliver of the true cross

    c. the staff carried by Jesus as he traveled to Jerusalem

    d. a mythic talisman sought by the knights of the Round Table

29. The Garden of Eden represents

    a. a state of innocence

    b. the path to righteousness

    c. life after death

    d. the uninterrupted dream

30. In the story of Cain and Abel, Cain

    a. was slain by Abel, who denied the deed

    b. killed his brother out of jealousy

    c. was the only son of Adam and Eve

    d. sacrified Abel to the Lord out of piety

31. What was the title given to Siddhartha Gautama?

    a. Huitzilopochti

    b. Apostle

    c. Buddha

    d. Krishna

32. Martin Luther is known for

    a. working with the civil rights movement

    b. founding the Church of England

    c. leading the Protestant Reformation

    d. ruling the Holy Roman Empire

33. What do these names have in common: Elohim, Allah, Brahma?

    a. They are all names of prophets.

    b. They are all names for God.

    c. They are all found in the Bible.

    d. They are all found in the Koran.

34. The Ten Commandments given to Moses by God include

    a. laws forbidding murder and theft

    b. freedom of speech

    c. prophecies about the coming of Christ

    d. descriptions of the apocalypse

35. In Greek and Roman mythology, Phoebus Apollo was

    a. the god of music and of light

    b. the ruler of the underworld

    c. the brother of Zeus (Jupiter)

    d. the motherless god of wisdom

36. The phrase *Immaculate Conception* refers to

    a. the belief that Jesus was the son of God

b. the concept that true believers can be saved

c. the idea that Mary was free from Original Sin

d. a movement of mystics and alchemists in the 1700s

37. According to Islam, Muhammad was

   a. the last of the prophets, following Abraham, Moses, and Jesus

   b. the one true god, whom all Muslims must obey without question

   c. the eighth incarnation of the great god Vishnu

   d. the author of the *Tao-te-ching*

38. What was the kingdom of the god Poseidon?

   a. the heavens

   b. the land of the dead

   c. the ocean

   d. none of the above

39. Sodom and Gomorrah were

   a. wicked people

   b. cities

   c. prophets

   d. Hindu gods

40. Eros was the god of

   a. athletic ability

   b. art

   c. peace

   d. love

41. What do these names have in common: Leviticus, Deuteronomy, Ruth?

   a. They are all names of prophets.

   b. They are all apostles of Christ.

   c. They are books of the Old Testament.

   d. They are characters in the New Testament.

42. The phrase *Achilles' heel* refers to

    a. the fulfillment of a prophecy despite a person's will

    b. a traitorous act against a former friend or leader

    c. the tendency to follow a leader blindly into battle

    d. a point of vulnerability on an otherwise strong person

43. When Pandora's box was opened,

    a. the first woman was created

    b. the Muses were set free

    c. evil was released into the world

    d. the winds and clouds flew out

44. What is the goal of Hinduism?

    a. divine assistance

    b. freedom from rebirth and suffering

    c. spiritual ecstasy

    d. worldwide recognition of the power of prayer

45. What is Ramadan?

    a. the festival of lights in Jewish tradition

    b. a manifestation of the Great Spirit of the Sioux

    c. the largest Mayan temple, dedicated to Kulkulcán

    d. the ninth month of the Muslim year

46. Daedalus designed

    a. the Minotaur and the Gorgons

    b. the Parthenon

    c. a labyrinth and a method of flight

    d. the palace of the gods

47. The story of David and Goliath represents

    a. the triumph of the slave over his oppressor

    b. the power of the righteous against all odds

    c. the discovery of an honorable man

    d. the loss of innocence and the building of an empire

48. Because of her beauty, Helen of Troy

    a. was stolen from her husband and precipitated a war

    b. displeased the goddess Athena and was condemned to die

    c. became the symbol of unrequited love

    d. was adored by Lancelot and caused the fall of a kingdom

49. The story of the prodigal son is a parable about

    a. a child who shows remarkable talent in music

    b. the unforgiving nature of man and God

    c. predictions made by a soothsayer about a young prince

    d. a repentant sinner's return to his father's house

50. The adventures of Theseus included

    a. a war against the Amazons

    b. the killing of the Minotaur

    c. removing a sword from under a stone

    d. all of the above

TEST 7: Explanatory Answers

1. (c) Original Sin, according to Christian theology, is held by all people at birth and results from Adam and Eve's disobedience to God in eating the fruit of the Tree of Knowledge. Original Sin can be removed by baptism.

2. (a) Mecca, a city in what is now Saudi Arabia, was the birthplace of Muhammad and is the holiest city of the Islamic religion. Pious Muslims are urged to journey to Mecca at least once in their lifetimes. Muslims, when praying, face in the direction of Mecca.

3. (d) In Egypt the sun was venerated as the greatest god and was called Re. Osiris was the god of the funerary cult, a hero who had died and been resurrected. Isis was the wife and sister of Osiris; she was the patron goddess of mariners.

4. (b) John the Baptist, born to St. Anne late in her life, heralded the coming of Christ in his sermons in the wilderness. He baptized Christ, beginning his ministry. He was imprisoned by Herod Antipas for denouncing Herod's marriage to his brother's wife and was beheaded at the request of Salome, Herod's stepdaughter.

5. (c) On the border of Thessaly and Macedonia stands Mt. Olympus, 9,800 feet high, purported to be the home of the Greek gods. Asgard, on the other hand, is not a real place but is supposed to be the center of the universe, according to Norse mythology. The gods lived in its many halls and mansions, the most famous of which was Valhalla.

6. (a) Job was tested by Satan, who took his wealth and his children and afflicted him with boils; however, Job kept his patience and his faith, as God knew he would, and eventually God rewarded him.

7. (d) The Koran is considered by Muslims to be the word of God, revealed to Muhammad by the angel Gabriel. It has its basis in the Judeo-Christian tradition and was transmitted orally for hundreds of years before it was written down.

8. (a) Aphrodite (Venus in Roman mythology) was the Greek goddess of love and marriage. She was born from the foam that bubbled about the severed parts of the castrated Uranus. She was the wife of Hephaestus and the lover of Ares; her child was Eros. The gods of the other areas mentioned are Ares (Mars), Artemis (Diana), and Hestia (Vesta).

9. (b) John Wesley was the founder of Methodism, which began at Oxford University in the 1720s. The name was originally used derisively because the group of believers were so regular in their meetings and prayers. Presbyterianism is another Protestant sect, based on the Calvinist creed, which states that salvation is predetermined. The presbyters, or elders of the church, govern the church for the members. Unitarianism, also a Protestant sect, rejects the idea of the Trinity and holds that God is one being. It affirms reason, conscience, tolerance, and a belief in the universal brotherhood of man.

10. (d) Charon, the ferryman of the River Styx, ferried the dead to the fields of Elysium, a land of perfect happiness. Greek dead were customarily buried with a coin in their mouth, payment for Charon. The idea of crossing a river to reach the land of the dead is older than Greek mythology; it appears in Egyptian and Mesopotamian mythology as well.

11. **(c)** Noah, one of the few faithful left on earth, was told by God that civilization would be destroyed by a flood that would last forty days and nights. Noah built an ark and populated it with two of each kind of animal. His family rode out the flood with the creatures. Most religions and mythologies, including Hinduism and Babylonian, Greek, and Hittite mythology, have a flood story.

12. **(c)** The Norse god Thor was the son of Odin, leader of the gods. He was the most widely worshipped of Norse gods and was known as man's protector. The word *Thursday* comes from his name.

13. **(b)** The Torah is the first five books of the Old Testament. It is also the word used for the scroll, kept in every Jewish synagogue, on which these five books, or Pentateuch, are written. In Christianity, these five books are referred to as Genesis, Exodus, Leviticus, Numbers, and Deuteronomy.

14. **(a)** Born fully armed from the head of Zeus, Athena (Minerva in Roman mythology) was the goddess of war and helped to defeat the giants when they stormed Olympus. She was also the goddess of wisdom and of handicrafts. The city of Athens was named after her, and the Parthenon was dedicated to her.

15. **(c)** The evangelists who wrote the Gospels are generally supposed to have been different people from the original apostles and to have written their works up to seventy years after the crucifixion. The Gospel of Matthew is the most complete account of Jesus' sayings and is called the Gospel of the Son of David; the Gospel of Mark is an account of Jesus' actions and is called the Gospel of the Son of God. St. Luke wrote the *Acts of the Apostles* as well as a Gospel, which is called the Gospel of the Saviour; St. John's Gospel is the most spiritual of the four and is called the Gospel of the Word.

16. **(b)** Lazarus, a New Testament figure who was the brother of Mary and Martha of Bethany, died and was raised from the dead by Jesus four days later.

17. **(a)** The phoenix, a mythical Arabian bird, builds a pyre every five hundred years and immolates itself. A new phoenix then rises from the ashes and, some say, flies with the remains of its parent to Heliopolis in Egypt. The idea of a bird that burns

itself and is reborn also appears in myths of the Aztecs and Mayans, the Chinese, and the Japanese.

18. **(d)** The story of the Tower of Babel is a Biblical explanation for the differences among languages. Determined to reach heaven and see God, Noah's descendants built a huge tower; but God, displeased with their presumption, struck all mankind with the inability to understand one another's speech.

19. **(c)** Dionysius, or Bacchus in Roman mythology, was the son of Zeus and a mortal woman. He introduced wine to the world, but when driven mad by Hera, he wandered the earth inciting his followers to wild, drunken revelry.

20. **(b)** The story of the Good Samaritan is a parable from the Gospel of St. Luke. It tells of a man stripped and wounded by thieves and of the Samaritan who found and took care of him. Jesus' message after the parable was "Go and do thou likewise." Nowadays, "Good Samaritan" is a phrase that describes anyone who helps someone in need.

21. **(d)** Zeus (Jupiter or Jove in Roman mythology) was the king of the gods. He was the son of Chronos and Rhea, husband to Hera, and father, by various goddesses and humans, of the Graces, Persephone, Apollo, Artemis, Athena, Ares, Hermes, Dionysius, Heracles, Perseus, Helen, and Clytemnestra.

22. **(d)** Yom Kippur, the Day of Atonement, falls on the tenth day of the seventh month in the Jewish calendar. It is the last of ten days of atonement, which begin on Rosh Hashanah, the Jewish new year.

23. **(a)** St. John the Divine, a prisoner on the Greek island of Patmos, had a vision in which he saw the Day of Judgment. This prompted him to write the Book of Revelation, a description of the end of the world and the triumph of Christ. Before Judgment Day the forces of good and evil will fight on the plain of Armageddon.

24. **(c)** The Muses, the nine daughters of Zeus and Mnemosyne, were Calliope, muse of the epic; Clio, muse of history; Erato, muse of erotic poetry; Euterpe, muse of lyric poetry; Melpomene, muse of tragedy; Polyhymnia, muse of hymns; Terpsichore, muse of dance; Thalia, muse of comedy; and Urania, muse of astronomy.

25. **(b)** Judas Iscariot, one of Christ's disciples, betrayed Jesus for thirty pieces of silver by identifying him with a kiss in the

Garden of Gethsemane. As a result, Jesus was arrested, tried, and crucified; in remorse, Judas returned the money and hanged himself. The story of the betrayal at Gethsemane is told in the gospels of Mark and Matthew.

26. **(a)** Baal was the name of various gods of the Canaanites, gods who required human sacrifice. Denounced by the prophets as false gods, Baal became equated with evil. *Beelzebub*, from *Baal*, is a name for the devil.

27. **(b)** Narcissus was a beautiful and vain young man. When he rejected the love of the nymph Echo, she pined away until only her voice remained. In punishment he was forced by a goddess to fall in love with his own reflection. He too pined away for love, leaving only a small flower in his place.

28. **(d)** There are many theories about the Grail. Once it was assumed to be the chalice from which Christ drank at the Last Supper. Joseph of Arimathea caught some drops of the crucified Christ's blood in the chalice, and it sustained him through imprisonment and hardship. The chalice then passed through various hands until at last it reached Sir Galahad of King Arthur's Round Table. More recent theories claim that the Grail was an ancient fertility symbol. Whatever its origin, the quest for the Grail is one of the great Western literary themes, appearing in works from Chrétien de Troyes' *Perceval* (c. 1185) to T. S. Eliot's *The Waste Land* (1922).

29. **(a)** Adam and Eve were placed by God in the Garden of Eden and told to eat freely of all of the trees but the Tree of Knowledge of Good and Evil. The serpent convinced Eve that to eat of that tree would not harm her but would make her "like God, knowing good and evil." Eve ate the fruit and gave some to Adam. God recognized their sin, cursed them, and expelled them from the garden.

30. **(b)** Cain was the first son of Adam and Eve, and Abel was their second son. Abel was a shepherd, while Cain farmed and grew crops. Abel sacrified a lamb to God, thereby satisfying the requirement of a blood sacrifice that proved true faith. Cain offered the fruits of his harvest, but his offering was rejected. In fury Cain killed Abel, was cursed, and was driven east of Eden and marked for life. Cain thus was the first murderer and Abel the first martyr, according to Judeo-Christian tradition.

31. (c) *Buddha*, meaning "the enlightened one," was the title given to Siddhartha Gautama, founder of the Buddhist religion. Siddhartha, who lived about the sixth century B.C., gave up his princely position and wandered for six years seeking enlightenment. While meditating he achieved his goal, and he went on to instruct others in the path he had taken. The basic tenets of his philosophy are four: the idea that existence is suffering; that suffering is caused by desire; that nirvana, or an end to suffering, is possible; and that there is a path leading to nirvana that involves right action, right resolve, and right concentration.

32. (c) Trained as a lawyer, Luther (1483–1546) became a priest after a religious awakening. Disgusted by the church's sale of pardons for sin (called *indulgences*), Luther protested and was excommunicated. After the Diet of Worms called for his imprisonment, Luther found sanctuary with the Elector Frederick III of Saxony. He continued to write and preach, and his followers, the Protestants, grew in number. His teachings were challenged by John Calvin and Huldreich Zwingli, and the Protestant movement split into factions. However, the Lutherans remained a vital force in northern Europe.

33. (b) Elohim is one of several forms of the name for God in the Old Testament. Allah is the name of God in the Koran. Brahma is the creator in the Hindu trinity.

34. (a) When Moses met God on Mount Sinai, he was given the Law, which listed the principles that were to govern the life of the faithful. Among the commandments were laws that forbade killing, adultery, and theft.

35. (a) Phoebus Apollo, a son of Zeus, was the god of archery and prophecy as well as music. Although Helios was the sun god, Apollo is often associated with the sun, and various myths depict him driving his sun-chariot across the heavens.

36. (c) In Christian thought all people are born with the taint of Original Sin, which can be removed only through baptism. The idea that Mary was free from such taint has been argued through the ages (with noted resistance coming from Thomas Aquinas), but Pope Pius IX made the idea formal Roman Catholic dogma in 1854.

37. (a) The founder of Islam named himself Muhammad in order to fulfill certain prophecies in the Old Testament. His teachings and those revelations made to him by Allah are set down in the Koran, the holy book of Islam. Islam is considered a theocracy; thus, the ruler of an Islamic nation should be a spiritual leader as well as head of government, and division between civil and religious law is negligible. In the first few centuries after Muhammad's death in 632, battles over his succession led to a division of Islam into Sunni and Shiite sects. The Wahabi sect of Sunni Islam is the religion of Saudi Arabia. Shiite Islam is the predominant religion of Iran.

38. (c) Poseidon (Neptune in Roman mythology) was the god of the sea and the brother of Zeus and Hades. He was also in charge of horses. The Greeks feared his nasty temper, which manifested itself in earthquakes and storms at sea. It was Poseidon's wrath that kept Odysseus so long at sea in the *Odyssey.*

39. (b) God determined to destroy the cities of Sodom and Gomorrah because of their wicked inhabitants. Abraham asked that the cities be spared if ten good men could be found. When that proved impossible, Lot and his family were the only people allowed to escape. At the last moment Lot's wife looked back at the burning cities and was turned into a pillar of salt.

40. (d) Early myths claim that Eros (Cupid) was born at the same time as Earth, but the more common tale is that he was the son of Aphrodite, goddess of love. He is often pictured as a child with a bow and a quiver of arrows.

41. (c) The books of the Old Testament are Genesis, Exodus, Leviticus, Numbers, Deuteronomy (the Books of Moses); Joshua, Judges, Ruth, I Samuel, 2 Samuel, 1 Kings, 2 Kings, 1 Chronicles, 2 Chronicles, Ezra, Nehemiah, Esther, Job, Psalms, Proverbs, Ecclesiastes, Song of Solomon, Isaiah, Jeremiah, Lamentations, Ezekiel, Daniel, Hosea, Joel, Amos, Obadiah, Jonah, Micah, Nahum, Habakkuk, Zephaniah, Haggai, Zechariah, and Malachi. Some books are named after their authors (e.g., Ezekiel), some are named after the main characters (e.g., Jonah), and others are named for the main plot points (e.g., Exodus). *Leviticus* means "about the Levites"; *Deuteronomy* means "repetition of the law." *Ruth* tells the story of Ruth and her mother-in-law, Naomi.

42. (d) In the *Iliad*, Achilles was a hero who fought against Troy in the Trojan War. At birth his mother had dipped him in the River Styx, which made him invincible everywhere except on the heel by which she held him. After Achilles killed Hector in battle, Hector's brother Paris shot Achilles in the heel, killing him.

43. **(c)** Prometheus' brother, Epimetheus, was supposed to bestow attributes on man and other animals. He ran out of gifts by the time he reached man, and he called on Prometheus to suggest something. Prometheus went to heaven and brought back the gift of fire to give to man. This gift made man stronger than the other animals, and Prometheus' recklessness enraged Zeus so much that he created the first woman, Pandora. Zeus gave Pandora a box that she was to present to the man she married. Epimetheus married Pandora and opened the box, releasing all of the evils that plague man. Other versions of the story claim that Pandora's curiosity led her to open the box. This story may be compared with that of the Garden of Eden.

44. **(b)** Many religions are covered by our term *Hinduism*, but the primary tenets of these religions are similar. The results of people's actions are their *karma*, and these control their lives in the next stage of rebirth. Pure acts lead to the possibility of *moksha*, or freedom from the cycle. The goal is attained through pilgrimage, worship, mental exercises, and clean living.

45. **(d)** This is the Muslim Holy Month, commemorating the revelations of the Koran to Muhammad. Muslims are expected to fast from sunrise to sundown every day during this period.

46. **(c)** After Daedalus completed the labyrinth in which the Minotaur was to be kept, he and his son were imprisoned by King Minos so that they would not give away the secrets of the maze. Daedalus made wings from feathers and wax for himself and Icarus, and they flew from Crete and headed for Sicily. In his pride at being able to fly, Icarus flew too close to the sun, which melted the wax in his wings. He fell into the sea and was killed.

47. **(b)** The Philistine giant Goliath challenged the Israelites, but only David agreed to fight. Saul gave him a sword and armor, but David was not used to them and chose to fight with only his sling and five stones. Armed with these and his faith, he struck Goliath in the forehead and killed him. This began an intense rivalry between Saul and David that ended only with Saul's death.

48. **(a)** Helen was half-divine, being the daughter of Zeus and Leda. In legend, she was stolen from her husband, Menelaus, by Paris. The kidnapping sparked the Trojan War. Helen's legendary beauty led Christopher Marlowe to refer to her as "the face that launched a thousand ships" (1604).

49. **(d)** One of Christ's parables tells of the sinning son who returns to his father's house to find forgiveness and love awaiting him. The meaning of the parable is clear: forgiveness of the repentant sinner is possible in the house of the Father.

50. **(d)** Theseus was probably a real king of Athens, but the myth that surrounds him far outweighs any real contributions he made. According to the story, he was brought up by his mother, who led him to a rock under which the sword and sandals of his father lay. When he could move the rock and take the sword and sandals, he would be worthy of presentation to his father, the king. Theseus was finally able to move the rock, and he set out for Athens, having many adventures along the way. Once he had been recognized by his father, Theseus resolved to save Athens from the Cretan Minotaur, to whom fourteen young Athenians were sacrificed each year. With the help of Ariadne, daughter of King Minos of Crete, he was able to find his way through the labyrinth and kill the half-man, half-bull monster. Theseus unheroically abandoned Ariadne and sailed for home, but his father, thinking him dead, leaped from a cliff to his death. King Theseus then did battle with the Amazons, women warriors from the Black Sea region. He defeated them and made their queen, Hippolyta, his bride.

A Well-Turned Phrase: Quotes, Phrases, and Aphorisms

A word is dead
When it is said,
Some say,
I say it just
Begins to live
That day.

—*EMILY DICKINSON*

1. If a speaker talks *ad infinitum*, he or she

   a. goes on without limit

   b. speaks off the cuff

   c. appeals to a listener's heart rather than head

   d. talks between main presentations

2. In his "I Have a Dream" speech, Martin Luther King, Jr. refers to

   a. violence as the correct response to oppression

   b. the struggle between the rights of commoners and of kings

   c. a world in which children are judged by character, not color

   d. a light "which shines over all the land and sea"

3. What is the Golden Rule?

   a. "As ye would that men should do to you, do ye also to them likewise."

   b. "To everything there is a season, and a time to every purpose under heaven."

   c. "It is better to light one candle than curse the darkness."

   d. "God loves to help him who strives to help himself."

4. "A bird in hand is worth two in the bush" is equivalent in meaning to

   a. "They will turn and bite the hand that fed them."

   b. "Good words are worth much, and cost little."

   c. "Hope is the thing with feathers."

   d. "He is a fool who leaves things close at hand to follow what is out of reach."

5. The phrase "fiddle while Rome burns" may be applied to people who

   a. respect higher learning and reward intellectualism

   b. ignore human misery while indulging themselves

   c. prefer the arts to affairs of state

   d. lose hope in the face of disaster

6. To express optimism in times of disaster, you might say,

   a. "Every cloud has a silver lining."

   b. "He who hesitates is lost."

   c. "Still waters run deep."

   d. "A rolling stone gathers no moss."

7. "Actions speak louder than words" means

   a. words outlast deeds

   b. deeds are meaningful; talk is cheap

   c. a bad action will not go unpunished

   d. never act without weighing the consequences

8. Who said, "The only thing we have to fear is fear itself"?

   a. Abraham Lincoln

   b. Winston Churchill

    c. John F. Kennedy

    d. Franklin D. Roosevelt

9. "Let sleeping dogs lie" means

    a. you can't teach an old dog new tricks

    b. never listen to the advice of strangers

    c. don't ask for needless trouble

    d. old ways are better

10. If a transaction is *bona fide*,

    a. it favors one party

    b. it is made in good faith

    c. no one can break the agreement

    d. the payment is in cash

11. A person who has the Midas touch

    a. cannot make friends

    b. has a firm handshake

    c. is cold and distant

    d. makes money easily

12. In his soliloquy that begins "To be, or not to be," Hamlet weighs the pros and cons of

    a. fidelity

    b. poetry

    c. suicide

    d. power

13. What is a *non sequitur*?

    a. a statement that does not follow logically from prior remarks

    b. a person who is not affiliated with a particular religion

    c. the failure to honor a contract or personal obligation

    d. an idea that is absurd or unintelligible

14. To "steal (people's) thunder" is to

    a. poke fun mercilessly and make them look bad

   b. cajole them out of a very bad mood

   c. avoid them at all costs

   d. use their ideas without giving credit

15. If you wished to remark on familial closeness, you might say,

   a. "Happy families are all alike."

   b. "Have no friends not equal to yourself."

   c. "Blood is thicker than water."

   d. "Familiarity breeds contempt."

16. To perform a deed "by hook or by crook" is to do it

   a. by any means possible

   b. carelessly and without forethought

   c. in an unlawful manner

   d. with malicious intent

17. Something that is run-of-the-mill is

   a. coarse

   b. ordinary

   c. peculiar

   d. refined

18. "Hobson's choice" refers to

   a. a choice between two equally terrible events

   b. no choice at all

   c. an obvious decision

   d. an overabundance of options

19. If people meet briefly and never encounter each other again, they are like

   a. "little, nameless, unremembered acts"

   b. "two hearts that beat as one"

   c. "partners in crime"

   d. "ships that pass in the night"

20. The phrase *e pluribus unum*, found on the seal of the United States, means

   a. "in God we trust"

   b. "from many, one"

   c. "united we stand"

   d. "liberty and equality"

21. If you promise to turn over a new leaf, you aim to

   a. read more in the coming year

   b. set aside youthful passions

   c. alter your behavior

   d. "cultivate (your) garden"

22. When you tell someone, "You can't have your cake and eat it, too," you mean to say,

   a. "Sweet things never last."

   b. "Don't put off your work until tomorrow."

   c. "Finish one thing before starting another."

   d. "You must make a decision."

23. To warn someone of the foolishness of relying on future gains, you might say,

   a. "Don't count your chickens before they are hatched."

   b. "Slow and steady wins the race."

   c. "Prepare today for the wants of tomorrow."

   d. "Beware lest you lose the substance by grasping at the shadow."

24. If you "walk the straight and narrow," you

   a. follow a course laid out by fate

   b. lead the "life of Riley"

   c. do not stray from righteousness

   d. give up everything for love

25. You might use the phrase "The grass is always greener on the other side of the fence" to describe

   a. discontented people who seek their fortunes far from home

    b. politicians who promise followers "a chicken in every pot"

    c. farmers who prefer planting crops to harvesting them

    d. happy children who enjoy the out-of-doors

26. If you "bury the hatchet," you

    a. ignore an insult

    b. spend too much money

    c. hide the evidence of a crime

    d. make peace

27. When you claim that "the road to hell is paved with good intentions," what do you mean?

    a. Good intentions do not guarantee a good deed.

    b. Good men as well as bad go to hell.

    c. Sin can mask itself as good.

    d. The devil tempts us to forget our good intentions.

28. When someone works or plays too hard, you say he or she

    a. makes hay while the sun shines

    b. takes the bitter with the sweet

    c. burns the candle at both ends

    d. can't make a silk purse out of sow's ear

29. What does "an eye for an eye" mean?

    a. An act of violence should be punished with equal violence.

    b. Sight is the most precious of man's senses.

    c. People must strive to look at life in the same way.

    d. Any part of you that is not pleasing in God's eyes should be struck off.

30. Those who separate the wheat from the chaff

    a. use advanced methods in farming

    b. separate people by race or religion

    c. pick the winners in horse races

    d. decide what is important or valuable

31. The incident or thing that finally causes you to lose control is

    a. "the lunatic fringe"

    b. "the last straw"

    c. "the most unkindest cut of all"

    d. "Pandora's box"

32. Who are the *hoi polloi*?

    a. the news media

    b. the common masses

    c. the aristocracy

    d. royalty

33. Who originally advised men to "turn the other cheek"?

    a. Moses

    b. Jesus

    c. Mahatma Gandhi

    d. Martin Luther King, Jr.

34. Who said, "Give me liberty or give me death," and under what circumstances?

    a. Patrick Henry, addressing the Virginia Convention

    b. Nathan Hale, before his execution for spying

    c. George Washington, addressing troops at Valley Forge

    d. Thomas Jefferson, after the reading of the Declaration of Independence

35. What is "the American Dream"?

    a. returning to the land of one's ancestors

    b. the possibility of bettering oneself through individual enterprise

    c. spreading democracy throughout the world

    d. being the first country to put a station in space

36. People who injure themselves trying to wreak revenge on another are said to

   a. grin like a Cheshire cat

   b. be guilty by association

   c. speak softly and carry a big stick

   d. cut off their noses to spite their faces

37. Who is "the Grim Reaper"?

   a. Jesus

   b. Death

   c. Satan

   d. God

38. The phrase "Fourscore and seven years ago" is the opening to what speech?

   a. Franklin D. Roosevelt's address to Congress asking for a declaration of war

   b. Winston Churchill's "Blood, Sweat, and Tears" speech

   c. Abraham Lincoln's Gettysburg Address

   d. King Edward VIII's abdication speech

39. What is a vicious circle?

   a. the symbol of something precious and valuable

   b. a chain of events in which the solution to a problem creates a worse problem

   c. the solution to a problem found in one brilliant move

   d. a spectacular display made without effort

40. A person who is warned, "*Caveat emptor!*" should be aware that

   a. there is a vicious dog on the premises

   b. he or she should seize the opportunity to enjoy life

   c. the goods or services purchased are not guaranteed by the seller

   d. he or she should be careful of what is said and to whom

41. Who claimed that "no man is an island"?

   a. John Donne, in "Devotions upon Emergent Occasions"

   b. William Shakespeare, in Sonnet 97

   c. Andrew Marvell, in "A Dialogue between the Soul and Body"

   d. John Milton, in "How Soon Hath Time"

42. What is the difference between the abbreviations *e.g.* and *i.e.*?

   a. After using e.g. you quote; after using i.e. you paraphrase.

   b. E.g. refers to years before the birth of Christ; i.e. refers to years after the birth of Christ.

   c. E.g. is used in footnotes; i.e. is used in bibliographies.

   d. After using e.g. you list examples; after using i.e. you explain or expand.

43. When you see the handwriting on the wall, you

   a. are the means of your own defeat

   b. are warned of your approaching ruin or defeat

   c. leave potential problems undisturbed

   d. ignore an act of vandalism or violence

44. If you are convicted of a crime *in absentia*, you

   a. were sick at the time of the conviction

   b. were innocent of the crime

   c. were not present at the conviction

   d. fought against the conviction

45. When you are advised not to look a gift horse in the mouth, you

   a. take what is offered with gratitude and without question

   b. try to brighten a gloomy situation

   c. acknowledge the positive features of someone you
   dislike

   d. leave troublesome issues undisturbed

46. Who advised Americans to "ask not what your country
can do for you; ask what you can do for your country"?

   a. Franklin D. Roosevelt

   b. John F. Kennedy

   c. Martin Luther King, Jr.

   d. Ronald Reagan

47. If you play the devil's advocate, what are you doing?

   a. finding fault with an idea or person supported by
   someone else

   b. going along with the crowd

   c. arguing against organized religion

   d. blaming someone for the wrongdoing of others

48. A man with a chip on his shoulder is

   a. confused about a situation

   b. suffering from a crippling disease

   c. entirely with hope

   d. angry for no apparent reason and ready to fight

49. What is a wolf in sheep's clothing doing?

   a. pretending to love animals

   b. masking ill will with an outward show of good nature

   c. showing a liking for parties and fun

   d. running away from danger

50. If a family has a nasty secret that they keep hidden,
you say they

   a. are on the horns of a dilemma

   b. are riding for a fall

   c. have a skeleton in their closet

   d. have a fly in the ointment

TEST 8: Explanatory Answers

1. **(a)** From the same root as the word *infinity*, the Latin phrase *ad infinitum* means "without end or limit."

2. **(c)** This speech was the culmination of the March on Washington in 1963. Drawing on texts from the Old Testament and lyrics of spirituals, King called for a world where black and white were equal partners and racism was nonexistent.

3. **(a)** Christ says this in his Sermon on the Mount, which sets forth his definitions of righteousness, his interpretations of the commandments, and his rules for religious observances.

4. **(d)** The first quotation is from Cervantes (1547–1616); citation *d* is from Plutarch (c. 46–120 A.D.), who said it some fifteen hundred years before Cervantes.

5. **(b)** The emperor Nero blamed Christians for the fire that destroyed most of Rome in 64 A.D. It is believed that he himself set the fire in order to have a reason to persecute the Christians. Nero thought of himself as a great artist and musician. The image of his playing a fiddle while Rome burns is used to illustrate callous disregard for human suffering.

6. **(a)** Its use in two popular songs of the early 1900s kept the "silver lining" metaphor in the public vocabulary. Lena Ford's "Keep the Home Fires Burning" (1915) and P.G. Wodehouse's "Look for the Silver Lining" (1920) both refer to the silver lining that hints at the sun behind every cloud.

7. **(b)** In *Henry VIII* Shakespeare wrote, " 'tis a kind of good deed to say well: And yet words are no deeds." The implication is that talking is easy, but actions are all that matter. The phrase "easier said than done" is ascribed to Plautus (254–184 B.C.).

8. **(d)** Roosevelt said this in his first inaugural address in 1933. The quote reflects Proverbs 3:25: "Be not afraid of sudden fear." The biblical reference had been paraphrased by many writers, including Montaigne and Thoreau, before being used by Roosevelt in perhaps its most famous wording.

9. **(c)** Dickens uses this phrase in *David Copperfield*, but in *Troilus and Criseyde*, Chaucer writes, "It is nought good a slepyng hound to wake." The maxim had probably been around for years before Chaucer so recorded it in the late fourteenth century.

10. **(b)** *Bona fide* is Latin for "good faith," meaning "without deceit." The phrase is often used to mean "genuine" or "authentic."

11. **(d)** This phrase, ironically, has come to mean something positive, but its original connotation was extremely grave. In Greek mythology Midas was a Phrygian king who asked for and received the power to turn all he touched to gold. He delighted in his gift until he found that he could neither eat nor drink, and he turned his beloved daughter into a cold, lifeless statue. In despair he asked for the power to be removed, and he lived out the rest of his life quietly in the country.

12. **(c)** In Shakespeare's play, Hamlet, a man of thought rather than action, is driven to despair by the murder of his father by his uncle and his uncle's subsequent marriage to his mother. In this famous speech Hamlet wonders whether it is better to "suffer the slings and arrows of outrageous fortune" or to die. He decides that the fear of what lies after death keeps most people from taking their own lives.

13. **(a)** *Non sequitur* is Latin for "it does not follow." In logic it refers to a kind of fallacy, or inference that does not follow from a given premise. In ordinary speech it refers to any statement that is not a logical part of the conversation.

14. **(d)** According to Bartlett's *Familiar Quotations*, in 1709 the playwright John Dennis invented a special effect for a play that was badly received. At a performance of *Macbeth* some time later, Dennis heard his special effect in use, whereupon he cried, "See how the rascals use me! They will not let my play run, and yet they steal my thunder!"

15. **(c)** John Ray lists this maxim in *English Proverbs* in 1670. It is used to describe the connection between even the most spiritually distant relatives.

16. **(a)** In the late fourteenth century this phrase appeared in *Controversial Tracts* by John Wycliffe, but it had probably been in use for a while. It is thought to stem from methods of gathering firewood—using a hooked pole or a scythe.

17. **(b)** Henry James speaks of a person "ground in the very mill of the conventional" in *The Portrait of a Lady* (1881). Something that is run-of-the-mill is just like everything else ground in the mill—average.

18. (b) According to Bartlett's *Familiar Quotations*, Hobson was a liveryman who forced his customers to take whichever horse stood nearest the door. The phrase thus refers to lack of choice.

19. (d) Henry Wadsworth Longfellow (1807–1882) penned this image in a poem in *Tales of a Wayside Inn* (1863–1874):
Ships that pass in the night, and speak each other in passing,
Only a signal shown and a distant voice in the darkness;
So on the ocean of life we pass and speak one another,
Only a look and a voice; then darkness again and silence.

20. (b) This Latin phrase, also found on many U.S. coins, refers to the idea that from people of great diversity was forged a single nation.

21. (c) "Turning over a new leaf" (as in "book," not "tree") was mentioned by Cervantes in *Don Quixote* (1605–1615). It appears earlier in works by Roger Ascham (1570) and Gabriel Harvey (1593). The metaphor relates to starting over on a blank page.

22. (d) "Wouldst thou both eat thy cake and have it?" asked George Herbert in 1633. The proverb was already probably in common usage as a way to point up the impossibility of having things both ways and the need to make a choice.

23. (a) All of these quotations are morals from Aesop's fables, set down about the sixth century B.C. Aesop warns his readers that expecting all of their eggs to hatch may prove foolish.

24. (c) In the Sermon on the Mount, Christ tells his listeners about the path to everlasting life: "Wide is the gate, and broad is the way, that leadeth to destruction, and many there be which go in thereat: Because strait is the gate, and narrow is the way, which leadeth unto life, and few there be that find it." André Gide used this ironically in *Strait Is the Gate* (1909), a story of a girl who sacrifices her worldly happiness to that of her sister, only to die without achieving spiritual or earthly joy.

25. (a) This maxim tells of the futility involved in assuming that things are better somewhere else—no matter where you are, the grass is always greener elsewhere.

26. (d) Burying the hatchet was an American Indian tradition signifying peace. Washington Irving used the phrase in *Cap-*

tain Bonneville (1837) to describe a peaceful meeting among Indian chiefs.

27. **(a)** In 1150 Bernard of Clairvaux claimed that "Hell is full of good intentions or desires," meaning that a person's deeds do not necessarily reflect his or her intentions. The idea of the road to hell being "paved" with good intentions wasn't used until Samuel Johnson spoke of it in 1775.

28. **(c)** To burn (or light) a candle at both ends was a phrase used by Thomas Bacon in 1592; he meant it to express wasted time. The idea of burning a candle at both ends to mean living too hard wasn't used until 1857 when, in a novel called *Two Years Ago* by Charles Kingsley, a character is described as burning "the candle of life at both ends."

29. **(a)** In Exodus, God tells Moses that "thou shalt give life for life, eye for eye, tooth for tooth, hand for hand," informing him that an act of violence should be punished in equal measure.

30. **(d)** Those who separate the wheat from the chaff do what farmers have done for centuries: dispose of what is not useful or true and set aside that which is. In the Gospel of St. Matthew, John the Baptist predicts that Jesus will "burn up the chaff," that is, send the wicked to hell.

31. **(b)** "The last straw" is a shortened form of "the last straw that breaks the camel's back," first used by Charles Dickens in *Dombey and Son*. The phrase refers to the last incident or piece of information that a person can bear before breaking down in sorrow, anger, or exhaustion.

32. **(b)** *Hoi polloi* is a Greek phrase meaning "the many." *Hoi polloi* are the masses.

33. **(b)** In the Gospel of St. Matthew, Jesus says, "Whosoever shall smite thee on thy right cheek, turn to him the other also." This means that violence should not be met with violence, an idea that translated itself into the passive resistance movements led by Gandhi and Martin Luther King, Jr.

34. **(a)** On March 23, 1775, Patrick Henry addressed the Virginia Convention in Richmond, urging them to fight for their freedom from Great Britain.

35. **(b)** The American Dream is based on the concept of America as a new Eden, a land where people can redefine themselves, free of the restrictions of society. Such an idea is easily

corrupted; F. Scott Fitzgerald's *The Great Gatsby* is one of the best illustrations of how the American Dream can be debased.

36. **(d)** In *A Classical Dictionary of the Vulgar Tongue*, Francis Grose defines "he who cut off his nose to be revenged of his face" as one who, "to be revenged of his neighbour, has materially injured himself."

37. **(b)** The Grim Reaper is Death, who mows down men with his scythe. He is described by Henry Wadsworth Longfellow in his poem "The Reaper and the Flowers"(1839): "There is a reaper whose name is Death."

38. **(c)** In 1863, after the battle at Gettysburg, Pennsylvania, President Abraham Lincoln gave a speech honoring the dead who fell defending the Union. The speech ended, "government of the people, by the people, for the people, shall not perish from the earth."

39. **(b)** A vicious circle is a chain of events in which the solution to a problem causes another problem, and the solution to that problem causes still another problem, and so on.

40. **(c)** *Caveat emptor* is Latin for "Let the buyer beware." It is a rule of law that stipulates that a purchaser rather than a vendor is responsible for goods or services purchased, except for what is specified in a sales contract.

41. **(a)** "No man is an island, entire of itself; every man is a piece of the continent, a part of the main" was written by John Donne in 1624. In the same "Meditation," Donne wrote, "Never send to know for whom the bell tolls; it tolls for thee." Both statements stress the idea that people are linked together and that each person's actions affect others.

42. **(d)** E.g. is the abbreviation for *exempli gratia*, Latin for "for example"; after using it you would list examples. I.e. is the abbreviation for *id est*, or "that is," after which you would explain or expand on what you were saying.

43. **(b)** The original handwriting on the wall, "Mene, mene, tekel upharsin," was drawn by God on the wall of Belshazzar's palace in Babylon. In the Old Testament tale, Daniel interpreted the writing, which foretold the ruin of Belshazzar, who had dined from the sacred vessels from the temple of the Israelites.

44. **(c)** *In absentia* is Latin for "in one's absence." Whatever happens to you *in absentia* occurs while you are absent.

45. (a) A horse's age can be determined by looking at its teeth. Literally, "Don't look a gift horse in the mouth" means "Refrain from insulting the giver by checking the horse's age." In general, the saying means that any gift or offering should be accepted without question.

46. (b) In his inaugural address of 1961, John F. Kennedy urged Americans to act for their country rather than waiting for their country to act for them. The thought comes from a speech made by Oliver Wendell Holmes in 1884, in which he stated that the citizenry should recall "what our country has done for each of us, and to ask ourselves what we can do for our country in return."

47. (a) The devil's advocate was originally a churchman who had the job of arguing against the sainthood of someone nominated for canonization.

48. (d) If you have a chip on your shoulder, you are ready for a fight. In an 1857 *Harper's Magazine* an anonymous contributor wrote, "A provocation to a fight . . . is placing a chip upon a man's shoulder and daring another to knock it off."

49. (b) The original wolf in sheep's clothing was an invention of Aesop, who used the fable, written around 550 B.C., to show that appearances can be deceiving. The idea also appears in the Gospel of St. Matthew, who wrote, "Beware of false prophets, which come to you in sheep's clothing, but inwardly they are ravening wolves."

50. (c) William Makepeace Thackeray (1811–1863) was the first to use the idea of a skeleton to symbolize a shameful secret. He claimed that "there is a skeleton in every house."

Of Thee I Sing: American Literature

> *By American literature ... we ought to mean literature written in an American way, with an American turn of language and an American cast of thought.*
>
> —STEPHEN BUTLER LEACOCK

1. Who wrote *Cat on a Hot Tin Roof, A Streetcar Named Desire*, and *The Glass Menagerie*?

   a. Eugene O'Neill

   b. Sam Shepard

   c. Tennessee Williams

   d. Edward Albee

2. Langston Hughes was a writer of

   a. poetry

   b. novels

   c. plays

   d. all of the above

3. A black writer known for his antiracist essays and novels of black life is

   a. Imamu Amiri Baraka

   b. Thomas Pynchon

    c. Norman Mailer

    d. James Baldwin

4. The novel for which Nathaniel Hawthorne is best known is

    a. *The Scarlet Letter*

    b. *The Deerslayer*

    c. *Maggie: A Girl of the Streets*

    d. *Sister Carrie*

5. The novelist who satirized small-town life, the scientist's search for truth, and evangelism is

    a. Saul Bellow

    b. Sinclair Lewis

    c. Nathanael West

    d. John Dos Passos

6. One of the major themes of *The Great Gatsby* is

    a. the corruption of American innocence through the pursuit of wealth

    b. the prejudices and injustices of Americans toward American Indians

    c. the acceptance of death as a part of nature

    d. the loss of faith and the triumph of science

7. The book that made Ralph Ellison famous is the story of

    a. life in the Chicago stockyards

    b. a boy who is sent to reform school

    c. a black man's search for identity in the 1930s

    d. a drummer and drug addict in the slums of Chicago

8. Ezra Pound was known for

    a. his novels of social conscience

    b. his pro-Communist essays

    c. his deeply religious poems and short stories

    d. his poetry, criticism, and political views

9. Of what kind of poetry are these lines characteristic?

   "I arise from rest with movements swift / As the beat of the raven's wings."

   a. Southern poetry

   b. American Indian poetry

   c. Haiku

   d. Romantic poetry

10. A Nobel Prize winner known for his mystical tales of Jewish life and folklore is

    a. Isaac Bashevis Singer

    b. Frederik Pohl

    c. Saul Bellow

    d. Henry Miller

11. What are Jack London's best-known novels?

    a. *Seize the Day* and *Herzog*

    b. *Babylon Revisited* and *Tender Is the Night*

    c. *The Call of the Wild* and *The Sea Wolf*

    d. *The Naked and the Dead* and *Armies of the Night*

12. When you think of E. E. Cummings, what stylistic eccentricity comes to mind?

    a. his use of obscenity in poetry

    b. his use of onomatopoeia in poetry

    c. his use of dissonance in poetry

    d. his use of only lowercase letters in poetry

13. Who is the author of the novels *Ethan Frome* and *The House of Mirth*?

    a. Edith Wharton

    b. Alice James

    c. Alice Walker

    d. Carson McCullers

14. Eugene O'Neill is the author of

   a. *Waiting for Lefty, Awake and Sing!* and *Golden Boy*

   b. *The Emperor Jones, A Long Day's Journey Into Night,* and *The Iceman Cometh*

   c. *American Buffalo, The Woods,* and *Glengarry Glen Ross*

   d. *True West, Fool for Love,* and *Buried Child*

15. A nineteenth-century writer known for his Romantic poetry and macabre stories is

   a. Washington Irving

   b. James Fenimore Cooper

   c. Edgar Allan Poe

   d. Bret Harte

16. Who was Emily Dickinson?

   a. a nineteenth-century novelist who explored women's sexual and emotional dependence

   b. a nineteenth-century poet who used the imagery of nature to explore human consciousness

   c. a twentieth-century poet who experimented with unusual stanza forms

   d. a twentieth-century writer who explored the black Midwestern experience

17. Eudora Welty, Flannery O'Connor, and Carson Mc-Cullers are all

   a. poets who focused on the struggle for female independence

   b. novelists who wrote satires of midwestern life

   c. playwrights who explored the isolation of modern women

   d. novelists who wrote about the American South

18. Winner of both the Pulitzer Prize and the Nobel Prize, John Steinbeck wrote

   a. *V* and *Gravity's Rainbow*

    b. *The Grapes of Wrath* and *Of Mice and Men*

    c. *A Death in the Family* and *Let Us Now Praise Famous Men*

    d. *Ragtime* and *Loon Lake*

19. What is the major theme of Thornton Wilder's play *Our Town*?

    a. Even the smallest moments in life have great value and meaning.

    b. Life in big cities is spiritually degrading.

    c. Children are the means of humankind's immortality.

    d. The American Dream has become meaningless.

20. Why is Walden Pond an important location in American literary history?

    a. It is the body of water in which Virginia Woolf drowned herself.

    b. It is the body of water around which the Lake poets lived.

    c. It is where Henry Thoreau lived and recorded his impressions.

    d. It is the setting for Charles Kingsley's *The Water Babies*.

21. Who wrote the lines: "The woods are lovely, dark, and deep, / But I have promises to keep, / And miles to go before I sleep"?

    a. Anne Sexton

    b. Robert Frost

    c. A. R. Ammons

    d. Robert Lowell

22. What is transcendentalism?

    a. a movement led by Alfred Jarry that stressed the lack of reason in human existence

    b. a movement led by Jean-Paul Sartre that stated that existence precedes essence

   c. a movement led by Tristan Tzara that tried to negate all traditional values in the arts

   d. a movement led by Ralph Waldo Emerson that stressed the divinity of man

23. What do Dashiell Hammett, Raymond Chandler, and Mickey Spillane have in common?

   a. They are poets in the modernist tradition.

   b. They are all writers of detective fiction.

   c. They wrote novels of rural life in the Southeast.

   d. They are biographers of famous literary figures.

24. Who was the creator of the characters Huckleberry Finn, Tom Sawyer, and Pudd'nhead Wilson?

   a. Herman Melville

   b. Hart Crane

   c. Thomas Wolfe

   d. Samuel Clemens

25. What belief did the Naturalist movement in America stress?

   a. the importance of conservation of land and animal life

   b. the innocence and virtue of man in the state of nature

   c. the limitations of social conditions and heredity on man's capacity to change

   d. the free and spontaneous act of literary composition

26. Washington Irving created which of the following characters?

   a. Diedrich Knickerbocker and Rip van Winkle

   b. Meg, Beth, Amy, and Jo

   c. Little Eva and Topsy

   d. Billy Budd and Queequeg

27. Willa Cather is perhaps best known for her

   a. stories of life on the New England coast

b. novels that celebrate the American past

c. poems about spiritual growth and doubt

d. essays on the rights of women

28. *The Sound and the Fury* and *Absalom, Absalom!* are two novels by

  a. Robert Penn Warren

  b. William Faulkner

  c. Booth Tarkington

  d. Katherine Anne Porter

29. What is a "tall tale"?

  a. a short novel set on the prairie

  b. any tale whose main characters are animals with human traits

  c. an exaggerated anecdote about frontier life

  d. a stream-of-consciousness story by Edgar Allan Poe

30. Herman Melville is famous for his

  a. tales of life along the Mississippi River

  b. poems about the simple pleasures of sport and competition

  c. novels about sea voyages

  d. adventure stories about explorers and pirates

31. *The Waste Land* and *Four Quartets* are poems by

  a. Edna St. Vincent Millay

  b. Wallace Stevens

  c. Carl Sandburg

  d. T. S. Eliot

32. *Uncle Tom's Cabin* was an important influence on

  a. the Abolitionist movement

  b. American isolationists

  c. the carpetbaggers

  d. the colonial militia

33. Which of these people wrote in prerevolutionary times?

    a. Mary Mapes Dodge and William Dean Howells

    b. Waldo Frank and Josephine Herbst

    c. Sarah Orne Jewett and George Washington Cable

    d. Anne Bradstreet and Jonathan Edwards

34. Which of these plays are by Arthur Miller?

    a. *Death of a Salesman* and *The Crucible*

    b. *Sweet Bird of Youth* and *The Night of the Iguana*

    c. *Who's Afraid of Virginia Woolf?* and *The Zoo Story*

    d. *Our Town* and *The Skin of Our Teeth*

35. Ernest Hemingway's writing style is characterized by

    a. flowing imagery and poetic diction

    b. biting wit and sarcastic humor

    c. terseness and understatement

    d. sentimentality and use of symbolic structure

36. Louisa May Alcott is known for her

    a. somewhat moralistic novels for children

    b. unique educational philosophy and ideas for school reform

    c. illustrated children's stories about animals

    d. strong antislavery sentiment and political speech-writing

37. Which of these works are by Richard Wright?

    a. *Notes of a Native Son* and *The Fire Next Time*

    b. *The 42nd Parallel* and *Manhattan Transfer*

    c. *Native Son* and *Black Boy*

    d. *Bronzeville Boys and Girls* and *The Bean Eaters*

38. Which of these lines is attributable to Henry Wadsworth Longfellow?

    a. "This is the forest primeval. The murmuring pines and the hemlocks."

b. "Life is real! Life is earnest! / And the grave is not its goal."

c. "Listen, my children, and you shall hear, / Of the midnight ride of Paul Revere."

d. all of the above

39. *Slaughterhouse-Five* and *Cat's Cradle* are novels by

a. Thomas Pynchon

b. Kurt Vonnegut

c. William Styron

d. Joseph Heller

40. Henry James's influence on later writers stems from his

a. attention to point of view and psychological realism

b. use of regional dialect and historical settings

c. emphasis on heroic traits in handicapped or impoverished characters

d. all of the above

41. What do Sherwood Anderson and Edgar Lee Masters have in common?

a. Both wrote about small towns in the Midwest.

b. Both started literary magazines in Boston.

c. Both published tales based on Cajun legends.

d. Both satirized New York and European society.

42. Which of these authors are known for their science fiction?

a. Arthur Schlesinger, Daniel Boorstein, Frances Fitzgerald

b. Ray Bradbury, Ursula LeGuin, Isaac Asimov

c. A. R. Gurney, Lanford Wilson, Beth Henley

d. Marjorie K. Rawlings, John Hersey, Pearl Buck

43. Upton Sinclair, Ida Tarbell, and Lincoln Steffens were part of

a. the Puritan tradition

    b. the school of regionalism

    c. the Transcendentalist movement

    d. the muckraking movement

44. Walt Whitman's poetry was among the first in America to

    a. concentrate on rural themes

    b. eliminate regular metrical structure

    c. apply medievalism to American art

    d. emphasize form over emotion

45. *Rabbit, Run* and *The Centaur* are novels by

    a. Mary McCarthy

    b. Robert Coover

    c. John Updike

    d. Bernard Malamud

46. Which of these writers are associated with the Beat movement?

    a. John Crowe Ransom, Allen Tate, John Gould Fletcher

    b. Gregory Corso, Jack Kerouac, Allen Ginsberg

    c. Eugene Debs, Norman Thomas, Robert La Follette

    d. Abbie Hoffman, Jerry Rubin, Eldridge Cleaver

47. Marianne Moore is known for her

    a. plays satirizing "the rat race"

    b. biographies of famous American women

    c. ironic poems on everyday subjects

    d. financial support of "Lost Generation" writers

48. Dorothy Parker, E. B. White, and James Thurber were all

    a. poets

    b. playwrights

    c. expatriates

    d. humorists

49. Who wrote *Common Sense* and *The Rights of Man?*
   a. Thomas Paine
   b. John Adams
   c. Thomas Jefferson
   d. Henry Adams

50. *Lolita, Pnin,* and *Pale Fire* are novels by
   a. Donald Barthelme
   b. Edna Ferber
   c. Vladimir Nabokov
   d. John Barth

TEST 9: Explanatory Answers

1. (c) Tennessee Williams (1911–1983) is thought by many to be the best modern American dramatist. He was awarded the Pulitzer Prize for both *A Streetcar Named Desire* (1947) and *Cat on a Hot Tin Roof* (1955); his characters often suffer from loneliness and sexual anxiety that erupts into violence.

2. (d) Langston Hughes (1902–1967) was one of the foremost members of the Harlem Renaissance, a movement of black writers that included Zora Neale Hurston, Countee Cullen, and Richard Wright. He was mainly known for his poetry, but he also wrote plays, novels, humorous sketches, short stories, and a two-volume autobiography. His use of black dialect led to a revolution in black writing, influencing later generations of writers up to the present.

3. (d) James Baldwin (1924–1987) was the author of *Notes of a Native Son* (1955) and *The Fire Next Time* (1963), collections of essays condemning American race discrimination. His novels *Giovanni's Room* (1956), *Another Country* (1962), and *Just Above My Head* (1979) are moving stories of black life in America and abroad.

4. (a) Nathaniel Hawthorne (1804–1864) was a New Englander, a writer of short stories and novels, among which are *The House of the Seven Gables* (1851) and *The Blithedale Romance* (1852). His story of Puritan America, *The Scarlet Letter*

(1850), is his masterpiece; it tells of the illicit romance between a married woman and a minister and explores the themes of sin, guilt, and hypocrisy. The other novels mentioned are by James Fenimore Cooper, Stephen Crane, and Theodore Dreiser.

5. **(b)** Winner of the Nobel Prize in 1930, Sinclair Lewis was a satirist who targeted small-town America in *Main Street* (1920), scientists in *Arrowsmith* (1925), and evangelists in *Elmer Gantry* (1927). *Arrowsmith* was awarded the Pulitzer Prize, but Lewis turned it down because the award was given to the work that best presented "the wholesome atmosphere of American life."

6. **(a)** *The Great Gatsby* (1925) is the story of the rise and fall of Jay Gatsby, a man without a real past or emotional ties, and his effect on Tom and Daisy Buchanan and on the story's narrator, Nick Carraway. The novel is set during the 1920s and shows the emptiness of the lives of those who lived and prospered in the Jazz Age.

7. **(c)** *The Invisible Man* (1952), winner of the National Book Award, charts the journey of a black man from the South to Harlem and his search for personal and racial identity. A poll of two hundred authors and critics taken in 1964 named the book "the most distinguished single work published in the last twenty years."

8. **(d)** Ezra Pound (1885–1972) was a controversial poet, critic, and essayist. Early in his career he promoted the school of imagism, which stressed metaphor and image. Later he became involved in the Fascist movements of Hitler and Mussolini, broadcasting propaganda from Italy. After World War II he was arrested and committed to an asylum, but he continued to write poetry and essays until his death.

9. **(b)** This line is from an Eskimo poem in *Beyond the High Hills: A Book of Eskimo Poetry*. Like other Native American poetry, it uses simple, clear images of nature to express emotions and thoughts about life.

10. **(a)** Isaac Bashevis Singer (1904–1992), born in Poland, emigrated to the United States in 1935. He wrote novels such as *The Family Moskat* (1950), memoirs, and collections of stories for children, the best known of which is *The Fools of Chelm* (1973). His tales, most of which were originally written in Yiddish, reflect Jewish culture and folklore. In 1978 he won the Nobel Prize for literature.

11. **(c)** Jack London (1876–1916) was known for his stories of Alaska, where he lived during the Klondike gold rush. His books stress the theme of survival against all odds. He was a socialist and author of many essays promoting socialism, but his Alaska novels are his true legacy. The other works mentioned are by Saul Bellow, F. Scott Fitzgerald, and Norman Mailer.

12. **(d)** Although E. E. Cummings (1894–1962) is most often remembered for using only lowercase letters in his poetry, this was only part of his experimentation with the visual form of the poem. He worked with line fragments, unusual punctuation, and verse shapes as well. He also wrote a novel, *The Enormous Room* (1922) and a play, *Him* (1927), and was the author of numerous essays.

13. **(a)** Edith Wharton (1862–1937) was called "the great and glorious pendulum" by Henry James, perhaps because of the way she moved between society life and the intellectual life that produced her novels, including *The House of Mirth* (1905) and *Ethan Frome* (1911). The former revealed the hypocrisies of high society, while the latter is an almost legendary tale of a couple who live outside society.

14. **(b)** Eugene O'Neill (1888–1953) was America's first major playwright. He was a four-time Pulitzer Prize winner (in 1920 for *Beyond the Horizon*, in 1921 for *Anna Christie*, in 1928 for *Strange Interlude*, and in 1956 for *A Long Day's Journey Into Night*) and the only American dramatist to win a Nobel Prize. His theater group, the Provincetown Players, staged his early plays in Greenwich Village, but soon O'Neill's work moved to Broadway. He wrote more than thirty plays, most of which explore the raw, primitive self beneath man's civilized veneer. The other plays mentioned are by Clifford Odets, David Mamet, and Sam Shepard.

15. **(c)** Edgar Allan Poe (1809–1849) became famous with the publication of his poem "The Raven" (1845), which many critics consider an imitation of the British romantic style. His tales of the grotesque, however, established him as an important writer, one who has influenced such later greats as William Faulkner and Vladimir Nabokov.

16. **(b)** Emily Dickinson (1830–1886) was a New England poet who in her later years became a recluse. She wrote almost two thousand poems, only seven of which were published in her

lifetime. Her short verses, characterized by her use of dashes as punctuation, explored themes of love, death, and immortality.

17. **(d)** Eudora Welty, born in 1909, is a native of Jackson, Mississippi. Her stories and novels, including *Delta Wedding* (1946) and the Pulitzer Prize-winning *Optimist's Daughter* (1972), tell of small-town life in the South. Flannery O'Connor (1924–1964) set most of her short stories and novels in the South. She blended religious faith with the grotesque in her novel *Wise Blood* (1952) and the story collection *A Good Man Is Hard to Find* (1955). Carson McCullers (1917–1967) was a Georgian whose novel *The Heart Is a Lonely Hunter* (1940) and collection of stories *The Ballad of the Sad Cafe* (1951) were set in the South and explored human loneliness.

18. **(b)** John Steinbeck (1902–1968) wrote primarily about the disadvantaged in America. His best-known novel, *The Grapes of Wrath* (1939), is the story of the Joads, an Oklahoma family driven from their dustbowl farm and forced to become migrant workers in California. The other novels mentioned are by Thomas Pynchon, James Agee, and E. L. Doctorow.

19. **(a)** *Our Town* (1938), which won the Pulitzer Prize, takes place in a small New England town and traces the daily lives of several inhabitants. The play treats themes of love, marriage, birth, and death, and stresses the value of seemingly insignificant moments in life.

20. **(c)** *Walden* (1854) was written by Henry David Thoreau (1817–1862) during the two years he lived alone in a cabin on the banks of Walden Pond. In the book, Thoreau urges readers to simplify their lives and look to nature for meaning and clarity in life.

21. **(b)** Robert Frost (1874–1963) was not well known as a poet until he reached his forties. He wrote in traditional verse forms and developed themes of rural life and nature.

22. **(d)** Transcendentalism was a movement that began in New England in the nineteenth century. It had its roots in the philosophy of Plato and stressed intuition as the means to understanding reality. Emerson, the leader of the movement, called for Transcendentalists to trust only direct experiences; their belief in man's divinity was the key to reliance on self rather than on an external God. The other movements mentioned are absurdism, existentialism, and dadaism.

23. (b) Raymond Chandler (1888–1959) created the detective Philip Marlowe, who solved crimes in *The Big Sleep* (1939), *Farewell My Lovely* (1940), and *The Long Good-bye* (1954). Mickey Spillane, born in 1918, wrote novels of violence and sex starring detective Mike Hammer, such as *I, the Jury* (1947) and *Kiss Me Deadly* (1952). Dashiell Hammett (1894–1961) created detectives Sam Spade in *The Maltese Falcon* (1930) and Nick Charles in *The Thin Man* (1932).

24. (d) Samuel Clemens (1835–1910), who wrote under the pen name Mark Twain, created characters that reflected purely American traits and habits. His greatest character, Huck Finn, is a boy whose adventures on the Mississippi with Jim, a runaway slave, are a social commentary that condemns slavery and reveals the corruption of the American South.

25. (c) Naturalism, a literary movement that came to America from France at the turn of the century, emphasized the subordination of characters to their environments. Stephen Crane's novel *Maggie: A Girl of the Streets* (1896), Frank Norris's *McTeague* (1899), and Theodore Dreiser's *Sister Carrie* (1900) are examples of naturalist fiction.

26. (a) Washington Irving (1783–1859) grew up as a wealthy member of New York society, which he satirized in *History of New York*, a burlesque that he claimed was by the historian Diedrich Knickerbocker. The word *knickerbocker* is now used to name any resident of New York State, particularly one descended from the early Dutch settlers. Rip van Winkle is the hero of one tale in *Sketch Book of Geoffrey Crayon, Gent.*, usually considered to be the first collection of short stories in America. Rip falls asleep for twenty years. When he wakes, an old man, he finds his wife dead and the British colonies replaced by the United States. The other characters listed are from works by Louisa May Alcott, Harriet Beecher Stowe, and Herman Melville.

27. (b) The novelist Willa Cather (1876–1947) grew up in Nebraska, and the prairie country is the setting for many of her works. Her best-known novels deal with pioneers and immigrants in the Midwest—*O Pioneers* (1913), *The Song of the Lark* (1915), and *My Àntonia* (1918) among them. Although *Death Comes for the Archbishop* (1927) is set in the Southwest, it also focuses on the American past.

28. (b) The decadence and slow destruction of the Old South are major themes of the novels of William Faulkner (1897–1962).

His important works take place in a mythical county in Mississippi and involve several fictional families whose lives interweave. *The Sound and the Fury* (1929) tells the story of the disintegration of the Compson family. The narrative is in four distinct parts, the first three being the stream of consciousness of the three sons, one of whom is retarded. *Absalom, Absalom!* (1936) has multiple narrators, who tell of Thomas Sutpen and his doomed attempts to become a Southern aristocrat in the years preceding the Civil War.

29. **(c)** Distinguished by rampant exaggeration and humor, tall tales are folk tales of the American frontier. Some, such as the tales of Davy Crockett, have characters based on real heroes. Most, including stories of Pecos Bill and Paul Bunyan, simply celebrate pioneer traits of courage, strength, and inventiveness.

30. **(c)** Herman Melville (1819–1891) went to sea at the age of eighteen. For the next eight years, he alternated life aboard ships with life as a schoolteacher. Most of his writing is based on his experiences on whalers in the South Pacific. Novels include *Typee* (1846), *Omoo* (1847), *White-Jacket* (1850), and the powerful *Moby-Dick* (1851), which integrates a symbolic tale of man and fate with realistic scenes of whaling and discussion of its history.

31. **(d)** Thomas Stearns Eliot (1888–1965) wrote criticism and plays, but he is best known for his poetry. *The Waste Land*, written after World War I, evokes the related legends of the primitive Fisher King and the Holy Grail in its depiction of a sterile and amoral modern world. *Four Quartets* (1943) includes "Burnt Norton," "East Coker," "The Dry Salvages," and "Little Gidding." Through memories of these places, the poet explores time, mortality, and the creative process.

32. **(a)** *Uncle Tom's Cabin* is a morality tale about life on a plantation. The evil Simon Legree, a Northerner, oversees the slaves and treats them cruelly. Harriet Beecher Stowe (1811–1896) wrote the book in support of the Abolitionist cause, and Abraham Lincoln referred to her as "the little woman who started (the Civil) war." Her book was wildly popular and controversial, and a year after its publication in 1852, she was forced by doubting readers to write *A Key to Uncle Tom's Cabin*, a list of facts about slavery and plantation life.

33. **(d)** Anne Bradstreet (c. 1612–1672) traveled from England to Massachusetts at the age of eighteen. The first collection of

her poems was published in 1650 in England under the title *The Tenth Muse Lately Sprung Up in America*. She is remembered chiefly for short poems on life in New England, including "On the Burning of Her House" and "To My Dear and Loving Husband." She also wrote an autobiography, *Religious Experiences*. Jonathan Edwards (1703–1758), a pastor and missionary in Massachusetts, is known for his "fire-and-brimstone" sermons, notably "Sinners in the Hands of an Angry God." His evangelicism led to the religious movement known as "The Great Awakening" in 1740–1750, which culminated in a split between Edwards's followers and more liberal churchgoers.

34. **(a)** *Death of a Salesman* won Miller a Pulitzer Prize in 1949. Its hero is Willy Loman, the quintessential common man, whose seemingly petty failures are raised to the level of tragedy. *The Crucible* was written at the height of the McCarthy era (1953) and told of the Salem witchcraft trials. The other plays listed are by Tennessee Williams, Edward Albee, and Thornton Wilder.

35. **(c)** In short stories such as "The Snows of Kilimanjaro" (1938) and novels such as *The Sun Also Rises* (1926) and *For Whom the Bell Tolls* (1940), Ernest Hemingway (1899–1961) used a spare, unemotional style punctuated by terse dialogue. His themes include courage, cynicism, and the loss of liberty.

36. **(a)** The daughter of Bronson Alcott, a noted educator and friend to Thoreau and Emerson, Louisa May Alcott (1832–1888) grew up in a poor household surrounded by books and learned people. She wrote melodramas to make ends meet, and became editor of a children's magazine in 1867. Her most popular novels are based on her own family life and include *Little Women* (1869), *Little Men* (1871), *Rose in Bloom* (1876), and *Jo's Boys* (1886).

37. **(c)** Richard Wright (1909–1960) achieved recognition with a collection of short stories called *Uncle Tom's Children*, which won a prize in 1938 as the best work submitted by a member of the Federal Writers' Project. The stories dealt with racial discrimination in the South. *Native Son* (1940) brought Wright lasting fame with its depiction of Bigger Thomas, a Chicago slum-dweller whose environment is directly linked to his fate. *Black Boy* (1945) is an autobiographical account of Wright's Southern boyhood. The other works listed are by James Baldwin, John Dos Passos, and Gwendolyn Brooks.

38. (d) Henry Wadsworth Longfellow (1807–1882) was a prolific poet who helped to create and maintain many American legends in poems such as *The Song of Hiawatha* (1855) and *The Courtship of Miles Standish* (1858). The lines quoted are from *Evangeline* (1847), "A Psalm of Life" (1839), and "Paul Revere's Ride" from *Tales of a Wayside Inn* (1874).

39. (b) Kurt Vonnegut was born in 1922 and worked as a freelance writer in the early 1960s before gaining attention as a science fiction novelist. Works such as *Cat's Cradle* (1963) and *Slaughterhouse-Five* (1969), although still concerned with science fiction themes, were atypical of the genre in their use of absurdism and satire.

40. (a) The quintessential novelist, Henry James (1843–1916) is considered one of the greatest technicians of the form. Many of his works treat the "international theme"—the contrast of American and European characters and values. He strove to hone the point of view in his novels and stories so that revelations and insights belong to his characters rather than to an omniscient narrator. Characterization is therefore subtly and deliberately revealed over the course of the narrative. Among his most important works are *The Portrait of a Lady* (1881), *The Wings of the Dove* (1902), *The Ambassadors* (1903), *The Golden Bowl* (1904), and the novella *The Turn of the Screw* (1898).

41. (a) Sherwood Anderson (1876–1941) is best known for his collection of stories of small-town life titled *Winesburg, Ohio* (1919). The book focuses on the psychological dramas behind the scenes of a fictional town. The extraordinary dreams of ordinary people is also the theme of *Spoon River Anthology*, a collection of blank verse by Edgar Lee Masters (1868–1950).

42. (b) Among the popular works of Ray Bradbury (b. 1920) are *The Martian Chronicles* and many short stories. Ursula LeGuin (b. 1929) wrote *Left Hand of Darkness*, *City of Illusion*, and many other science fiction and fantasy works for children and adults. Isaac Asimov (1920–1992) wrote *I, Robot* and the *Foundation* trilogy, among hundreds of works of fiction and nonfiction.

43. (d) *Muckrakers* was a term used by Theodore Roosevelt to label people concerned with uncovering corruption in business and government. The movement began in 1902 and lasted until World War I. Among the major works of protest to emerge from the movement were Upton Sinclair's *The Jungle* (1906), an exposé of the meat-packing industry; Ida Tarbell's *History of the Standard Oil Company* (1904); and Lincoln Steffens's *Shame of the Cities* (1904).

44. (b) Walt Whitman (1819–1892) wrote poetry that fit natural speech patterns rather than regular metrical structure. His most important work, a collection of poems called *Leaves of Grass* (1855), underwent many revisions and additions during the poet's lifetime. At first ignored by the critics, the book became controversial in time, and Whitman lost a job with the Department of the Interior because of his "immoral" writing. In his celebration of the human body, egalitarianism, and the sexual self, he was certainly ahead of his time.

45. (c) John Updike (b. 1932) is a poet and essayist as well as a fiction writer. His subjects tend to be suburbanites, and although his short stories are quite popular, it is novels such as *Rabbit, Run* (1960) and *The Centaur* (1963) that made his reputation.

46. (b) The Beat movement of the 1950s involved a complicated combination of Eastern mysticism, social nonconformity, sexual freedom, and drug use. Many of the writers associated with the movement were poets, with Allen Ginsberg (b. 1926) and Gregory Corso (b. 1930) among the best known. Jack Kerouac (1922–1969) was a novelist, whose *On the Road* (1957) typifies the rambling style of all of the Beats, poets and fiction writers alike.

47. (c) The poems of Marianne Moore (1887–1972) are unusual in their focus on the whole stanza rather than the line, which makes them read at times like prose rather than poetry. For her subjects she chose animals, machines, buildings, and people, examining each with a scientific eye for detail.

48. (d) Dorothy Parker (1893–1967) wrote acerbic drama reviews for *Vanity Fair* and *The New Yorker* and poems and short stories full of irony and bitter humor, but she is remembered more for her bon mots, one-liners culled from her writing or conversation. These include "Men seldom make passes / At girls who wear glasses" from "News Item" (1927) and "runs the gamut of emotions from A to B" from a drama review. Elwyn Brooks White (1899–1985) was a columnist for *The New Yorker*, a writer of children's books, a poet, and an essayist. He collaborated with James Thurber (1894–1961) on the book *Is Sex Necessary?* (1929). Thurber worked at *The New Yorker* as well. He wrote "The Secret Life of Walter Mitty," a number of other stories, essays, and a play.

49. **(a)** A radical pamphleteer, Thomas Paine (1737–1809) believed in the need for reform through revolution. *Common Sense* (1776) called for the secession of the colonies from England and led to the drafting of the Declaration of Independence. *The Rights of Man* (1792) was written in defense of the French Revolution and led to Paine's trial in England as a traitor. He lived in France until he was imprisoned during the Reign of Terror, and he later died in poverty in the United States.

50. **(c)** Vladimir Nabokov (1899–1977) was born in Russia and moved to the United States in 1940. *Lolita* (1958) is a darkly comic novel about a man's obsessive desire for a very young girl. The title character in *Pnin* (1957) is a semiautobiographical portrait of a professor of Russian literature at an American university. *Pale Fire* (1962) is an experiment in narrative structure, a novel disguised as a poem and commentary.

TEST 10

Mightier Than the Sword: World Literature

> *World literature is . . . a kind of*
> *collective body and a common*
> *spirit, a living unity of the heart*
> *which reflects the growing*
> *spiritual unity of mankind.*
>
> —*ALEXANDER SOLZHENITSYN*

1. *Crime and Punishment* and *The Brothers Karamazov* are novels by
   a. Leo Tolstoy
   b. Aleksandr Pushkin
   c. Fyodor Dostoevsky
   d. Nikolai Gogol

2. Which of the following plays is *not* by George Bernard Shaw?
   a. *Man and Superman*
   b. *Major Barbara*
   c. *Pygmalion*
   d. *Antony and Cleopatra*

3. The poems of William Wordsworth can best be described as
   a. comic and rhetorical

    b. lyrical and romantic

    c. epic and didactic

    d. sentimental and dramatic

4. James Joyce created which of the following characters?

    a. Molly Bloom and Stephen Dedalus

    b. Little Nell and Samuel Pickwick

    c. Adam Bede and Dorothea Brooke

    d. Jean Valjean and Fantine

5. A cave wherein prisoners see only shadows cast by a fire is a central simile in a work by

    a. Plato

    b. Aristotle

    c. Spinoza

    d. Descartes

6. Which of these poets is associated with Irish nationalism and Celtic mythology?

    a. William Butler Yeats

    b. John Dryden

    c. Rudyard Kipling

    d. Elizabeth Barrett Browning

7. "Of man's first disobedience, and the fruit / Of that forbidden tree" is the opening to

    a. *The Fairie Queene* by Edmund Spenser

    b. *The Pilgrim's Progress* by John Bunyan

    c. *The Vision of Delight* by Ben Jonson

    d. *Paradise Lost* by John Milton

8. Which of these characters does *not* appear in *David Copperfield*?

    a. Uriah Heep

    b. Mr. Micawber

    c. Barkis

    d. Pip

9. Gothic novels generally feature
   a. romantic settings and happy endings
   b. gloomy settings and supernatural occurrences
   c. exotic settings and a young boy's coming-of-age
   d. historic settings and characters based on real people

10. *Beowulf* is the oldest existing English
   a. novel
   b. epic
   c. play
   d. historical document

11. Who was Jorge Luis Borges?
   a. a Spanish novelist of the sixteenth century
   b. a Mexican poet and diplomat
   c. an Argentine short-story writer
   d. a Chilean playwright

12. The hero of *Gulliver's Travels*
   a. visits a land of tiny people and a land of philosophers
   b. is shipwrecked on an island with only one inhabitant
   c. travels around the world in a hot-air balloon
   d. has a series of comical adventures in America

13. Who wrote *The Rime of the Ancient Mariner* and *Kubla Khan?*
   a. Edgar Allan Poe
   b. Samuel Taylor Coleridge
   c. Edward Fitzgerald
   d. Robert Burns

14. Marcel Proust is famous for writing
   a. a collection of poems called *The Flowers of Evil*
   b. a hymn to the joys of unconventionality and sexuality
   c. a seven-part novel about memory and time
   d. all of the above

15. What do Alfred, Lord Tennyson; T. H. White; and Sir Thomas Malory have in common?

   a. They all wrote during the Victorian era.

   b. They all left England to live in France.

   c. They all wrote poetry on mythical subjects.

   d. They all wrote about the Arthurian legend.

16. Which of these works is *not* by Samuel Beckett?

   a. the novel *Malone Dies*

   b. the play *Waiting for Godot*

   c. the play *Endgame*

   d. the play *The Maids*

17. Which of these plays are by Anton Chekhov?

   a. *Ghosts, The Master Builder, When We Dead Awaken*

   b. *The Sea Gull, Uncle Vanya, The Cherry Orchard*

   c. *Miss Julie, The Dance of Death, The Father*

   d. *Misalliance, Heartbreak House, Arms and the Man*

18. John Locke, Voltaire, and Jean Jacques Rousseau were

   a. seventeenth- and eighteenth-century philosophers

   b. nineteenth-century politicians

   c. sixteenth- and seventeenth-century novelists

   d. eighteenth- and nineteenth-century poets

19. Among the themes in Franz Kafka's work are

   a. divine love and the achievement of mystical union with God

   b. war and hope expressed through the earth's return to a natural state

   c. alienation and the impossibility of human interconnection

   d. sexual dependence and the role of women in society

20. Which British poet is *not* matched correctly with his work?

   a. William Blake, "To a Mouse"

    b. George Gordon, Lord Byron, *Don Juan*

    c. Percy Bysshe Shelley, "Ozymandias"

    d. John Keats, "La Belle Dame sans Merci"

21. Who wrote *Heart of Darkness* and *Lord Jim?*

    a. E. M. Forster

    b. Rudyard Kipling

    c. Joseph Conrad

    d. Sir Walter Scott

22. Who was Victor Hugo?

    a. a leader of the French Protestants in the sixteenth century

    b. a leading playwright in Victorian England

    c. the deformed hero of *The Hunchback of Notre Dame*

    d. a key figure in the Romantic movement in France

23. Alan Paton, Nadine Gordimer, and Athol Fugard are

    a. South African writers

    b. founders of the school of New Criticism

    c. twentieth-century black dramatists

    d. journalists who have received Pulitzer Prizes

24. The Epic Theater of Bertolt Brecht attempts to

    a. shock the audience and force them to react

    b. involve the audience intellectually rather than emotionally

    c. create a sustained illusion that arouses pity and terror

    d. convey the meaningless of existence through illogical dialogue

25. Miguel de Cervantes' most important work was

    a. *El Cid*

    b. *Life Is a Dream*

    c. "The Death of a Bullfighter"

    d. *Don Quixote*

26. What is the legend of Faust?

    a. the story of a woman who unleashed a box full of evil on the world

    b. the story of a king whose three daughters betray him

    c. the story of a man who sells his soul to the devil in return for youth, knowledge, and power

    d. the story of a deformed man whose love for a gypsy is set against the backdrop of medieval Paris

27. In what genre did the Brothers Grimm, Charles Perrault, and Hans Christian Anderson chiefly write?

    a. fairy tales

    b. novels of social protest

    c. one-act plays

    d. sonnets

28. What happens in the play *Romeo and Juliet?*

    a. A Moorish general kills his wife in the belief that she was his lieutenant's lover.

    b. A leader of the state is murdered in a political conspiracy.

    c. A troubled prince plots against the king to avenge his dead father.

    d. A boy and girl from feuding families fall in love and die while trying to flee together.

29. Who is the author of *Hedda Gabler, A Doll's House,* and *The Wild Duck?*

    a. Henrik Ibsen

    b. Bertolt Brecht

    c. Emile Zola

    d. August Strindberg

30. Which siblings wrote *Jane Eyre* and *Wuthering Heights?*

    a. William and Henry James

    b. Edmond and Jules de Goncourt

    c. Emily and Charlotte Brontë

    d. Thomas and Heinrich Mann

31. Who created the characters of the Wife of Bath, the Prioress, and the Pardoner?

    a. Geoffrey Chaucer

    b. William Shakespeare

    c. Chrétien de Troyes

    d. Thomas Malory

32. Which of these novelists created the desperate, sentimental housewife, Madame Bovary?

    a. Stendahl

    b. Honoré de Balzac

    c. Victor Hugo

    d. Gustave Flaubert

33. A modern novelist for whom man's rediscovery of sexual vitality was the clue to his salvation is

    a. D. H. Lawrence

    b. Thomas Mann

    c. E. M. Forster

    d. Günter Grass

34. Who was the author of *Jude the Obscure, The Return of the Native,* and *The Mayor of Casterbridge?*

    a. L. P. Hartley

    b. Peter Handke

    c. Thomas Hardy

    d. Winifred Holtley

35. Who was George Eliot?

    a. a novelist; she wrote *Middlemarch* and *Daniel Deronda*

    b. a poet; he wrote "Gerontion" and *Old Possum's Book of Practical Cats*

    c. a novelist; he wrote *Parktilden Village* and *Muriel*

    d. a novelist; she wrote *Indiana* and *Consuelo*

36. Who wrote the story of Ulysses, a sailor who faced danger and adventure on his way home from the Trojan War?

    a. Sophocles

    b. Homer

    c. James Joyce

    d. Cicero

37. Who is the Nobel Prize–winning novelist who wrote *Buddenbrooks*, *The Magic Mountain*, and *Death in Venice*?

    a. Thomas Mann

    b. Anton Chekhov

    c. Nikolai Gogol

    d. Isak Dinesen

38. What happened to Robinson Crusoe?

    a. He was orphaned and forced to steal for a living.

    b. He fought for the freedom of the Jewish maiden, Rebecca.

    c. He was shipwrecked on a deserted island.

    d. He roamed the world, surviving misadventures, with Dr. Pangloss.

39. Jean-Paul Sartre, André Malraux, and Martin Buber are all

    a. romantics

    b. existentialists

    c. expressionists

    d. illuminists

40. Which characters were created by Henry Fielding?

    a. Felix Krull and Gustav von Aschenbach

    b. Roderick Random and Humphrey Clinker

c. Pamela Andrews and Clarissa Harlowe

d. Tom Jones and Joseph Andrews

41. For which novels is Jane Austen known?

a. *Villette* and *Shirley*

b. *Pride and Prejudice*, *Emma*, and *Persuasion*

c. *Felix Holt*, *Silas Marner*, and *Adam Bede*

d. *Cousin Bette* and *Lost Illusions*

42. Which Russian novelist wrote sweeping sagas of historical and moral crises?

a. Leo Tolstoy

b. Ivan Turgenev

c. Fyodor Dostoyevsky

d. Isaac Babel

43. A British novelist and critic who experimented with stream of consciousness and interior monologue was

a. Malcolm Lowry

b. D. M. Thomas

c. Virginia Woolf

d. Lytton Strachey

44. A Renaissance poet who wrote of a trip through Hell, Purgatory, and Heaven was

a. Geoffrey Chaucer

b. John Milton

c. Dante Alighieri

d. Giovanni Bocaccio

45. Of what is this poem an example?

Snow, softly, slowly,
settles at dusk in a dance
of white butterflies.
    —*Harry Behn*

a. a sonnet

b. a haiku

c. an epic

d. a ballad

46. Which of these plays is *not* by August Strindberg?

   a. *A Dream Play*

   b. *Miss Julie*

   c. *The Dance of Death*

   d. *Six Characters in Search of an Author*

47. Which of these authors made the year 1984 famous?

   a. George Orwell

   b. Aldous Huxley

   c. H. G. Wells

   d. all of the above

48. Who created the characters of the Cheshire Cat, Tweedledee and Tweedledum, and the Mad Hatter?

   a. Joseph Jacobs

   b. Charles Dodson

   c. J. R. R. Tolkien

   d. Edward Lear

49. For what is Ovid primarily known?

   a. his poetry and discourses on love and art

   b. his tragic plays

   c. his epic poem about Aeneas

   d. his philosophy of government

50. Which of these plays is *not* a Greek tragedy?

   a. *Oedipus the King*

   b. *Electra*

   c. *The Clouds*

   d. *Antigone*

TEST 10: Explanatory Answers

1. **(c)** Fyodor Mikhailovich Dostoevsky (1821–1881) had a career plagued by hostile reviews and mental imbalance. His father's murder by his serfs in 1844 may have precipitated Dostoevsky's preoccupation with murder and patricide, a theme that permeates his work. *Crime and Punishment* (1866) is the story of Raskolnikov, an impoverished student who kills an old pawnbroker. No sooner does he commit the crime than he begins to torment himself by uncovering his unconscious motives. *The Brothers Karamazov* (1880) has a complicated plot surrounding the death of a father and the evidence that implicates his four sons. The plot is perhaps secondary to the themes involving ethics and agnosticism.

2. **(d)** *Antony and Cleopatra* is a play by William Shakespeare. In 1899 Shaw (1856–1950) wrote a play based on a work by Plutarch and called it *Caesar and Cleopatra*. Shaw is known as an advocate of social reform as well as a writer of witty, satiric plays.

3. **(b)** One of the English Romantic poets, William Wordsworth (1770–1850) is remembered for his focus on natural scenes, simple people, and the mystical power of memory. His theory that the language of poetry should arise from common speech was a turning point in English poetry. Such poems as "Lines Composed a Few Miles above Tintern Abbey" and "I Wandered Lonely as a Cloud" are prime examples of romanticism.

4. **(a)** Stephen Dedalus is the protagonist of *Portrait of the Artist as a Young Man* (1916) and a major character in *Ulysses* (1922), in which Molly Bloom figures as well. James Joyce (1882–1941), considered the finest English-language novelist of the twentieth century, experimented with a huge variety of narrative techniques and used symbols from such disparate sources as Greek mythology, Catholic theology, Irish history, and popular songs. The other characters listed are from works by Charles Dickens, George Eliot, and Victor Hugo.

5. **(a)** In his *Republic*, Plato (c. 428 B.C.–348 B.C.) discusses the question "What is philosophy?" He defines it as the "vision of truth" and sees those people with no philosophy as prisoners chained in a cave, with a fire behind them throwing shadows on the wall in front. The prisoners see only shadows, but since they know no other reality, they think of the shadows as real.

Should a prisoner escape, see the outside world, and return to describe it to the others, that escapee will find that the shadows no longer seem clear to him or her. The escapee will find it difficult to convert the others, who still see the shadows clearly. Most of Plato's work is in the form of a dialogue between the philosopher Socrates and a pupil. Other works include the *Apology, Phaedrus, Gorgias,* and *Symposium.*

6. **(a)** William Butler Yeats (1865–1939) was a central figure in the Irish Renaissance, a movement designed to restore Irish culture in the wake of a rise in nationalism. He helped to found the Abbey Theatre, which gained fame through production of controversial plays by Sean O'Casey, John Millington Synge, and Yeats himself. His plays, which include *The Countess Cathleen* (1891) and *The Herne's Egg* (1938), often mix Irish legend with Eastern mysticism. He is better known for his poetry, particularly such late works as "Sailing to Byzantium."

7. **(d)** *Paradise Lost* is a twelve-part epic by John Milton (1608–1674) about the expulsion of Satan from Heaven and Adam and Eve from the Garden of Eden. It is notable for its detailed characterization of biblical figures, its sustained tension, and its ringing, dramatic tone.

8. **(d)** Pip is the hero of *Great Expectations* (1861). *David Copperfield* (1850), like most of the novels by Charles Dickens (1812–1870), was originally serialized. It tells the tale of young David, who lives with his stepfather and whose only comfort in his childhood is his nurse, Clara Peggotty, who later marries Barkis. David is sent by his stepfather to London to fend for himself. He lives with the Micawbers and works in a warehouse before finding work with a lawyer, whose clerk is Uriah Heep, an obsequious man who blackmails his employer. With the help of Mr. Micawber, David at long last removes the threat posed by Uriah Heep. Like most of Dickens's work, the book aims at raising social consciousness by exposing the cruelty of society to the poor and helpless. Unlike his other work, this book is supposed to be at least partly autobiographical.

9. **(b)** A gory book called *The Castle of Otranto* (1764) by Horace Walpole is probably the first English novel in the Gothic genre. Gothic novels were extremely popular and somewhat scandalous in their time—from the late eighteenth to the early nineteenth century. Other works in the genre include *The*

Mysteries of Udolpho (1794) by Ann Radcliffe, *The Monk* (1795) by Matthew Lewis, and *Frankenstein or the Modern Prometheus* (1818) by Mary Wollstonecraft Shelley. Typical of Gothic novels were violent plots, supernatural occurrences, and medieval settings.

10. **(b)** *Beowulf* (c. 700) is a long epic poem in Old English about a Danish hero and his defeat of the monster Grendel. It is assumed to be based in part on Norse legend and in part on Danish history. Each of the more than three thousand lines has four stressed syllables, at least two of which are alliterative (begin with the same sound).

11. **(c)** Jorge Luis Borges (1899–1986) wrote poetry and essays before turning to narrative fiction. His stories, some of which are translated in a collection called *Labyrinths* (1962), feature experimental structures and highly compressed symbolic patterns.

12. **(a)** In *Gulliver's Travels* (1726) the hero goes on four excursions. One takes him to the land of Lilliput, where the residents are extremely small. One takes him to the land of Brobdingnag, where the residents are giants. He also visits the land of Laputa, whose people are "wise" men and philosophers, and Houyhnhnmland, where horses keep Yahoos (who look suspiciously like humans) in servitude. The author, English satirist Jonathan Swift (1667–1745), used the novel to denounce human pettiness, self-styled philosophers, and European society in general.

13. **(b)** *The Rime of the Ancient Mariner* (1798) and *Kubla Khan* (1797) are among the most frequently quoted of all English poems. The latter was written in an opium-induced haze and was never finished. Samuel Taylor Coleridge (1772–1834) was a critical essayist of great importance and one of the leaders of the English romanticists. With Wordsworth he published *Lyrical Ballads* (1798), which contained *The Rime of the Ancient Mariner* and a treatise by Wordsworth that set forth the credo of romantic literature. *The Rime of the Ancient Mariner* contains the often-misquoted lines: "Water, water, everywhere / Nor any drop to drink."

14. **(c)** *Remembrance of Things Past* (1913–1927) is the masterwork of French novelist Marcel Proust (1871–1922). The narrator's memory is involuntarily triggered by inanimate objects, and he also deliberately scrutinizes his past to make

sense of experiences he had no way of understanding at the time. The author explores the disappointing nature of love, the hypocrisy behind the aristocratic façade, and the need to transcend time to find essential meaning. The other works alluded to are by Charles Baudelaire and André Gide.

15. **(d)** Arthur was probably a Celtic chieftain of the sixth century, but he may instead have been a Celtic deity from much earlier. The Arthurian legends were passed down in Wales and England for centuries before being collected and written down by Thomas Malory in *Morte d'Arthur* (c. 1469). In these eight tales King Arthur is presented as the son of Uther Pendragon and the husband of Guinevere. Merlin the magician incorporates druidic rites into the legend as Arthur's teacher and aide. *Idylls of the King* (1859–1885), a series of poems by Alfred, Lord Tennyson, interprets the legend in a more Christian spirit, focusing on the introduction of sin into Camelot through the adultery of Guinevere. Terence Hanbury White wrote four epics based on the legend under the title *The Once and Future King* (1958). This version came to the stage as the musical *Camelot*.

16. **(d)** Samuel Beckett (b. 1906) is known for his plays about the overwhelming desire to communicate in the face of human disintegration. He has also written several novels, many using a stream-of-consciousness narrative. *Malone Dies* (1951) is told through the thoughts of a dying tramp. *Waiting for Godot* (1952) features two tramps, dependent on each other though despising each other, who wait endlessly for someone who never comes. *Endgame* (1957) focuses on a blind man, his parents who are imprisoned in ashcans, and his servant, from whom he derives all information about the disappearing outside world. *The Maids* (1948) is by French playwright Jean Genêt.

17. **(b)** Anton Pavlovich Chekhov (1860–1904) was a short-story writer as well as one of the greatest playwrights in any language. *The Sea Gull* (1896) tells of a writer and his love for Nina, a would-be actress. When she prefers a successful writer to him, he kills a sea gull and offers it to her as a symbol of his destroyed happiness. The successful writer leaves her, and Nina returns, but there is no hope of reconciliation. In *Uncle Vanya* (1899) Vanya gives up his own happiness to make his brother-in-law happy because he considers him a genius. When the brother-in-law proves to be less than Vanya imagines,

Vanya unsuccessfully attempts to murder him and kill himself. *The Cherry Orchard* (1904) is about a family that is helpless in the face of bankruptcy and the loss of their estate. Themes of despair, inability to communicate, and loss of idealism are mitigated by flashes of humor and Chekhov's deep understanding of human behavior. The other plays listed are by Henrik Ibsen, August Strindberg, and George Bernard Shaw.

18. **(a)** John Locke (1632–1704) was an English philosopher who wrote on the origin of ideas and knowledge in "An Essay Concerning Human Understanding." Locke's political theories are even more important; he was the father of modern liberalism, and his ideas are found in the constitutions of France and the United States, among others. François Marie Arouet (Voltaire) (1694–1778) helped bring Locke's ideas to France. He was a prolific writer of poems, dramas, allegories, essays, and histories, believing firmly that only a philosopher could write a history that was meaningful and thus creating a new way of looking at the past. Jean Jacques Rousseau (1712–1778) rejected the rationalism of both Locke and Voltaire and strove to create a climate in which people could respond to life through emotion rather than intellect. Nature and the individual were key elements of the school of thought that became romanticism.

19. **(c)** The Czech writer Franz Kafka (1883–1924) is known especially for his unfinished novels (*The Trial, The Castle, and Amerika*) and the story "Metamorphosis" (1915), in which the protagonist, Gregor Samsa, turns into a giant cockroach. His works feature strained and problematic relationships among guilt-ridden people and plots that range from hilarious to terrifying.

20. **(a)** "To a Mouse" is by the Scottish poet Robert Burns. Lord Byron (1788–1824), Percy Bysshe Shelley (1792–1822), and John Keats (1795–1821) were all English poets in the romantic tradition. *Don Juan* (1819–1824) features a thinly disguised Byron in the role of the Spanish profligate. "Ozymandias" (1818) is a sonnet by Shelley, and "La Belle Dame sans Merci" is a ballad by Keats, who is also known for his odes on melancholy, a nightingale, and a Grecian urn.

21. **(c)** Joseph Conrad (1857–1924) is remembered for his tales of adventure and moral dilemmas. *Heart of Darkness* (1902) tells of the exploitation perpetrated on the natives of the

Belgian Congo by Kurtz, a white trader. The title character in *Lord Jim* abandons ship in his youth, leaving his passengers to die. They survive to tell the tale, and Jim spends the rest of his life trying to regain his lost honor. Both the short story and novel are narrated by Marlow, whose analysis of the events is as vital to the work as the events themselves.

22. **(d)** Victor Hugo (1802–1885) was one of the best-known poets in France and a leader of the Romantic movement, but English-speaking audiences know him for his novels. *The Hunchback of Notre Dame* (1831) and *Les Miserables* (1862) feature sweeping, melodramatic plots.

23. **(a)** Alan Paton (1903–1988) is the author of *Cry, the Beloved Country* and other novels about racism. Nadine Gordimer (b. 1923) is also a novelist and short-story writer whose works have at times been banned in South Africa. Athol Fugard (b. 1932) is an actor and playwright, whose *Blood Knot* (1961) was the first play to be performed in his country with a mixed-race cast.

24. **(b)** Rather than telling one story from beginning to end, Epic Theater is generally episodic. The audience is alienated from the action via such unexpected effects as direct address by the actors and the use of placards and slides. By removing the possibility of emotional connection, Brecht (1898–1956) hoped to cause the audience to think and learn. The other techniques mentioned are typical of Artaud's Theater of Cruelty, the classical theory of tragedy espoused by Aristotle, and the Theater of the Absurd.

25. **(d)** *Don Quixote* (1615) is the story of a somewhat demented romantic who believes that he is a knight. He chooses the practical peasant, Sancho Panza, to be his squire, and the two travel abroad, with Don Quixote's vivid imagination providing endless adventures and misadventures. The work, by Miguel de Cervantes (1547–1616), marks a milestone in the history of the novel. The other items listed are a historic character whose exploits formed the basis for works by Pierre Corneille and Lope de Vega, a play by Pedro Calderón de la Barca, and a poem by Federico García Lorca.

26. **(c)** Based on the life of fifteenth-century magician Georg Faust, the legend of the man who sold his soul to the devil has been treated by many, including Christopher Marlowe in his play *The Tragical History of Dr. Faustus* (1588), Goethe in his play

Faust (1808), and indirectly by Thomas Mann in his novel *Doktor Faustus* (1947).

27. **(a)** The brothers Grimm, Jacob (1785–1863) and Wilhelm (1786–1859), wrote and collected German legends and fairy tales, including "Rapunzel" and "Snow White and Rose Red." They were also known for their studies of the German language. Charles Perrault (1628–1703) was a French critic as well as a writer of fairy tales, including "Sleeping Beauty" and "Puss in Boots." Hans Christian Andersen (1805–1875) was a Dane who wrote novels, poetry, and plays as well as fairy tales, among which are "The Ugly Duckling," "The Little Mermaid," and "The Emperor's New Clothes."

28. **(d)** One of William Shakespeare's best-known tragedies, *Romeo and Juliet* (c. 1596) tells of the warring Montague and Capulet families of Verona, and how Romeo, a Montague, and Juliet, a Capulet, fall in love, are secretly married, and plot to flee Verona after Romeo kills Juliet's cousin. A misunderstanding leads Romeo to believe that Juliet is dead; he kills himself, and on seeing his dead body, Juliet also kills herself. The other plots mentioned are those of *Othello, Julius Caesar,* and *Hamlet.*

29. **(a)** Henrik Ibsen (1828–1906) was a Norwegian playwright much of whose work focuses on the social problems of his time, such as the role of women, explored in *A Doll's House* (1879) and *Hedda Gabler* (1890), and the weakness of human idealism, treated in *The Wild Duck* (1884). Many of his plays were examples of realism, a style that presents life without idealization, but he also wrote fantasy plays such as *Peer Gynt* (1867) and highly symbolic dramas such as *When We Dead Awaken* (1900).

30. **(c)** Charlotte Brontë (1816–1855) and Emily Brontë (1818–1848) were sisters raised in Yorkshire, England. Charlotte Brontë's best-known novel is *Jane Eyre* (1847), the story of a poor governess and her domineering, obsessive employer. Emily Brontë's masterpiece, *Wuthering Heights* (1847), tells of the intense and unfulfilled love between Heathcliff and Catherine.

31. **(a)** Geoffrey Chaucer (1343–1400) was the author of *The Canterbury Tales*. It is the story of a group of pilgrims journeying to Canterbury, each of whom tells a tale. In the

telling, the tales reveal much about the characters who are speaking and about Chaucer's time.

32. (d) Gustave Flaubert (1821–1880) was known for his detailed, precise style. *Madame Bovary* (1856), a masterpiece of craftsmanship, is the story of the life of a bourgeois woman and the despair that drives her to suicide.

33. (a) D. H. Lawrence (1885–1930) was the son of a miner, a profession on which he focuses in his early novel *Sons and Lovers* (1913). Other well-known novels are *The Rainbow* (1915), *Women in Love* (1920), *Aaron's Rod* (1922), and the controversial *Lady Chatterley's Lover*, which was censored in England until 1960.

34. (c) Thomas Hardy (1840–1928) was an English novelist in the naturalist tradition who wrote of characters trapped by fate and their environment in stories such as *The Return of the Native* (1878), *The Mayor of Casterbridge* (1886), and *Jude the Obscure* (1896).

35. (a) George Eliot is the pen name of Mary Ann Evans (1819–1880). One of the foremost Victorian novelists, she explored the moral and social problems of her era in novels such as *The Mill on the Floss* (1860), *Middlemarch* (1871), and *Daniel Deronda* (1874). The other writers mentioned are T. S. Eliot, George Elliot, and George Sand.

36. (b) Homer, supposed to have been a blind poet who lived in Greece in the ninth century B.C., may or may not have composed the *Odyssey*, the story of Ulysses' journey from Troy to Ithaka, and the *Iliad*, the story of certain episodes during the Trojan War. The stories themselves were handed down orally before appearing in written form, and after their writing they were further edited and changed until the second century B.C.

37. (a) Thomas Mann (1875–1955) wrote novels, novellas, and short stories, many of which are explorations of the artistic temperament. His greatest novel, *The Magic Mountain* (1924), reflects his growing concern with the political state of Europe; in 1933 he was exiled from Germany by Hitler, and he became an American citizen in 1944.

38. (c) Daniel Defoe (1660–1731) wrote *Robinson Crusoe* when he was nearly sixty. The story is taken from the true story of Alexander Selkirk, who lived for five years on a deserted island.

Defoe is also the author of *Moll Flanders* (1722) and *A Journal of the Plague Year* (1722). The other plot summaries are of *Oliver Twist* (1837), *Ivanhoe* (1819), and *Candide* (1759).

39. **(b)** The Existential movement was at its peak in France in the 1940s. Influenced by the philosophers Kierkegaard and Nietzsche, it postulated that existence precedes essence, that man is nothing but what he becomes by acting. Self-honesty is the key to moral life because no absolutes exist by which to make decisions or judgments.

40. **(d)** Henry Fielding's (1707–1754) best-known character is Tom Jones, the hero of his story about a foundling who grows into a headstrong young man and meets with many adventures before claiming his birthright. Fielding also wrote *Joseph Andrews* (1742), the tale of another young man, this one supposed to be the brother of Samuel Richardson's character, Pamela. The other characters mentioned are inventions of Thomas Mann, Tobias Smollett, and Samuel Richardson.

41. **(b)** Jane Austen (1775–1817) was the author of six complete novels: *Sense and Sensibility* (1811), *Pride and Prejudice* (1813), *Mansfield Park* (1814), *Emma* (1815), *Northanger Abbey*, and *Persuasion*, the last two published in 1818 after her death. Her novels, which feature ordinary characters in ordinary surroundings, are brilliantly comic studies of human nature. The other novels mentioned are by Charlotte Brontë, George Eliot, and Honoré de Balzac.

42. **(a)** Count Leo Tolstoy (1828–1910) is best known for his immense historical novel *War and Peace* (1864), set during the Napoleonic Wars, and his story of an adulteress punished, *Anna Karenina* (1873). After writing *Anna Karenina*, Tolstoy underwent a religious conversion that resulted in his belief in passive resistance and his rejection of wealth and property. As well as novels and short stories, he wrote religious pieces and essays criticizing the czarist regime.

43. **(c)** Virginia Woolf (1882–1941) was the author of many novels and short stories, among which are *Mrs. Dalloway* (1922), *To the Lighthouse* (1927), and *The Waves* (1931). Her work incorporates experimental techniques and focuses on the psychological lives of her characters.

44. **(c)** *The Divine Comedy* (1321), Dante's masterwork, is an epic poem describing the author's journey, under the guidance of the Roman poet Virgil and the author's beloved, Beatrice,

through Hell and Purgatory to Heaven. The poem is a condemnation of the corrupt Catholic church and a criticism of the Florentine political situation as well as a description of the state of human nature and an allegory of the movement of the soul toward God.

45. (b) A haiku is a Japanese poem of three lines, the first with five syllables, the second with seven syllables, and the third with five syllables. The poems usually contain figurative language to suggest aspects of nature.

46. (d) August Strindberg (1849–1912) was a Swedish playwright whose emotional life deeply influenced his work. Bitter because of an unhappy marriage and accusations of blasphemy for his short stories, he wrote *Miss Julie* (1888) and *The Dance of Death* (1901), plays detailing sexual and emotional torment between men and women. He suffered a nervous breakdown in 1896, and his later plays, including *A Dream Play* (1902), are mystical in nature. He is often considered a forerunner of the Expressionist movement.

47. (a) George Orwell (1903–1950) was the author of the horrifying futuristic novel *1984* (1949), which looked toward a future in which life was controlled by an all-seeing Big Brother. He also wrote *Animal Farm* (1945), a novel in which farm animals revolt against the farmer who owns them. Both books are satires directed against the Communist regime in the Soviet Union under Joseph Stalin.

48. (b) Charles Dodson (1832–1898), who wrote under the pen name Lewis Carroll, was the author of *Alice's Adventures in Wonderland* (1865) and *Through the Looking Glass* (1872), written for a young girl whom he idolized. The stories follow the adventures of Alice, who falls down a rabbit hole and meets many bizarre and fascinating characters. The books have been closely examined by Freudians and are sometimes called surrealistic.

49. (a) Ovid (43 B.C.–17 A.D.) was a Roman poet whose most famous work, *The Metamorphoses* (c. 8 A.D.), is a series of poems that tell of historical and legendary figures from the creation of the world to the time of Augustus. His *Art of Love*, when revived in the Middle Ages, became the basis of the medieval ideal of courtly love.

50. **(c)** *The Clouds* (423 B.C.) by Aristophanes is a comedy, the butt of which is Sophocles, whom the playwright mocks. *Oedipus the King* (c. 427 B.C.) and *Antigone* (413 B.C.) are tragedies by Sophocles; the first is about a man who, through misunderstanding and mistaken identity, kills his father and marries his mother. Antigone, Oedipus' daughter, sacrifices her own life to bury her brother. *Electra* (413 B.C.) is a tragedy by Euripides in which Electra seeks revenge on her mother, Clytemnestra, for the murder of her father, Agamemnon; she and her brother, Orestes, murder Clytemnestra, and Orestes goes mad.

The Birds and the Bees: Life Science

Beyond plants are animals,
Beyond animals is man,
Beyond man is the universe.

—*JEAN TOOMER*

1. If a desert tortoise spends the summer or the dry season in a burrow, what is it doing?

   a. regenerating

   b. lactating

   c. hibernating

   d. estivating

2. Who was Gregor Mendel?

   a. a British physician who discovered how blood circulates

   b. an Austrian monk who pioneered the study of genetics

   c. a Russian chemist who formulated the periodic table of elements

   d. a Dutch scientist who classified members of the insect family

3. What does the theory of natural selection state?

   a. A plant or animal can return to the characteristics of its ancestors.

   b. A population of animals will move from one region to another.

   c. Those organisms that are best adapted to the environment will survive.

   d. All organisms are made up of cells.

4. Which of these pairs of animals can interbreed?

   a. cats and dogs

   b. horses and donkeys

   c. rats and mice

   d. none of the above

5. What is the chemical change that produces alcohol in wine?

   a. fermentation

   b. distillation

   c. hydrolysis

   d. condensation

6. What is osmosis?

   a. the removal of waste products

   b. the movement of molecules of liquid through a membrane

   c. the maintenance of a balanced environment

   d. the clumping together of cells

7. If a man with pure dominant genes for six fingers and a woman with recessive genes for five fingers have a child, how many fingers will the child have on each hand?

   a. six

   b. five

   c. six on one hand, five on the other

   d. eleven

8. What is the best definition of a cell?

   a. the site of protein synthesis

    b. the material that makes up genes

    c. the unit of structure and function of all living things

    d. any living plant or animal

9. What is the role of chromosomes?

    a. They contain enzymes that release energy in respiration.

    b. They propel organisms.

    c. They control all of the functions of a cell.

    d. They contain the genes that will determine the characteristics of an organism.

10. What is the difference between instinct and conditioning?

    a. Instinct is a reaction of hunger; conditioning is a reaction of fear.

    b. Instinct is innate behavior; conditioning is learned behavior.

    c. Instinct is learning in early youth; conditioning is learning later in life.

    d. Instinct is possessed by the higher animals; conditioning is possessed by lower animals.

11. What do the amoeba, the paramecium, and the euglena have in common?

    a. They are all sessile.

    b. They are all one-celled organisms.

    c. They are all types of algae.

    d. They are all types of mold.

12. The thorns of the rose, the shape of the walking stick insect, and the coloration of the chameleon are examples of

    a. adaptation

    b. mimicry

    c. metamorphosis

    d. substitution

13. In what substance is nitrogen found?

    a. carbon dioxide

    b. water

    c. protein

    d. sugar

14. To what classes do salamanders and snakes belong?

    a. Salamanders are reptiles and snakes are amphibians.

    b. Snakes are reptiles and salamanders are amphibians.

    c. Both are reptiles.

    d. Both are amphibians.

15. In order, which animals are herbivores, carnivores, and omnivores?

    a. alligator, anteater, hedgehog

    b. skunk, elephant, pig

    c. dog, horse, eagle

    d. sheep, lion, human

16. An animal undergoing metamorphosis is

    a. changing from cold-blooded to warm-blooded

    b. moving from one location to another

    c. changing from one developmental stage to the next

    d. mutating in a beneficial manner

17. For what are James Watson and Francis Crick known?

    a. establishing the function and structure of DNA

    b. discovering how plants get nourishment

    c. recognizing the similarities between primates and humans

    d. discovering the function of gills in aquatic animals

18. Why do certain trees have needles instead of leaves?

    a. The needles provide protection against bark-eating animals.

    b. The needles do not taste good to predatory insects.

    c. The needles contain the seeds that allow the trees to reproduce.

    d. The needles allow the trees to exist in colder temperatures and with less water.

19. What is homeostasis?

    a. the loss of water from a cell

    b. the maintenance of a balanced internal environment

    c. the process during which sex cells are formed

    d. the sudden appearance of a new, inheritable trait

20. What was Charles Darwin's major contribution to the scientific world?

    a. the refutation of the existence of God

    b. the discovery of the age of the earth

    c. the formulation of a viable theory of evolution

    d. the invention of the microscope

21. Which of the following is *not* true of birds?

    a. They are vertebrates.

    b. They are warm-blooded.

    c. They have a four-chambered heart.

    d. They have functional teeth.

22. What is the correct order of stages in the life cycle of a butterfly?

    a. caterpillar → larva → butterfly

    b. egg → larva → pupa → imago

    c. egg → imago → caterpillar → butterfly

    d. larva → imago → pupa → butterfly

23. Why are identical twins studied to determine the effects of heredity and environment on personality?

    a. Identical twins consist of a male and female.

    b. Identical twins are usually treated the same way by parents.

     c. Identical twins have identical genetic makeup.

     d. Identical twins share the same environment in the womb.

24. In chemistry, what is a bond?

     a. a tiny particle in the nucleus of an atom

     b. the unit used to measure the amount of a substance

     c. a molecule made up of only one atom

     d. the force that holds atoms together to form molecules

25. Which of these animals are invertebrates?

     a. lobsters, crabs, and shrimp

     b. salmon, eels, and trout

     c. frogs, toads, and salamanders

     d. snakes, lizards, and turtles

26. The term *scientific method* refers to

     a. a system in which numbers are expressed as products of a one-digit number and a power of 10

     b. the classification and labeling of organisms

     c. a process involving hypothesizing, collecting data, and testing the hypothesis

     d. the belief that science can explain social and cosmic disorders

27. To be classified as a mammal, an animal must

     a. live on land

     b. have hair and be warm-blooded

     c. have a three-chambered heart

     d. all of the above

28. How is aerobic respiration different from anaerobic respiration?

     a. One is internal; one is external.

     b. One involves oxygen; the other does not.

     c. One is performed by animals; the other is performed by plants.

     d. One applies to living matter; the other does not.

29. The process of germination involves

    a. the beginning of growth in a plant embryo

    b. the dispersal of seeds by wind or water

    c. a variation in the genes of an organism

    d. the spread of contagion from one organism to another

30. What is DNA?

    a. a series of genes that determine a specific characteristic

    b. a pair of chromosomes found in the nucleus of a cell

    c. the product of the joining of a male and female gamete

    d. a chain of nucleotides containing genetic information

31. When you refer to an organism's habitat, you mean

    a. the behavior it exhibits

    b. the relationship between it and its environment

    c. the type of region in which it lives

    d. the population of its community

32. Which list gives the correct order for the classification of living things?

    a. kingdom, phylum, class, order, family, genus, species

    b. kingdom, phylum, family, class, order, species, genus

    c. kingdom, class, phylum, order, genus, species, family

    d. kingdom, order, class, phylum, family, genus, species

33. Which statement about symmetry is *not* true?

    a. Only animals with backbones are bilaterally symmetrical.

    b. A hydra and a sea anemone are radially symmetrical.

    c. An earthworm and a spider are bilaterally symmetrical.

    d. Taxonomists use symmetry as a classifying trait.

34. An example of a food chain might be

    a. carbohydrate → protein → fat

    b. fungus → oak → robin

    c. algae → fish → heron

    d. salivary gland → stomach → small intestine

35. The reptiles known today as dinosaurs roamed the earth

    a. about 1 million years ago

    b. at the same time as the first birds and mammals

    c. at the same time as Cro-Magnon man

    d. for about five thousand years

36. Meiosis and mitosis are both processes of

    a. cell division

    b. human digestion

    c. phototropism

    d. liquid absorption

37. What is an enzyme?

    a. a kind of virus that attacks bacteria

    b. the part of the red blood cell that carries oxygen

    c. a protein that activates chemical conversions

    d. a ductless gland found in mammals and birds

38. Which of these steps is *not* part of the carbon cycle?

    a. Animals release carbon dioxide through respiration.

    b. Plants use carbon dioxide in photosynthesis.

    c. Microorganisms break down carbon compounds.

    d. Incomplete combustion forms carbon monoxide.

39. What is a protein?
   a. the nucleus of the hydrogen atom
   b. the water and other cells in a living organism
   c. any of a certain class of single-celled organisms
   d. a molecule made up of chains of amino acids

40. Which of the following is an example of a parasitic relationship?
   a. mistletoe growing on a cottonwood tree
   b. cellulose-digesting microorganisms in a deer's stomach
   c. wolves attacking a herd of caribou
   d. a cattle egret eating insects stirred up by a cow

41. Which of these animals is likely to migrate?
   a. elk
   b. whale
   c. bald eagle
   d. all of the above

42. Bacteria differ from most single-celled organisms in that
   a. they lack a nuclear membrane
   b. they cause numerous diseases
   c. they have no means of locomotion
   d. they do not reproduce

43. The French naturalist Jean-Baptiste de Lamarck was responsible for a theory stating that
   a. molecules of ATP are formed during cellular respiration
   b. plants produce a substance that restores air
   c. organisms can pass on traits acquired during their lifetimes
   d. genetic material can move from one bacterium to another

44. When a chemist refers to *synthesis*, he or she means

   a. change that does not alter the chemical composition of a substance

   b. creation of a complex compound through combining of elements or simple compounds

   c. separation of combined liquids into individual liquids

   d. chemical decomposition of a substance into simpler substances

45. Which of the following statements is *not* true of mutations?

   a. They can be caused by radiation.

   b. They are caused by a change in DNA.

   c. They invariably are passed on to offspring.

   d. They may be harmful or beneficial.

46. The reproductive organs of certain plants are contained in the

   a. fruit

   b. flower

   c. stem

   d. root

47. What is the difference between organic and inorganic chemistry?

   a. Organic chemistry is concerned with physical properties of materials.

   b. Inorganic chemistry is the study of energy; organic chemistry is the study of entropy.

   c. Organic chemistry focuses on carbon compounds.

   d. Inorganic chemistry deals with living organisms.

48. What takes place during photosynthesis?

   a. Chlorophyll converts light energy into food.

   b. Carbohydrates break down and release energy.

    c. A new plant is formed from an existing plant part.

    d. Roots respond to water in the soil by growing downward.

49. *Ecology* may best be defined as the study of

    a. distribution of resources

    b. natural interrelationships

    c. technological advances

    d. toxic substances

50. How is AIDS transmitted?

    a. by contact between skin and skin

    b. by exchange of body fluids

    c. by bacterial infection

    d. by an airborne virus

TEST 11: Explanatory Answers

1. (d) When an animal estivates, as when it hibernates, its metabolism slows and its body temperature drops. Animals estivate or hibernate in response to extremes in temperature or lack of food or water. The difference is that hibernation takes place during the cold weather months, while estivation is a response to heat and lack of water.

2. (b) Mendel (1822–1884) was an Augustinian monk who conducted experiments on garden vegetables. His conclusions about pollination led to the development of the theories of heredity that make up the basis of genetics today. In particular, Mendel concluded that any inherited characteristic is the result of the combination of hereditary units from both parents. His conclusions were lost for thirty-five years; it was not until 1900 that they were rediscovered.

3. (c) Natural selection is a part of Darwin's theory of evolution. Because there is a struggle for existence among organisms, only those best suited to their environment will survive. Any favorable changes that develop—through mutation, for example—will be transmitted to offspring to aid further in survival.

4. **(b)** Horses and donkeys, although they are of different species, can interbreed, producing mules (the offspring of a male donkey and a female horse) and hinnies (the offspring of a female donkey and a male horse). Usually, these offspring are sterile. Deciding what determines a species is a point of scientific controversy. Speciation can be based on interbreeding, genetic makeup, shape and form, geographic location, and behavior. Usually, animals that can interbreed and produce viable offspring are said to be of the same species, but, as horses and donkeys illustrate, there are exceptions even to that rule.

5. **(a)** Fermentation, the breaking down of simple sugars, produces either lactic acid or ethyl alcohol and carbon dioxide. The fermentation of grapes or malt can result in an alcoholic beverage—wine or beer. In winemaking, the yeasts found on grape skins come into contact with fruit sugars when the grape is crushed and convert those sugars into alcohol.

6. **(b)** When a semipermeable membrane, such as a cell wall, divides two levels of a solvent, the molecules from the greater concentration of solvent will pass through the membrane until equilibrium is reached; this movement is called osmosis and helps to control the movement of liquids in and out of cells.

7. **(a)** In this purely theoretical speculation, the six-finger gene is dominant, and if one partner has two six-finger genes and one has two five-finger genes, the child produced will have one dominant, six-finger gene and one recessive five-finger gene. Since the dominant gene determines the physical characteristic, the child will have six fingers on each hand.

8. **(c)** The Cell Theory, developed by scientists working in many countries, states that cells are the units of structure of all plants and animals, cells are the units of function of all plants and animals, and all living cells come only from other living cells. Cells carry out the essential processes that produce energy and sustain life.

9. **(d)** Chromosomes are found in the nuclei of cells. Each species has a specific number of chromosomes in all cells. Most chromosomes come in pairs, except for those found in sex cells, which have only half the usual number of chromosomes.

10. **(b)** Innate behavior is that which does not have to be learned; it includes biorhythms and instincts, which are not based on previous experience. Learned behavior includes conditioning,

which occurs as a result of associating a response with a stimulus; imprinting, which is a type of learning that occurs early in life; and reasoning, which is finding solutions to previously unencountered problems.

11. **(b)** All life arose from a single-celled ancestor. Among the single-celled organisms that are considered plants are algae and plankton. Protozoa, including amoebae and paramecia, are single-celled animals. Euglena is a single-celled organism that has characteristics of both plants and animals.

12. **(a)** Living things must adapt to survive in their environments. Adaptations are changes made by organisms to increase their chances of survival. The rose developed thorns for protection, the walking stick looks like a stick to blend in with its environment, and the chameleon changes its color for safety as its environment changes.

13. **(c)** Because organisms cannot use free nitrogen from the air, they must secure the element from compounds. Plants obtain nitrogen from nitrates that are dissolved in water in the soil. Animals obtain it from plant proteins or from other animals that have gotten nitrogen from plants. Decaying animals or animal wastes in the soil are broken down by bacteria, replacing the soil's nitrogen. Other bacteria change the nitrogen to nitrates, and the nitrogen cycle goes on.

14. **(b)** Reptiles are animals that usually breathe through lungs, usually have a three-chambered heart, and lay eggs in leathery shells. Turtles, snakes, alligators, lizards, and crocodiles are reptiles. Amphibians are animals that breathe through gills in the larval stage and through lungs as adults; they undergo a complete metamorphosis to reach adulthood. Frogs, salamanders, and newts are amphibians.

15. **(d)** Herbivores are animals that eat only plants, such as many fish, cows, and most rodents. Carnivores are flesh-eating animals, such as seals, wolves, and cats. Omnivores eat both plants and meat; humans are omnivores.

16. **(c)** Animals metamorphose when they move from one state to the next in their growth cycle. A frog, for instance, begins as an egg that hatches into a gilled tadpole. It then develops legs and lungs and absorbs its tail and finally emerges as an adult frog.

17. **(a)** Francis Crick, born in 1916, and James Watson, born in 1928, are biologists who won the 1962 Nobel Prize in physiology

for discovering the double helix form of DNA, the material that makes up genes.

18. **(d)** Most evergreens have needlelike leaves that require less water than regular leaves and are more resistant to cold. Evergreens tend to keep their leaves all year, except for the larch and a few other species. The sequoias, evergreens that grow in California, are among the oldest living things on earth.

19. **(b)** Homeostasis can be defined as the maintenance of equilibrium within an internal environment. Such factors as osmosis, temperature adjustment, and maintenance of constant pH values contribute to homeostasis.

20. **(c)** Charles Darwin (1809–1882) worked as a naturalist aboard the HMS *Beagle*. During his five-year voyage he observed nature intently, and his thoughts about animal development led to his theory of natural selection, which postulated that evolution occurs through the survival of the fittest individuals in a population.

21. **(d)** Birds, which are warm-blooded animals with feathers, grind their food in their gizzards to help digestion. They have small brains and a poor sense of smell, but their eyesight is very good. Not all birds can fly; penguins and ostriches are land-bound, and penguins are also able to swim.

22. **(b)** The metamorphosis of the butterfly occurs in several stages. An egg hatches into a larva, which is often a caterpillar. In the next stage, the larva pupates within a chrysalis, or cocoon. Finally, an imago, or full-grown butterfly, emerges.

23. **(c)** Deciding what personality traits are influenced by heredity and what traits are influenced by environment is very difficult and controversial. One way of determining which characteristics are genetic is to compare identical twins and fraternal twins in terms of a personality trait. If the trait is inherited, identical twins should be much more similar regarding the trait than fraternal twins. The study of identical twins who have been separated since birth also provides much information about which traits are inherited and which are the result of environmental influences.

24. **(d)** A chemical bond is the union of atoms by the transfer or sharing of electrons. When electrons are shared, the bond is called covalent; when an electron is transferred from one atom to the other, the bond is called ionic.

THE BIRDS AND THE BEES: LIFE SCIENCE

25. **(a)** Invertebrates are animals that have no backbone or internal skeletons. They range from simple, one-celled protozoa to the complex insect. Arthropods such as the lobster, tick, and centipede are equipped with exoskeletons, or external skeletons.

26. **(c)** The scientific method is a label for a system in which a problem is formulated, a hypothetical answer is suggested, data about the problem are collected through observation or experimentation, and the hypothesis is tested and accepted or rejected.

27. **(b)** A mammal has a four-chambered heart, is warm-blooded, and has hair. Most female mammals bear live young, which they feed with milk produced in their mammary glands. Examples of mammals include dogs, humans, whales, and elephants.

28. **(b)** Both aerobic and anaerobic respiration are internal; that is, each takes place within a cell. In aerobic respiration, oxygen is used to break glucose into carbon dioxide and water. In anaerobic respiration, yeast or bacteria may change glucose into ethanol and carbon dioxide in a process called *fermentation.* In animals a lack of oxygen may cause enzymes to break down glucose into lactic acid in the muscles. Energy is released with each change.

29. **(a)** The seed of a plant contains an embryo. Given the correct external conditions, growth begins in the embryo, and a new plant develops. Many seeds remain dormant in the ground until conditions involving heat and water are correct for germination.

30. **(d)** A nucleic acid is a chain of nucleotides, bonded chemically, that control cellular activity. There are two kinds of nucleic acid: DNA and RNA. DNA is made up of nucleotides that contain deoxyribose, a sugar; phosphoric acid; and one of the following bases: adenine, guanine, cytosine, or thymine. The bases bond with bases in other nucleotides to form a structure called a *double helix.* Genes are made up of DNA. RNA is made by DNA and plays a role in the synthesis of protein.

31. **(c)** A habitat is the kind of place in which an organism lives. The term may refer to a large natural area such as a desert, rain forest, or tundra; or it may be more specific—a riverbed, hillside, or swamp may also be a habitat.

32. (a) *Taxonomy* is the term for the classification of living organisms according to traits and relationships. When an organism is referred to by its "scientific name," that name is made up of the genus and species classifications. For example, human beings are *Homo sapiens.* The classifications for humans from kingdom down are as follows: kingdom—Animal; phylum—Chordata; subphylum—Vertebrata; class—Mammalia; order—Primates; family—Hominidae; genus—*Homo*; species—*sapiens.*

33. (a) Organisms that are radially symmetrical have similar parts arranged around a central axis, much like the spokes of a wheel. Organisms that are bilaterally symmetrical have similar parts arranged along a median axis, with one half more or less mirroring the other. All vertebrates and many invertebrates are bilaterally symmetrical.

34. (c) The term *food chain* refers to the sequence of energy transfer among organisms. Plants,which make up 90 percent of visible living organisms, get their food energy from sunlight. When they are eaten by herbivores (plant-eating animals) or omnivores (plant- or meat-eaters), they pass some of this energy on. Herbivores in turn pass on their energy to carnivores (meat-eaters) or omnivores. The energy from plants thus directly or indirectly sustains the remaining 10 percent of visible living things.

35. (b) Dinosaurs are classified as reptiles, although some appear to have been warm-blooded. Fossil records indicate that they first appeared about 200 million years ago, perhaps around the same time that the first mammals appeared. They died out about 150 million years later, and smaller reptiles, birds, and mammals dominated the earth. Cro-Magnons did not show up for another 50 million years or so. Many theories exist as to why the dinosaurs vanished; the likeliest involves changes in climate and geography.

36. (a) Mitosis is the normal process of cell division in animals and plants. First the chromosomes in the nucleus double. A centriole divides in two, and each half leads one set of chromosomes to one side of the nucleus as the membrane of the nucleus disappears. A new membrane forms around each group of chromosomes, creating two identical nuclei where only one had been. The end product is two identical cells. In meiosis two divisions take place. First the chromosomes double, and the doubled chromosomes line up in pairs. The pairs then separate. Next the separated pairs line up and divide as in mitosis. The end product is four sex cells, each containing half the number of chromosomes of the original nucleus. When sex cells combine during reproduction, they create a new cell containing the normal number of chromosomes, half from one parent cell and half from the other.

37. **(c)** Enzymes are proteins that catalyze chemical reactions. They are produced by cells in animals, plants, and bacteria. Most enzymes are keyed to a single type of chemical reaction, which means that cells must make a huge variety of enzymes. Some examples of human enzymes are pepsin, which breaks down proteins to produce peptides, and maltase, which breaks down maltose to produce glucose. As with any protein, an enzyme is made up of amino acids.

38. **(d)** Every living thing contains carbon. The movement of this element between living things and the environment is called the carbon cycle. Through photosynthesis plants convert carbon into carbohydrates and other molecules. Through respiration they release the carbon in the form of carbon dioxide and water. When plants die, microorganisms break down the carbon in them and release it. Animals gain carbon through consumption of plants; they release it through respiration and decay.

39. **(d)** Proteins perform a variety of tasks. For example, enzymes catalyze chemical changes, hemoglobin transports oxygen, hormones regulate metabolism, and antibodies control immunity. Each protein type is made up of a unique sequence of amino acids, linked together by peptide bonds to form long chains. DNA contains the genetic information for the sequence of amino acids for each protein. The information is first used to make a molecule of messenger RNA from which the protein sequence is derived.

40. **(a)** Living things survive through complex interactions with their environment and with other living things. In a parasitic relationship one organism lives off a host organism, occasionally destroying the host over time. The other relationships mentioned are examples of symbiosis or mutualism, in which both organisms benefit; predation, in which a free-living organism feeds an another; and commensalism, in which one organism benefits and the other is neither harmed nor helped.

41. (d) Animals migrate for a number of reasons, the primary one being the need to locate a breeding place. They may search for better climate in winter or summer; for example, geese flying south and north. They may return to a particular area to spawn, as salmon do. Excessive population may force a migration, as with lemmings.

42. (a) Bacteria are neither plants nor animals. Each of the three main forms—rod-shaped, spiral, and round—is a single-celled organism. The organism houses DNA but has no separate nucleus to contain it. Some forms move by means of hairlike appendages called flagella; others are unable to propel themselves. Bacteria reproduce most commonly through binary fission (splitting). As is true of many single-celled organisms, some bacteria cause diseases. More important is their extraordinary variation and the fact that they may have been the first organisms on earth.

43. (c) Lamarck (1744–1829) set forth a theory of evolution that was a forerunner of Darwin's theory. Unfortunately, his theory was based on eighteenth-century ideas about eggs and sperm. The belief then was that different body parts sent particles through the bloodstream to the sex cells. In this way, traits were passed on. Lamarck's classic application of this has to do with the giraffe.Giraffes started out with short necks, he posited reasonably. By stretching for leaves on high tree branches, they lengthened their necks. Two giraffes with stretched necks then mated, bearing longer-necked offspring. The theory of acquired characteristics was rejected only after the true nature of reproductive cells was determined. The other theories listed belong to Hans Krebs, Joseph Priestly, and Fred Griffith.

44. (b) When elements or simple compounds are combined, forming a new complex compound, the process is called synthesis. For example, sodium (Na) and chlorine (Cl) can be combined to form salt:

$$2Na + Cl_2 \rightarrow 2NaCl$$

45. (c) A change in DNA, brought on naturally or by chemical causes, neutron bombardment, or radiation, can spark a change in an organism called a *mutation*. In higher organisms, only mutations within sex cells may be passed on to offspring. Skin cancer is an example of a mutation that takes place only within body cells and thus is not transmitted to offspring. Some mutations cause improvements; most are harmful.

46. **(b)** In flowering plants the flower is the center of reproductive activity. The stamen produces pollen, the male sex cells, in a sac called the anther. Pollen is carried to the pistil, which contains the eggs. Some plants self-pollinate, moving pollen to their own pistils. Others rely on animals or wind to move the pollen to a flower of the same species.

47. **(c)** Organic chemistry is the study of compounds formed from carbon; it thus incorporates the study of living matter. Inorganic chemistry deals mainly with minerals—elements and compounds that do *not* contain carbon.

48. **(a)** Photosynthesis is the process through which green plants manufacture food. Energy from direct sunlight is trapped by a substance called *chlorophyll*. The energy converts carbon dioxide and water into a complex compound, glucose, which is stored as food. The oxygen released as a by-product of this process is necessary for respiration in plants and animals.

49. **(b)** Ecologists study the interrelationships of organisms and their environments. An ecosystem is a community in which plants and animals coexist in a physical environment that supplies the energy and water they require. An ecosystem that is truly self-perpetuating is a *climax community*. Generally, ecosystems evolve over time.

50. **(b)** AIDS (Acquired Immune Deficiency Syndrome) so far has been 100% fatal. The syndrome, or group of symptoms, is caused by a virus that attacks the immune system, breaking it down and making its bearer susceptible to any and all diseases. The HIV virus is transmitted through blood or semen. At first it primarily infected homosexual men, intravenous drug users, and hemophiliacs in this country, but heterosexual transmission is becoming increasingly common. By the year 2000 the number of cases among women is expected to equal the number of cases among men. The number of Americans with AIDS now exceeds 200,000 according to the Centers for Disease Control. The first 100,000 cases appeared in the years 1981–1989, and the next 100,000 were reported between 1989 and 1991. Pneumonia and a type of cancer called Kaposi's sarcoma are two common AIDS-caused diseases, but there are dozens of opportunistic diseases that may appear as a result of the infection. Recent findings indicate that a new, previously unknown virus may be responsible for certain AIDS-like cases.

A Swiftly Tilting Planet: Physical Science

*True science teaches us to doubt
and to abstain from ignorance.*

—CLAUDE BERNARD

1. What is a catalyst?
   a. the smallest constituent of matter
   b. a substance that controls the rate of a chemical reaction
   c. a violent geological change
   d. a substance that merges with an element to form a compound

2. The steady-state and big-bang theories are associated with
   a. the study of the creation and structure of the universe
   b. the initial construction of the hydrogen bomb
   c. the volatility of liquids such as ether and chloroform
   d. plate tectonics and the development of mountain ranges

3. According to quantum theory,
   a. energy is infinite

    b. forces that balance each other are in equilibrium

    c. force can be expressed as the acceleration it gives to an object

    d. energy is limited and discontinuous

4. The earth's atmosphere is

    a. primarily nitrogen, with smaller amounts of oxygen and argon

    b. primarily oxygen, with traces of nitrogen and carbon

    c. primarily carbon dioxide, with some helium and ozone

    d. primarily ozone, with traces of oxygen and carbon dioxide

5. Which of these concepts is *not* associated with Einstein's theory of relativity?

    a. Nothing can move faster than the speed of light.

    b. Energy and mass are equivalent.

    c. Mass and time change with increases in velocity.

    d. Although matter may alter in shape, it is never destroyed.

6. On the Celsius scale, the boiling point of water is

    a. 100°

    b. 212°

    c. 373 A

    d. 0°

7. In a lunar eclipse,

    a. the Moon comes between the Earth and the Sun

    b. the Sun comes between the Earth and the Moon

    c. the Earth comes between the Sun and the Moon

    d. none of the above

8. Both strong and weak nuclear forces have to do with

    a. atoms

    b. electromagnetism

    c. gravity

    d. engines

9. The three major classes of rocks are

    a. granite, pumice, and quartzite

    b. stratified, molten, and sedimentary

    c. igneous, basalt, and clay

    d. metamorphic, sedimentary, and igneous

10. What did Marie and Pierre Curie discover?

    a. radioactivity

    b. radium and polonium

    c. electrons

    d. X rays

11. What is a vacuum?

    a. a unit of measure of atmospheric pressure

    b. gaseous matter with a high concentration of ions

    c. a device that operates through hydraulic pressure

    d. space from which all matter has been removed

12. You would be most likely to read a seismograph report in

    a. a newspaper account of earthquake activity

    b. a *Scientific American* article on quarks

    c. a novel about life on other planets

    d. Einstein's early papers on inertia

13. What is a molecule?

    a. the smallest particle of matter

    b. the smallest particle of an element or compound that has all the properties of that substance

    c. a substance with the same atomic weight as a given element

    d. a particle made up of a single nucleus and orbiting electrons in multiples of three or five

14. When an object is in equilibrium,

    a. it is not being acted on by any forces

    b. it is resistant to gravitational forces

    c. it is being acted on by two or more balanced forces

    d. it is spherical or otherwise precisely symmetrical

15. According to Newton's law of inertia,

    a. a body at rest tends to remain at rest

    b. a body in motion tends to remain in motion

    c. an outside force can manipulate a body

    d. all of the above

16. To a physicist, conservation of energy means

    a. use of natural resources must be controlled

    b. during a physical change, total energy remains constant

    c. a cautious approach to particle bombardment is recommended

    d. solid-state rather than electron materials are used

17. Which of the following bodies is *not* a star?

    a. nova   **c.** comet

    b. white dwarf   **d.** pulsar

18. If a bar magnet is allowed to swing freely,

    a. it will attract any metallic object

    b. it will repel any metallic object

    c. it will point north and south

    d. it will display the properties of a pendulum

19. The most amazing thing about a black hole is its ability to

    a. attract   **c.** navigate

    b. expand   **d.** pulsate

20. The half-life of an element is

    a. equal to half of its atomic number

b. the time it takes half of a given amount to decay

c. half the number of years an atom takes to break down

d. the number of electrons dispersed over a six-month period

21. In the process of diffusion,

   a. molecules of a substance spread evenly through a gas, liquid, or solid

   b. molecules of a substance separate from a gas, liquid, or solid

   c. wind or water spreads molecules of a substance

   d. a molecule returns to its natural shape after being acted on by a force

22. What is acceleration?

   a. speed in a straight line

   b. the rate of increase in velocity

   c. the rate at which motion occurs

   d. the process of traveling from place to place

23. Which list gives the correct order of the planets in terms of average orbital distance from the Sun?

   a. Earth, Venus, Mars, Mercury, Saturn, Jupiter, Uranus, Neptune, Pluto

   b. Mercury, Venus, Mars, Earth, Jupiter, Saturn, Neptune, Uranus, Pluto

   c. Mercury, Venus, Earth, Mars, Saturn, Jupiter, Uranus, Pluto, Neptune

   d. Mercury, Venus, Earth, Mars, Jupiter, Saturn, Uranus, Neptune, Pluto

24. In a nuclear chain reaction,

   a. atoms explode, causing the air around them to explode

   b. neutrons split atoms, releasing neutrons that split other atoms

    c. electrons leap from atom to atom, destabilizing them

    d. the nucleus of a hydrogen atom enters an atom of uranium

25. What is a light-year?

    a. the amount of time it takes light from the Sun to reach Earth

    b. the length of time it takes Earth to revolve around the Sun

    c. the distance between the Sun and the Earth

    d. the distance light travels in one year

26. What is the difference between nuclear fission and nuclear fusion?

    a. Fission produces an explosion; fusion produces safe energy.

    b. In fission an atomic nucleus is split; in fusion two atomic nuclei are joined.

    c. In a fission explosion only living things are killed; in a fusion explosion all objects are destroyed.

    d. Much more energy is produced in fission than in fusion.

27. What is the difference between a solar system and a galaxy?

    a. A solar system is a star and its family of planets and other bodies; a galaxy is a mass of stars, dust, and gases.

    b. A solar system is a group of stars; a galaxy is a geographic location in the universe.

    c. A solar system is a group of stars that forms a pattern in the sky; a galaxy is a cluster of dust and gases.

    d. There is no difference.

28. What is the study of thermodynamics?

    a. the study of sound and its production and effects

b. the study of atomic nuclei and their properties and uses

c. the study of the properties and role of electrons

d. the study of heat and its conversion into other forms of energy

29. What does the law of gravitation state?

a. If an object is given momentum in one direction, another object will get an equal momentum in the other direction.

b. Molecules are in a continual state of rapid motion.

c. Any two bodies are attracted with a force inversely proportional to the square of their distance apart.

d. Force equals mass times acceleration.

30. What did Archimedes discover?

a. An object immersed in liquid appears to lose an amount of weight equal to the amount of water it displaces.

b. The volume of a confined gas at a constant temperature varies inversely with the temperature.

c. When a liquid flows through a horizontal tube, the amount of energy per kilo is unchanged.

d. Pressure applied to any part of an enclosed liquid is transmitted to every other part of the liquid.

31. What are the particles that make up an atom called?

a. molecules

b. protons, neutrons, and electrons

c. mitochondria and vacuoles

d. moles

32. What theory did Copernicus develop?

a. the first modern theory of heliocentric movement of the planets

b. the first modern theory explaining the phases of the Moon

    c. the theory that states that life can exist on other planets

    d. the theory that states that stars move

33. What is a quark?

    a. a type of mineral with the compound name SiO_2

    b. a faint blue starlike object that is receding from our galaxy

    c. a hypothetical particle with a fractional charge

    d. an alkaloid isolated from a tree of the genus *Cinchona*

34. If a chemical solution is neutral, what is its pH?

    a. 3   **c.** 4.5

    b. 7   **d.** 14

35. If the barometric pressure falls abruptly, what will happen?

    a. The sun will come out.

    b. The temperature will rise.

    c. There will be a storm.

    d. It will be windy.

36. For what is Galileo known?

    a. discovering a comet and studying sunspots and satellites

    b. theorizing about motion, inventing a telescope, and discovering the composition of the Milky Way

    c. observing the planets, discovering a supernova, and theorizing on the Moon's motion

    d. describing the revolutions of planets and calculating the duration of planetary orbits

37. What are the layers of the Earth, from center to outer layer?

    a. liquid core, solid core, plate, rock

    b. crust, rock, sediment, mantle

    c. core, basin, sediment, crust

    d. solid core, liquid core, mantle, crust

38. What are the four states of matter?

  a. solid, liquid, gas, plasma

  b. atom, molecule, cell, organism

  c. acid, basic, alkaline, neutral

  d. terrestrial, solar, cosmic, universal

39. What are the three means of movement of heat?

  a. ventilation, emission, absorption

  b. conduction, convection, radiation

  c. transfer, expansion, evaporation

  d. condensation, diffraction, propagation

40. What is an ion?

  a. an atom with a positive or negative charge

  b. an atom with a neutral charge

  c. a particle possessing a positive electrical charge

  d. an electron found in the outermost shell of an atom

41. What is the difference between a stalactite and a stalagmite?

  a. Stalactites hang down, and stalagmites grow upward.

  b. Stalactites are made of calcite, and stalagmites are made of quartzite.

  c. Stalactites grow upward, and stalagmites hang down.

  d. Stalactites are found in underground caves, and stalagmites are found in aboveground caves.

42. To possess superconductivity, a substance must

  a. surround a battery with an iron core

  b. lose all electrical resistance

  c. have a positive electrical charge

  d. be alkaline and contain hydrogen

43. What makes isotopes of a given element different from each other?

  a. the number of neutrons in the atom nucleus

b. the number of protons in the atom nucleus

c. the number of electrons in the atom nucleus

d. All elemental isotopes are the same.

44. What makes up the light spectrum?

    a. ultraviolet radiation, X rays, and gamma rays

    b. infrared radiation, microwaves, and radio waves

    c. transparent light, opaque light, and translucent light

    d. white light diffracted into violet, indigo, blue, green, yellow, orange, and red

45. How is hail formed?

    a. Raindrops pass through a layer of freezing rain and freeze partially.

    b. Water vapor becomes solid crystal at temperatures below freezing.

    c. Raindrops are blown up and down in a cloud, freezing and refreezing.

    d. Drops of water form around large dust particles and evaporate partially before hitting the ground.

46. What is the most important characteristic of X rays?

    a. their ability to produce heat

    b. their ability to produce an image by reflecting light

    c. their ability to magnify objects

    d. their ability to penetrate dense substances

47. What does the periodic table of elements show?

    a. the geological periods during which the different elements were formed

    b. rows of elements by atomic number, with elements sharing similar properties grouped in columns

    c. the atomic structure of the elements and their isotopes

    d. rows of elements, their symbols, atomic numbers, weight, melting point, and boiling point

48. What is a compound?

    a. a liquid mixture that includes water

    b. a liquid that produces gas bubbles

    c. a substance that dissolves when added to water

    d. a substance made of atoms of two or more elements

49. How do you calculate a wavelength?

    a. Divide the speed of the wave motion by its frequency.

    b. Measure the number of vibrations in a wave motion.

    c. Measure the distance between the top and the middle of a wave.

    d. Calculate the pitch of the sound the wave produces.

50. What is the identifying characteristic of crystal?

    a. It does not have a definite form.

    b. It conducts heat and electricity.

    c. It has a regular repeating arrangement of atoms.

    d. Its molecules can move about with no force holding them together.

TEST 12: Explanatory Answers

1. (b) A catalyst changes the amount of energy needed for a reaction to take place, thus affecting the rate of the reaction. A catalyst that slows down a reaction is an inhibitor. Enzymes are organic catalysts.

2. (a) Cosmology is the study of the universe. Hubble's law (1929) implied that the universe is expanding uniformly. This law led to the big bang theory, which states that an explosion created the expanding universe from a compact lump of energy and matter. The steady-state theory accepted the idea of an expanding universe but claimed that the universe has always existed and that new matter is created to fill the empty space left by receding galaxies.

3. (d) Max Planck (1858–1947) solved the problem of infinite energy by deciding that particles could only radiate at certain limited energy levels. These levels could be expressed as the frequency λ, times Planck's constant, h. In other words, energy is not produced continuously and without limit; the energy can exist only as whole-number multiples of $h\lambda$, discrete parcels of energy called *quanta*. Albert Einstein (1879–1955) applied this theory to light, proving that light does not truly travel in waves but in separated particles, which we now call photons. (Newton was actually the first to talk about particles of light; the quantum theory merged his theory with wave theory.) Niels Bohr (1885–1962) applied the quantum theory to the atom, creating a model that described the limited number of possible orbits for electrons and thus explained the relative stability of the atom.

4. **(a)** Nitrogen makes up over 78 percent of the earth's atmosphere, the gaseous mass surrounding the planet. Oxygen makes up a little over 20 percent, and argon and carbon dioxide make up less than 1 percent each. Trace amounts of helium, hydrogen, krypton, methane, neon, ozone, and xenon also exist. Water vapor and various pollutants also appear in the atmosphere.

5. **(d)** Item d is the law of conservation of matter. Einstein's theory was a direct descendant of many Newtonian principles and an attempt to solve problems that they did not illuminate. The primary assumption in relativity is that the speed of light is constant no matter how fast the observer moves or where the light originates. From that Einstein determined that nothing could move faster than light. He posited that events that seemed simultaneous to one observer would not necessarily appear that way to an observer with another frame of reference—that time was relative to the observer's location in the space-time continuum. "$E = mc^2$" is perhaps the most famous equation of all time. Translated, it says that "energy equals mass times the speed of light squared," or "if an object radiates energy E, its mass decreases by E divided by the speed of light squared." It thus implies that mass and energy are equivalent. Substituting real numbers for the variables proves that huge amounts of energy can be radiated by objects of minute mass—atoms, for example. Einstein also determined that as an object's velocity approaches the speed of light, time and the object's mass are altered.

6. **(a)** The Celsius scale is a centigrade scale; that is, the interval between freezing and boiling is divided into one hundred

degrees. On the scale, 0°C is the freezing point of water, and 100°C is the boiling point. The other two measures given are the boiling point of water on the Fahrenheit scale (212°F) and the boiling point of water on the Absolute scale.

7. **(c)** During an eclipse, light falling on a body in space is blocked by another body. In a lunar eclipse, no light reaches the Moon because the Earth stands in the way. In a solar eclipse, no light reaches the Earth because the Moon stands in the way. Eclipses can be partial, in which case some light still reaches the body, or they may be total, in which case the body is entirely dark.

8. **(a)** There are four forces of nature: gravity, electromagnetism, strong nuclear force, and weak nuclear force. The strong nuclear force is the force that holds the nucleus of an atom together. It is the strongest force in nature; not only does it hold neutrons and protons in the nucleus, but it also is responsible for particle creation when atoms meet in high-energy collisions. The weak nuclear force is an interaction that may lead to particle decay and emission or absorption of neutrinos.

9. **(d)** Rocks are classified according to their formation. Rocks that undergo a change inside the Earth due to heat or pressure are called metamorphic rocks. Marble and slate are two examples. Rocks that are formed through erosion of older rocks and deposit of sediment from that erosion are sedimentary rocks. Clay and limestone are sedimentary. Rocks that were originally molten matter inside the Earth are called igneous rocks. Basalt and pumice are two such rocks.

10. **(b)** Radioactivity is the tendency of an atomic nucleus to decay through the emission of particles. Three things may be emitted: alpha particles (each one being two protons and two neutrons), beta particles (each one being an electron or a positron), and gamma radiation. Antoine Becquerel (1852–1908) discovered radioactivity occurring naturally in uranium in 1896. Marie Curie (1867–1934) began to study uranium, and with Pierre Curie (1859–1906) she discovered the new elements polonium and radium, which also proved naturally radioactive. The Curies shared the Nobel Prize in physics with Becquerel in 1903 for work on radioactivity. After Pierre's death Marie won the Nobel Prize in chemistry in 1911 for the discovery of the two new elements. Radioactivity may be induced artificially in more stable elements through high-energy collisions.

11. **(d)** There is no such thing as a perfect vacuum, but if there were, it would be empty of matter. Space from which a high percentage of matter has been removed is known as a *high vacuum.*

12. **(a)** A seismograph is an instrument that measures the motion of the Earth. Seismographs are used to locate oil, to determine ocean depth, and to detect and measure earthquakes.

13. **(b)** A molecule is made up of atoms. The atoms may be all of one type: O_2 is the smallest particle of oxygen that can exist by itself; it contains two oxygen atoms. The atoms may be of different types: H_2O is a molecule of water; it is made up of two hydrogen atoms and one oxygen atom.

14. **(c)** An object in equilibrium is acted on by forces with no result; the forces themselves are in a state of balance, and the object remains at rest.

15. **(d)** Isaac Newton (1642–1727), probably the greatest physicist the world has ever known, was the first to express the relationship between force and motion. His first law of motion is the law of inertia. It states that bodies at rest or in motion tend to remain that way unless acted on by outside forces. The other two laws of motion state that the acceleration of a mass by a force is inversely proportional to the mass and directly proportional to the force and that for every action there is an equal and opposite reaction.

16. **(b)** The major conservation laws state that the values of mass, momentum, charge, and energy remain constant during a physical process. For example, if energy disappears in one form, it must reappear in another form. With the equivalence of mass and energy implied by Einstein's relativity theory, it becomes possible for mass to disappear and reappear as energy.

17. **(c)** A comet is a condensed body of gases and particles, believed to originate in a great cloud of material orbiting the solar system. A star is primarily hydrogen. It has a strong gravitational force, and the light and heat it emits come from nuclear energy. A nova is a star that suddenly bursts forth with a huge increase in light radiation and then fades again. A white dwarf is a very small star, about the size of Earth. A pulsar is a very dense star that emits pulses of radio waves.

18. **(c)** In ancient times the Greeks observed that certain kinds of iron attracted other material containing iron. Lodestones, natural magnets made of iron ore, were found to attract iron

to opposite sides of the magnet. There proved to be an invisible field surrounding the magnet; a similar field also surrounds Earth. Just as Earth has two poles, so does any magnet. The north pole of a magnet is attracted in the direction of Earth's north pole. A compass uses this aspect of a magnet as a navigational tool. Somewhat confusingly, the so-called north pole of a magnet is repelled by the north pole of another magnet and attracted to the south pole of the other magnet. If a magnet is broken in half, each half has a north and south pole. The implication is that the atoms themselves are magnets.

19. **(a)** A black hole is probably the dense matter left after the collapse of a star. Because of its density it has a gravitational pull strong enough to attract everything around, including light and all other radiation. Black holes would appear to astronomers as dark patches in space.

20. **(b)** The nuclei of radioactive elements break down over time, emitting particles and radiation as they do so. The time it takes half of a given amount of a substance to decay is called the substance's *half-life*. The half-life is used to identify elements, and geologists and archaeologists use it to compute the age of minerals.

21. **(a)** When particles of materials intermingle, moving randomly from areas of higher concentration to areas of lower concentration, the movement is called *diffusion*. Diffusion ends with the molecules spread evenly. The process is stimulated by heat.

22. **(b)** Acceleration can be expressed in this way:

$$\frac{\text{increase in velocity}}{\text{time}}$$

The other definitions listed are of velocity, speed, and motion.

23. **(d)** The approximate distance from the Sun for each planet is:

Planet	Distance from Sun
Mercury	36,000,000 miles
Venus	67,000,000 miles
Earth	93,000,000 miles
Mars	141,000,000 miles
Jupiter	480,000,000 miles
Saturn	900,000,000 miles
Uranus	1,800,000,000 miles

Planet	Distance from Sun
Neptune	2,800,000,000 miles
Pluto	3,600,000,000 miles

These figures show the average distance from the sun. In fact, some planets' orbits are extremely eccentric. Pluto, for example, is currently closer to the Sun than Neptune is, and it will remain that way until the turn of the century.

24. (b) During nuclear fission, neutrons split the nuclei of atoms, and the neutrons that are produced go on to split other nuclei in a self-perpetuating reaction. The nuclear chain reaction is the power behind fission bombs and nuclear reactors.

25. (d) A light-year is one unit of measure of distance in space. It measures the distance light travels in one Earth year and equals 5,870,000,000,000 miles. For technical reasons astronomers often use the *parsec* as a unit of measure. The parsec equals 3.258 light years.

26. (b) When an atom is split into two or more nuclei by the absorption of a neutron, a huge amount of energy is released. This is called fission; it is the basis of the atomic bomb and the nuclear reactor. In fusion, two atoms are joined. The amount of energy given off is several times that of fission. A temperature of 1 million degrees centigrade must be reached to initiate fusion.

27. (a) *Solar system* is a phrase usually used only to describe our sun and its attendant planets, asteroids, meteors, and comets. A galaxy is a huge mass of millions of stars, dust, and gases. There are millions of galaxies, and they are separated from one another by vast distances. Our galaxy is called the Milky Way.

28. (d) Thermodynamics is the study of heat and energy. The terms used to calculate heat are *calorie* (the quantity of heat required to raise one gram of water one degree centigrade) and *Btu* (the quantity of heat required to raise one pound of water one degree Fahrenheit). Thermodynamics explores the transfer of heat by conduction, convection, and radiation. The other sciences mentioned are acoustics, nuclear physics, and electronics.

29. (c) Postulated by Newton, the law of gravitation explains why the planets move as they do. It can be expressed as a formula:

$$F = \frac{Gm_1m_2}{d^2}$$

where F is the force of attraction, m_1 and m_2 are the two masses, and d^2 is their distance apart. G is a constant that equals 0.000000000033, which makes the force between the Earth and the Moon 15 million trillion tons. The other laws mentioned are Newton's third law of motion, the kinetic theory of matter, and the law of force.

30. (a) Archimedes' principle, purportedly discovered as its author sat in a bathtub, governs the forces of buoyancy and flotation. Archimedes (287 B.C.–212 B.C.) was a Greek physicist, mathematician, and inventor who calculated the value of pi, proved the law of the lever, and invented the Archimedes screw as well as developing the principle of buoyancy. The other laws mentioned are Boyle's law, Bernoulli's principle, and Pascal's law.

31. (b) An atom is the smallest unit of a chemical element that possesses the properties of that element. The nucleus of an atom consists of protons, which are positively charged particles, and neutrons, which are uncharged particles. Electrons, negatively charged particles, exist outside the nucleus; the number of electrons and protons in an atom is equal in a neutral atom. The number of protons in an atom determines its atomic number and its chemical nature; the total number of protons and neutrons makes up its atomic weight.

32. (a) Nicholas Copernicus (1473–1543) was a Polish astronomer who developed a shocking idea: that the planets move around the Sun. According to the Egyptian scientist Ptolemy, the Earth was the center of movement, and though Copernicus did not have the laws of gravity to back him up, he revolutionized astronomy—and the religious world, which believed, as the Bible said, that the solar system revolved around the Earth—with his theory.

33. (c) Quarks are hypothetical particles that make up particles called *hadrons*, which are members of the baryon class of particles, a class that includes protons and neutrons. In 1964 Murray Gell-Mann explained the properties of hadrons, which are only one of perhaps eighty varieties of particles. The name *quark*, which means "nothing" in German, comes from James Joyce's *Finnegan's Wake*.

34. (b) A chemical solution, or a liquid that consists of a solute dissolved in a solvent, has a pH value that tells whether the solution is acidic or alkaline. The pH value is based on the concentration of hydrogen ions and ranges from less than 0 to 14, with a lower pH being more acidic; 7 is neutral, and a higher pH is more alkaline.

35. (c) Atmospheric pressure is the pressure exerted by the atmosphere, which exists in several layers out to about forty thousand miles from the Earth's surface. A barometer measures the pressure, usually using mercury. In weather forecasting, falling barometric pressure indicates foul weather is coming, and rising barometric pressure indicates fair weather is on the way.

36. (b) Galileo Galilei (1564–1642) was an Italian astronomer whose theories of motion prepared the way for Isaac Newton's studies. He built the first astronomical telescope and with it discovered that the Milky Way is composed of stars. In 1633 he was brought before the Inquisition for heresy, based on his theories about the movement of the planets, and forced to renounce his astronomical beliefs.

37. (d) The Earth's crust, consisting of continents and ocean basins, varies from five to twenty miles in thickness. Temperatures can reach 1600° Fahrenheit. The mantle is a solid layer of rock that goes down about another eighteen hundred miles and increases in temperature to 4000° Fahrenheit. The outer core is about fourteen hundred miles thick and consists of iron and nickel; it can rise to nearly 9000° Fahrenheit. The center of the inner core, solid iron and nickel, lies four thousand miles below the surface and can be as hot as 9000° Fahrenheit.

38. (a) Matter in its physical states has mass, and it cannot be destroyed or manufactured, only changed. Some compounds, such as water, can be found in several states: liquid, solid (as ice), and gas (as steam). Plasma exists in the interior of stars and in stellar gas; because it is an electrical conductor, it is important in the manufacture of nuclear energy.

39. (b) Heat can be transferred by: conduction, the movement of heat through a solid object; convection, the movement of heat through a liquid or gas; and radiation, the movement of heat through space.

40. (a) An ion can be charged positively or negatively, depending on whether it gains or loses electrons. If it gains electrons, it has a negative charge and is called an anion. If it loses electrons, it has a positive charge and is called a cation.

41. **(a)** Stalactites are made of calcite that condenses in water from the roof of a cave; stalagmites are formed from calcite in ground water. Sometimes these dripstones are multicolored, a phenomenon caused by other mineral deposits in the cave water.

42. **(b)** When certain substances, such as zinc, magnesium, and lead sulfite, are cooled to absolute zero, they lose all electrical resistance and become what are called superconductors. This property is important because, if a way could be found to eliminate the need for very cold temperatures, superconductors could be the basis for a whole new generation of super-efficient electrical equipment. Recently scientists have discovered that certain ceramic compounds possess superconductivity at temperatures well above absolute zero.

43. **(a)** Atoms of a given chemical element must contain the same number of protons but can contain different numbers of neutrons, giving them different masses. These atoms are called *isotopes*. Chlorine atoms, for example, have seventeen electrons and seventeen protons, but can have either eighteen or twenty neutrons. Most chemical elements have more than one isotope.

44. **(d)** The visible spectrum consists of white light, or colorless sunlight, refracted into colors. Newton's experiments on light proved this, showing that color depends on wavelength. Beyond the visible spectrum lie electromagnetic waves: gamma rays; X rays; ultraviolet radiation at wavelengths shorter than those of visible light; and infrared radiation, microwaves, and radio waves at wavelengths longer than those of visible light.

45. **(c)** Hail can occur at any time during the year. When raindrops are blown upward to the coldest part of a cloud, they freeze, then sink and are coated with more water, blown up and refrozen, and so on until they are heavy enough to drop.

46. **(d)** Because X rays, electromagnetic waves that are invisible and very short, can penetrate thick material, they are useful in medicine. The rays in an X-ray machine are produced by heating a filament to provide a stream of electrons that bombard an anode. Bone absorbs more X rays than does muscle or skin; that is why X-ray machines can take pictures of the skeletal structure.

47. **(b)** The periodic table arranges elements (substances that cannot be decomposed chemically) in horizontal rows called periods, by their atomic number, or number of protons. The elements form vertical columns that reflect the periodic recurrence of chemical or physical properties.

48. **(d)** A compound contains two or more elements in a constant proportion. Chemical bonds hold the elements together. Compounds can be given formula names: H_2O is the formula for the compound water; CO_2 is the formula for the compound carbon dioxide.

49. **(a)** Waves are the transfer of energy by vibration. A wavelength, the distance between a point on one wave and the same point on another, is measured by dividing the speed of the waves by their frequency.

50. **(c)** Crystals are solid substances with a regular geometric shape that reflects the arrangements of atoms within. They are formed by the solidification of an element, compound, or mixture and are often used, according to their physical characteristics, in various sectors of industry or as jewelry.

The Wave of the Future: Technology

Technology ... the knack of so arranging the world that we don't have to experience it.

—MAX FRISCH

1. A battery works by
   a. connecting to an outside source of electricity
   b. converting chemical energy to electrical energy
   c. warming up a wire to the point that it generates heat
   d. changing neutrons into electrons

2. What does a laser do?
   a. It focuses heat rays.
   b. It blocks the visible spectrum.
   c. It amplifies a beam of light.
   d. It converts electrons into light.

3. You would be likely to use Mach numbers if you were a
   a. test pilot
   b. electrician
   c. nutrition expert
   d. anthropologist

4. Orville and Wilbur Wright
   a. designed a motorized aircraft that flew in 1903
   b. piloted a successful glider in 1896
   c. started the first commercial airline in 1925
   d. flew the first transatlantic flight in 1927

5. Microwaves that are used in cooking work by
   a. radiating infrared waves (heat)
   b. causing molecules to vibrate and generate heat
   c. bouncing heat rays off the metallic sides of the oven
   d. amplifying waves of light to produce heat

6. Cyrus McCormick and John Deere contributed inventions that improved the working life of the
   a. housewife
   b. athlete
   c. driver
   d. farmer

7. A semiconductor is material that
   a. conducts electricity better than most metals
   b. insulates better than most minerals
   c. does not conduct electricity
   d. has limited conductivity at room temperature

8. What does a television transmitter transmit?
   a. radio waves
   b. television waves
   c. light waves
   d. sound waves

9. Johann Gutenberg was probably the first European to use
   a. explosives
   b. carbon dating
   c. movable type
   d. hydroelectric power

10. What is the difference between a ballistic missile and a guided missile?

   a. the former carries nuclear warheads

   b. the latter can be redirected in flight

   c. the former is designed as an antiaircraft weapon

   d. the latter is launched from an aircraft

11. Some people involved with the invention of the telegraph include

   a. Savery, Newcomen, and Watt

   b. Oersted, Henry, and Morse

   c. Benz, Daimler, and Diesel

   d. Daguerre, Herschel, and Land

12. An electrode is the same as a

   a. terminal

   b. battery

   c. electron

   d. circuit

13. What did George Eastman invent?

   a. motion pictures

   b. the Kodak camera

   c. the telescope

   d. magnifying lenses

14. A photoelectric cell is stimulated by

   a. heat

   b. chemical change

   c. neutrons

   d. light

15. In an assembly line,

   a. each worker assembles a single product

   b. more than one product is assembled

   c. a product is assembled in steps

   d. each worker oversees a variety of processes

16. The hardware in a computer system

    a. controls the operation of the system

    b. may include programs for filing and storage

    c. may include keyboard and printer

    d. contains sequential instructions

17. Thomas Edison is known for his inventions dealing with

    a. sound and electricity

    b. flight and motion

    c. food production and storage

    d. light and weather

18. A silicon chip is part of a

    a. floppy disk

    b. microcomputer

    c. cassette

    d. teleprinter

19. You would use a particle accelerator to

    a. detect radiation leakage

    b. increase the rate at which an engine revs

    c. bombard atoms with parts of other atoms

    d. model theoretical changes in an environment

20. Alexander Graham Bell's major invention involved

    a. sending a code via electric circuits

    b. recording sound on two or more microphones

    c. recording information on strips of tape

    d. transmitting speech on waves of electricity

21. Robert Fulton is known as the inventor of the

    a. steamboat

    b. cotton gin

    c. elevator

    d. revolver

22. Which of these is a lever?

    a. ice tongs

    b. crowbar

    c. balance scale

    d. all of the above

23. What is the job of a sensor?

    a. It locates and maps a radioactive source.

    b. It tests the depth and bottom conditions of oceans or rivers.

    c. It translates external conditions into signals.

    d. It takes X rays in sequential patterns.

24. What is the path of visual signals in a television broadcast?

    a. camera → transmitter → antenna → antenna → receiver → cathode-ray tube

    b. camera → videotape → antenna → cathode-ray tube → receiver

    c. antenna → camera → transmitter → receiver → cathode-ray tube

    d. microphone → transmitter → receiver → speaker → cathode-ray tube

25. An integrated circuit

    a. is made of copper tubes

    b. does not contain wires

    c. is microscopic in size

    d. all of the above

26. What is the aim of the SDI system?

    a. to defend against nuclear attack

    b. to develop self-aimed ballistic missiles

    c. to protect against germ warfare

    d. to use lasers to aid in medical operations

27. How does a nuclear reactor work?

    a. Atomic nuclei are split, producing a self-perpetuating chain reaction.

    b. Alpha, beta, or gamma rays cause a discharge that produces a nuclear reaction.

    c. Coal is heated to such intensity that atomic nuclei fuse together.

    d. An atom absorbs energy and then emits a photon, causing intense heat.

28. What is the difference between radar and sonar?

    a. Radar is used to record sounds; sonar is used to make sounds.

    b. Radar records sounds at very high frequencies; sonar records very low frequency sounds.

    c. Radar uses electromagnetic waves; sonar uses sound waves.

    d. Radar absorbs echoes; sonar produces echoes.

29. Which of these devices use cathode-ray tubes?

    a. semiconductors, generators, and transformers

    b. microphones, cameras, and holographs

    c. anemometers, teleprinters, and microwave ovens

    d. television, radar, and computer terminals

30. What can a receiver produce?

    a. sound waves and pictures

    b. microwaves and audio frequencies

    c. holograms and infrared waves

    d. all of the above

31. In which of these are microprocessors *not* used?

    a. X-ray machines, lasers, and calculators

    b. floppy disks, turbojet engines, and incandescent lamps

    c. wristwatches, computers, and telescopes

    d. microscopes, mass spectrographs, and radar

32. For what is Guglielmo Marconi best known?

   a. the invention of the steam engine

   b. the development of the incandescent lamp

   c. the invention of the telephone

   d. the development of wireless telegraphy

33. What is the usual method for toxic waste disposal?

   a. burning

   b. sealing in metal drums and burying

   c. processing and dumping at sea

   d. recycling

34. What do these things have in common: coal, gas, oil, the sun, plutonium, water, and wind?

   a. They are all potential pollutants.

   b. They all provide safe, inexpensive heat.

   c. They all provide methods of combustion.

   d. They are all sources of energy.

35. What is a watt?

   a. a unit of power

   b. a degree of brightness

   c. a charge of electricity

   d. an open circuit

36. How does a turbine work?

   a. Steam moves a piston to and fro in a cylinder.

   b. A heavy wheel rotates, storing kinetic energy.

   c. A stream of fluid or air turns a shaft that drives machinery.

   d. A bar turns around a pivot.

37. Where would you be most likely to find a mainframe computer?

   a. a home

   b. a bank

    c. a college English department

    d. a high school

38. How does hydraulic machinery work?

    a. through liquid that expands and contracts

    b. through pressure exerted by heat

    c. through the movement of levers

    d. through pressure exerted on liquid

39. What did Anton van Leeuwenhoek invent?

    a. the thermometer

    b. the microscope

    c. the bifocal lens

    d. the telescope

40. How does a VCR record from a television?

    a. Electrical signals from the television are transmitted to magnetic tape.

    b. Sound and picture are transformed into printed messages on the television.

    c. Glass fibers pick up radio wave transmissions and record them on tape.

    d. A disk in the television reacts directly with magnetic tape, producing a recording.

41. How does a telescope work?

    a. Light is magnified.

    b. Objects are photographed and enlarged.

    c. Light is refracted or reflected and focused.

    d. Light is bounced back and forth between mirrors.

42. Why was the space shuttle an important technological advance?

    a. It could go farther than any other spacecraft.

    b. It was reusable.

    c. It could fly unmanned with great precision.

    d. all of the above

43. What is a robot?

   a. a machine in the shape of a human
   b. a machine controlled from a distance
   c. a machine that can think
   d. a machine that senses and then reacts

44. For what is a transistor used?

   a. playing music loudly
   b. amplifying an electrical current
   c. providing a connection between receiver and turn-table
   d. negating electrical current in a circuit

45. Where might you find an internal combustion engine?

   a. in a jet
   b. in a hovercraft
   c. in an automobile
   d. in a steamship

46. Where can computer data be stored?

   a. on a hard disk
   b. on a floppy disk
   c. on a tape
   d. all of the above

47. What is the purpose of isotope scanning, ultrasound, and electrocardiographs?

   a. diagnosis and control of disease
   b. cure of heart disease
   c. maintenance of a healthy fetus
   d. reduction of the size of a tumor

48. Which of these are satellites?

   a. Sputnik I
   b. the moon
   c. Ganymede
   d. all of the above

49. What is a hologram?
   a. a colorized picture of an object
   b. a three-dimensional image of an object
   c. a photograph that develops automatically
   d. a photograph taken from the moon

50. For what inventions is Benjamin Franklin known?
   a. the lightning rod and bifocals
   b. the marine torpedo and the steamship
   c. the calculating machine and the hydraulic press
   d. the phonograph and the wax record

TEST 13: Explanatory Answers

1. (b) Batteries come in many varieties, but all are made up of three things: a positive electrode, a negative electrode, and a chemical solution called an *electrolyte.* The positive and negative electrodes are placed in the solution and connected externally with a wire. Positive ions from the solution travel to the negative electrode, and electrons travel from the negative electrode through the wire and into the positive electrode, creating a circuit.

2. (c) Just as a nuclear pile sets up a chain reaction with neutrons, so does a laser set up a chain reaction with photons, the particles that make up light. The laser stimulates atoms so that a majority of them are at a higher energy level than usual. The difference in energy between high-energy atoms and normal atoms may be matched by the frequency of a photon. If that photon hits the excited atom, it causes the atom to release a photon of the same frequency as the first and return to a normal level of energy. The released photon then moves in the same direction as the first photon, and both continue to hit high-energy atoms as they travel. The result is a burst of radiation, which is reflected back and forth between the silvered ends of the laser. When the radiation is intense enough, it passes through one end of the laser. The light emitted is all one wavelength and is extremely intense. *Laser* is an acronym for light amplification by stimulated emission of radiation.

3. **(a)** A Mach number measures the ratio of an object's speed to the speed of sound. When the Mach number exceeds 1, the object is supersonic; it exceeds the speed of sound.

4. **(a)** The Wright brothers owned a bicycle shop, and they used bicycle parts to make the first successful motorized airplane. A biplane, it had two propellers and was powered by a gasoline engine. It made a sustained flight near Kitty Hawk, North Carolina, on December 17, 1903.

5. **(b)** Microwaves are radio waves with wavelengths between 300 mm and 1 mm, placing them between infrared and radio short waves on the electromagnetic spectrum. They are used in radar and certain communications devices as well as in ovens. In ovens the waves penetrate food, causing molecules of moisture to vibrate and produce heat. A substance containing no moisture will not be affected.

6. **(d)** Cyrus McCormick (1809–1884) invented a reaper in 1831 that mechanized the harvest for the first time. John Deere (1804–1886) invented the first steel plow and created the farm implement company that bore his name. These inventions revolutionized farming by making it possible for fewer people to cultivate more acreage.

7. **(d)** A conductor allows electricity to flow through it. An insulator prevents the flow of electricity. A semiconductor has conducting properties between the two. At high temperatures it conducts well; at low temperatures, it insulates. Impurities that add electrons to or take electrons away from a semiconductor can increase its conductivity. In a negative (n-type) semiconductor, electricity is carried by the electrons. In a positive (p-type) semiconductor, it is carried via the "holes" where electrons were removed.

8. **(a)** All waves have amplitude (height), length, and frequency (number of waves that pass a point in a given amount of time). In radio or television, sound or images are converted into electrical signals by a microphone or camera, and these signals are used to modulate (vary) the amplitude or frequency of radio waves produced by a transmitter. (*AM* stands for "amplitude modulation," and *FM* means "frequency modulation.")

9. **(c)** Movable type was used in printing presses in Korea in the fourteenth century. Johann Gutenberg (c. 1397–1468) was probably the first European to use the technique. His most important work was the Mazarin Bible, usually called the

Gutenberg Bible, completed in Mainz, Germany, in 1455. It was the first complete book printed in Europe. Gutenberg's press was a hand press. Letters were placed by hand in a form, and ink was rolled over them. The form was then pressed against a sheet of paper.

10. **(b)** Ballistic missiles follow a parabolic path once launched, and they fall freely after reaching the apex of their ascent. Guided missiles may have self-contained controls, or they may be controlled from the ground by radio. By these means, their paths may be altered as they fly.

11. **(b)** In 1819 the Danish physicist Hans Christian Oersted accidentally discovered that a current flowing through a wire makes the wire act like a magnet. His discovery led to William Sturgeon's construction of the first electromagnet. In 1831 Joseph Henry demonstrated that an electromagnet could gain and lose magnetism almost instantly even though the switch that completed and broke the circuit was a mile away. However, it took Samuel F. B. Morse to develop this notion into a practical telegraph (1844). In his telegraph an electromagnet in the receiver was activated when a circuit was completed by pressing a key in the transmitter. The intermittent current was received as audible clicks. The other inventors listed were involved with the steam engine, the internal-combustion engine, and photography.

12. **(a)** In an electric circuit current passes between metallic and nonmetallic conductors. An electrode, or terminal, makes the connection between the two kinds of conductors. A negative electrode is called a *cathode;* current passes through it on its way from a nonmetallic to a metallic conductor. A positive electrode is called an *anode;* current passes through it on its way from a metallic to a nonmetallic conductor. Most electrodes are made of metal, copper being one example.

13. **(b)** George Eastman (1854–1932) invented a new process of photography that led to his chief invention, the Kodak camera, in 1888. The dry-plate process allowed him to replace bulky photographic plates with roll film, another Eastman invention. In 1892 Eastman founded a company to mass-produce the camera, paving the way for photography to become an affordable hobby. In 1928 he invented a process for color photography.

14. **(d)** The cathode or the semiconductor of a photoelectric cell is coated with a material that is sensitive to light. When light

hits the material, electrons are emitted. This either completes a circuit, allowing current to flow, or it increases a current that is already flowing due to a battery hookup. The amount of current depends on the intensity of the light.

15. **(c)** The Industrial Revolution mechanized industry, enabling the owners of companies to increase profit by increasing the productivity of the labor force. The development of the assembly line led to even greater profit. Each worker on an assembly line has a specific task. Machines and workers are assigned to stations along the line, and a product proceeds from station to station until it is completed. Henry Ford (1863–1947) first applied the process to automobile manufacturing, and his venture was certainly one of the most profitable early attempts at mass production.

16. **(c)** The hardware in a system includes the physical system itself, which may be made up of a keyboard, a central processing unit (CPU), a monitor, and tapes or disks. The other features mentioned belong to software, the information that controls the computer's functioning.

17. **(a)** Among the inventions of Thomas Edison (1847–1931), in order of their invention, were the carbon microphone (1877), the record player (1878), the light bulb (1879), and the kinetoscope (1889), an early motion-picture machine. He worked with teams of researchers in one of the largest laboratories of the time, a precursor of today's gigantic industrial research laboratories.

18. **(b)** An integrated circuit does not use wires to complete the circuit; instead, it is constructed from one piece of semiconductor material. A chip contains a tiny integrated circuit. In a silicon chip, silicon is the semiconductor material used.

19. **(c)** The most common kind of particle accelerator is the cyclotron, for which Ernest Lawrence won the Nobel Prize in physics in 1939. The accelerator directs beams of atomic particles against a target, accelerating the particles through the use of electric fields or electromagnetic waves. Early accelerators were very long straight lines, and those are still the most efficient. The cyclotron bends the beam in an arc, enabling acceleration to take place in a smaller space.

20. **(d)** Alexander Graham Bell (1847–1922) worked with deaf students before designing the first telephone in 1876. In a telephone, vibrations in one microphone vary the flow of current into a circuit. When the current reaches a second microphone, it causes identical vibrations in it, vibrations that translate into sound waves. Bell used the money and influence he gained from his invention to help found the magazine *Science* and to support other scientists.

21. **(a)** Robert Fulton (1765–1815) stole John Fitch's thunder and received credit for producing the first steamboat in 1807, more than twenty years after Fitch's ship was built. Fulton's ship, the *Clermont,* traveled amid much publicity from New York City to Albany in record time. Although Eli Whitney invented one kind of cotton gin, the idea probably originated with a black slave in the mid-1700s. The other two inventions listed belong to Elisha Otis and Samuel Colt.

22. **(d)** A lever is one of the five types of simple machines, the others being the pulley, inclined plane, screw, and wheel and axle. A lever is a bar supported by a stationary fulcrum. Force is applied to a point along the lever to overcome resistance (lift a load) at another point. The locations of the fulcrum, resistance, and force determine the kind of lever. A balance has a fulcrum in the center. A crowbar and tongs have the fulcrum at the end. With the crowbar, force is applied at one end of the lever to lift a resistance in the center. With the tongs, force is applied in the middle of the lever to lift a resistance at the opposite end from the fulcrum.

23. **(c)** A sensor detects an external condition such as light, heat, movement, or pressure. It evaluates the condition and emits a signal (usually electrical) based on the amount of the condition it senses. Sensors are found in some elevator buttons, photographic light meters, and car alarms.

24. **(a)** Images are converted into electrical signals by a camera, and these signals are used to modulate radio waves produced by a transmitter. These waves are sent out via an antenna, and some of them are picked up by antennas that are hooked up to receivers. The receiver converts the waves back to electrical signals, and in the cathode-ray tube, electrons are projected onto a screen to re-form the image.

25. **(b)** The fact that an integrated circuit is formed entirely of one semiconductor material and contains no wires means that it is more reliable than an ordinary circuit; there is little chance of a short circuit or loose connections.

26. **(a)** SDI, or Strategic Defense Initiative, is a space defense system against nuclear weapons. It is based on the ideas of interception and destruction of enemy missiles, either above or in the atmosphere. Lasers would be the basis of the system, including a hard X-ray laser, which would have to be powered by a nuclear explosion. All of the lasers are in early developmental stages, and some scientists believe that SDI is an unrealistic dream.

27. **(a)** In a nuclear reactor, fuel, which is usually uranium or plutonium, is treated to cause the fission of atomic nuclei, setting up a chain reaction that is controlled by a substance such as graphite or cadmium metal. Heat is emitted and used to heat water and to provide steam. Fusion reactors are still in the experimental stage, since extremely high temperatures are needed to initiate the reaction.

28. **(c)** Radar (*radio detecting and ranging*) calculates the distance of an object by bouncing electromagnetic waves off the object and timing their return. Sonar (*sound navigation ranging*) detects objects underwater by bouncing a high-frequency sound wave off them and timing its return.

29. **(d)** Cathode-ray tubes are vacuum tubes in which electrons, accelerated by high voltages, are focused into a beam and projected onto a screen. Among their uses are the production of images on television screens, computer terminals, and radar screens.

30. **(a)** A receiver picks up electromagnetic waves and converts them into either sound waves, as in a radio, or pictures, as in a television, using a device that vibrates with varying electric current.

31. **(b)** A microcomputer uses a microprocessor, which is the integrated circuit that controls the other units in the computer. It usually consists of a single silicon chip and so can be used in very small appliances and other items.

32. **(d)** The Italian physicist Marconi (1874–1937) won the 1909 Nobel Prize for developing long-wave wireless telegraphy. This paved the way for the invention of radio and television, which convert electromagnetic waves into sound and/or pictures. The other inventions listed are by James Watt, Thomas Edison, and Alexander Graham Bell.

33. **(b)** Toxic waste, which consists of chemicals such as heavy metals, hydrocarbons, and poisonous solvents, is usually disposed of by sealing it in metal cans and burying it. Often the drums corrode, leaking toxic waste into the environment. The other waste disposal methods are used on solid wastes.

34. **(d)** Each of these sources of energy has its drawbacks. Coal, gas, and oil are not renewable and contribute to pollution. Plutonium, used in nuclear reactors, is dangerous, and the waste it produces is difficult to dispose of. Water, wind, and solar energy are nonpolluting, but they are often unavailable when they are most needed, and we do not yet possess the necessary technology to use these resources to their full potential.

35. **(a)** A watt is a unit of power equal to the rate of work represented by a current of one ampere under a pressure of one volt. An ampere is the unit of electrical current, and a volt is the unit of electrical potential. An ohm, another important term in electricity, is the unit of electrical resistance.

36. **(c)** A turbine engine uses a continuous stream of gas or liquid to turn a shaft. The other devices mentioned are a steam engine, a flywheel, and a lever.

37. **(b)** A mainframe computer is large and is usually used to operate a network of other computers. It would be most useful in a big business, unlike the smaller minicomputer or microcomputer.

38. **(d)** Hydraulic machinery operates under the aegis of Pascal's law, which states that pressure applied to any part of an enclosed liquid moves without diminishing to all parts of the liquid.

39. **(b)** Anton van Leeuwenhoek (1632–1723) was a Dutch scientist interested in natural history. He made microscopes that magnified organisms more than two hundred times. This allowed him to observe and describe one-celled organisms and bacteria. The thermometer and the telescope were invented by Galileo; the bifocal lens, by Benjamin Franklin.

40. **(a)** A VCR (video cassette recorder) records the electrical signals from television onto magnetic tape. There are tracks on the tape for audio and for video and a device to match the sound and picture so that they can be played back simultaneously.

41. **(c)** There are three kinds of telescope: the refracting telescope, which bends light through a lens so that it converges to a point; the reflecting telescope, which reflects and focuses light

in a mirror; and the catadioptric telescope, which focuses light using both lenses and mirrors.

42. (b) The first operational space shuttle flight took place in 1982, and flights continued until the explosion of the *Challenger* shuttle in 1986. The shuttle, a reusable spacecraft, lifts off like a rocket and lands like an airplane. It is used for scientific investigation and launching and repair of satellites. From 1986 to 1988 the shuttle program was closely evaluated, and in October of 1988 the program was restarted with the launch of the shuttle *Discovery*.

43. (d) A robot is a machine that can sense its environment—through vision, touch, or another sense—and act on it. Usually, robots are controlled by computers, and they are often used today in assembly-line production.

44. (b) A transistor uses semiconductor material to transmit and amplify electrical current. It was invented in 1948 and is used in radio receivers, computers, and other devices.

45. (c) In an internal combustion engine, chemical energy is converted into heat energy and then into mechanical energy by burning a mixture of fuel and air. In an automobile, fuel and air are mixed by the carburetor and drain into the cylinder as the piston strokes downward. As the piston rises, the compressed fuel and air are ignited by a spark: the hot gases drive the piston down, rotating the crankshaft, which drives the car.

46. (d) Some microcomputers use cassettes to store information. This is inexpensive but very slow; finding information on a tape must be done by moving through the whole tape, a process known as serial access. With floppy and hard disks, access is random; hard disks are faster and are usually used with larger computers.

47. (a) Isotope scanning shows where diseased tissue lies because this tissue takes up large amounts of compounds that contain radioactive isotopes. Ultrasound can identify problems in soft tissue by reflecting sound vibrations off the tissue. Ultrasound is also used to heal and to watch the movement of blood. The electrocardiograph picks up voltages from the heart and graphs them, allowing an observer to see whether the heart is contracting normally.

48. (d) A satellite is a body that orbits a planet. Natural satellites are often referred to as moons. Ganymede, for example, is one of Jupiter's moons. Artificial satellites are launched by rockets and can be used for communications, navigation, weather forecasting, military reconnaissance, and scientific investigation.

49. **(b)** Holography uses lasers to record an image on a photographic plate. Two beams are used: One is diffracted by the object being recorded and falls on the plate; the other falls directly onto the plate. The patterns produced are then recorded, and when the plate is illuminated by light of the same frequency, a three-dimensional image is viewed.

50. **(a)** Benjamin Franklin (1706–1790) was an inventor, printer, statesman, and scientist. He published *Poor Richard's Almanack*; set up a fire company, a hospital, and a library; invented bifocals and the Franklin stove; and experimented with electricity. He also signed the Declaration of Independence and helped negotiate the peace treaty of 1783 with England. The other inventions mentioned are by Robert Fulton, Blaise Pascal, and Thomas Edison.

The Queen of the Sciences and the Dismal Science: Mathematics and Economics

The pulse of modern life is economic.

—CH'EN TU-HSIU

1. Which of these could be considered an asset?

  a. income tax

  b. a checking account

  c. interest payments paid to a creditor

  d. a car that is rented or leased

2. Which of these figures is three-dimensional?

  a. a point

  b. a line

  c. a square

  d. a cylinder

3. In the graph on page 258, which country listed has the fewest nuclear reactors?

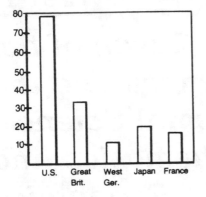

Number of nuclear reactors, 1982

a. the United States

b. West Germany

c. France

d. Great Britain

4. What is the Dow Jones Composite Average?

   a. the average of the closing prices of sixty-five stocks on the New York Stock Exchange

   b. the average of the closing prices of all the stocks on the New York Stock Exchange

   c. the average of the midday prices of all government bonds

   d. the average interest rates offered by banks

5. What is the primary job of the Federal Reserve Board?

   a. to oversee loans to foreign nations

   b. to regulate the federal budget

   c. to regulate money supply and interest rates

   d. to monitor the nation's store of gold

6. What is this number in Arabic numerals: MDCCLXVII?

   a. 1972   c. 1066

   b. 1552   d. 1767

7. In economics, what is a market?

   a. any context in which the sale and purchase of goods and services occurs

   b. a place where edible goods are sold

   c. an economic system that depends on price fluctuations

   d. activities associated with the sales and distribution of products

8. Who was Euclid?

   a. a Greek mathematician who calculated the value of pi

   b. a French philosopher who developed analytic geometry

   c. a Greek mathematician who developed the study of plane geometry

   d. a Greek mathematician who developed a formula for computing the area of a triangle

9. What was Thomas Malthus' conclusion about population growth?

   a. that population can be controlled by genocide

   b. that population will grow faster than food supply, leading to poverty

   c. that population will grow faster among lower classes than among upper classes

   d. that population will eventually decrease in wealthy European countries

10. 3 to the sixth power, or 3^6, equals

   a. 18   **c.** 81

   b. 9   **d.** 729

11. How is the gross national product measured?

   a. by monitoring investment in foreign markets

   b. by counting the money spent to buy, or received for producing, goods and services

    c. by measuring the change in the value of the dollar over time

    d. by measuring the gap between national consumption and national production

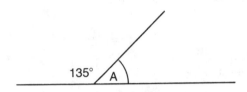

135° A

12. What is the size of ∢A?

    a. 90°   **c.** 45°

    b. 180°   **d.** 10°

13. Under what circumstances might bankruptcy be declared?

    a. if a person does not pay his creditors on a timely basis

    b. if a bank is robbed at gunpoint

    c. if the New York Stock Exchange is closed

    d. if a war or national emergency is declared by federal authorities

14. What is required to make mass production cost-effective?

    a. many factories producing the same item

    b. a large number of units being produced

    c. a city-dwelling workforce

    d. a growing population

15. What does the Pythagorean theorem state?

    a. The area of an equilateral triangle is one-fourth the square of a side multiplied by the square root of 3.

    b. The diagonal of any square is equal to the length of a side multiplied by the square root of 2.

    c. In any triangle the sum of the three angles is equal to 180°.

    d. In a right triangle the square of the hypotenuse is equal to the sum of the squares of the legs.

16. Which of these situations illustrates the laws of supply and demand?

    a. Prices of beef rise, and the demand for beef lessens.

    b. A large quantity of potatoes hits the market; the price of potatoes drops.

    c. As the price of wheat rises, suppliers bring more wheat to the market.

    d. all of the above

17. What is inflation?

    a. high interest rates on government securities

    b. an overall trend toward rising prices, occurring for reasons about which economists disagree

    c. economic stagnation caused by unemployment

    d. an overall trend toward rising wages, caused either by a shortage of workers or by the influence of trade unions

18. Why was the FDIC formed?

    a. to regulate the levels of income taxation

    b. to protect citizens against strikes by government employees

    c. to protect bank depositors from the effects of a depression

    d. to protect consumers against monopolization

19. How many inches are there in a yard?

    a. 12   **c.** 36

    b. 24   **d.** 8

20. Why might a country practice protectionism?

    a. because of high unemployment and large trade deficits

    b. because of efficient labor practices and low income taxes

    c. because of high foreign oil prices and a stable dollar

    d. because of inflation and high interest rates

21. What is the purpose of a mortgage?

    a. to protect the lender against nonpayment by the homeowner

    b. to protect the homeowner against property damage

    c. to pay for home improvements

    d. to enable homeowners to make downpayments

22. Why does a corporation consider an initial public offering?

    a. to avoid a takeover by a larger corporation

    b. to export goods through new joint ventures

    c. to raise capital

    d. to legalize business practices with its board of directors

23. What kind of income tax do Americans pay?

    a. proportional income tax

    b. progressive income tax

    c. regressive income tax

    d. value added income tax

24. When does a federal deficit exist?

    a. when the amount of taxes exceeds the amount of income

    b. when government salaries exceed government expenditures

    c. when government spending exceeds government revenues

    d. when actual income exceeds projected income

25. When is a stock market *bullish*?

    a. when recession threatens

b. when stock prices are fluctuating

c. when stock prices are rising and investment is up

d. when trading is heavy

26. An interest rate can be

   a. a percentage of an amount of money borrowed

   b. a tax on overseas investments

   c. a proportion of income paid to the federal government

   d. payment made after an initial down payment

27. According to Keynesian economics,

   a. government action can raise the level of national income

   b. productive labor includes service jobs as well as manufacturing

   c. population increases faster than resources

   d. the division of labor is necessary to production

28. If your company's profit is $5 billion, that is the same as

   a. five million million dollars

   b. fifty thousand million dollars

   c. five hundred million dollars

   d. five thousand million dollars

29. Which of these is generally *not* considered an economic resource?

   a. land   c. labor

   b. tools   d. money

30. The average height of three people is always

   a. the height of the one who is neither tallest nor shortest

   b. their height in inches divided by 12

   c. the sum of their heights divided by 3

d. the height of the shortest plus the height of the tallest

31. The consumer price index shows

    a. the price of a meal in various parts of the United States

    b. changes in costs of various essential goods and commodities

    c. the average wages of an American worker

    d. the percentage of wages spent on food and clothing

32. If a country's imports exceed its exports, it

    a. takes in more in sales than it loses in production

    b. imposes heavy tariffs on goods entering from overseas

    c. spends more on foreign goods than it makes selling its own goods abroad

    d. buys more foreign goods than other countries do

33. Pi is the ratio of

    a. the total cost to the number of units

    b. a circle's circumference to its diameter

    c. the length of a triangle's hypotenuse to the length of the side opposite the hypotenuse

    d. all of the above

34. Where a monopoly exists, there is no possibility of

    a. profit

    b. productivity

    c. increased demand

    d. competition

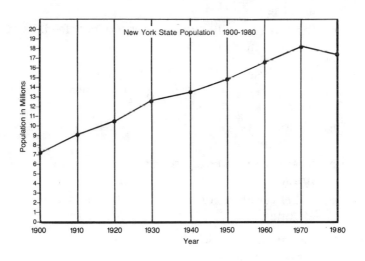

35. This graph shows
   a. a dramatic increase in population over time
   b. a dramatic decrease in population over time
   c. a decrease followed by a tapering off
   d. a steady increase followed by a downswing

36. A depression and a recession are both periods of
   a. high spending
   b. low business activity
   c. high prices
   d. increased production

37. What is the class struggle?
   a. the ratio of earnings between a boss and a worker
   b. a comparison between monarchies and democracies

    c. the historic tension between economic exploiters and the exploited

    d. the contrast in life-styles between middle-class workers and the underclass

38. The term *credit* refers to a promise

    a. to pay in the future for goods or services received now

    b. to add a percentage to every base price on every purchase

    c. to supply collateral on demand to a bank or credit union

    d. to deliver goods or services within a specified period of time

39. The most common kind of tariff is

    a. a form of income tax

    b. a price agreed on by two or more countries

    c. a tax on imports

    d. money paid to cover shipping costs

40. According to Adam Smith, the force of greed is counterbalanced in the economy by

    a. social conscience

    b. competition

    c. church dogma

    d. regressive taxation

41. William Haywood, John L. Lewis, and Samuel Gompers founded

    a. Standard Oil

    b. U.S. Steel

    c. labor federations

    d. the Federal Reserve

42. If a pole is two meters tall, it is

    a. less than two feet tall

    b. about three feet tall

    c. about four feet tall

    d. over six feet tall

43. In a purely capitalist economy,

    a. individuals are free to own property and the means of production

    b. government restrictions are limited

    c. individuals compete to provide goods and services for profit

    d. all of the above

44. Which shape is matched incorrectly to its number of sides?

    a. heptagon—six

    b. decagon—ten

    c. octagon—eight

    d. pentagon—five

45. Among the duties of the Federal Trade Commission is

    a. insuring people's savings in private loan associations

    b. licensing and regulating small businesses

    c. preventing unfair pricing or advertising

    d. administering disability insurance

46. What is a federal subsidy?

    a. assistance to an unprofitable service that benefits the public

    b. a tax added to a product to raise revenue for the state

    c. a business under the control of the federal government

    d. a division of the welfare system designed to aid families

47. If a baseball team's win-loss ratio is 4 to 1, the team
   a. must have played five games in all
   b. won four times as many games as they lost
   c. won three times as many games as they lost
   d. none of the above

48. The cost-of-living index measures the change in
   a. housing costs over a period of ten years
   b. prices of items needed to maintain a given standard of living
   c. cost of nonessential goods and services over time
   d. average wages from one year to the next

49. Which statement about lines is entirely true?
   a. Parallel lines never meet; perpendicular lines intersect once.
   b. Parallel lines never meet; perpendicular lines cross twice.
   c. Parallel lines intersect at a point; perpendicular lines form right angles.
   d. Parallel lines are perpendicular lines that never intersect.

50. Social security programs in the United States include
   a. maximum work hours, minimum wages, and child labor laws
   b. job placement for veterans and farm workers
   c. unemployment compensation, retirement insurance, and Medicare
   d. the Job Corps, VISTA, and neighborhood Youth Corps

TEST 14: Explanatory Answers

  1. (b) Assets are everything owned by an individual, a partnership, a corporation, or an estate and can include a sum of money, a piece of equipment, real estate, a claim on another, or even a patent.

2. **(d)** Two-dimensional figures have length and width. A three-dimensional figure takes up space as well; other examples are a cube, a pyramid, a sphere, and a cone. The study of two-dimensional figures is called plane geometry; the study of three-dimensional figures is solid geometry.

3. **(b)** A bar graph is a chart used to compare quantities. It uses rectangular lengths to represent the size of the quantities compared.

4. **(a)** The Dow Jones Composite Average is the mean of closing prices of thirty industrial stocks, fifteen public utility stocks, and twenty transportation stocks. These means are averaged together at the end of each day on the New York Stock Exchange to produce the Dow Jones Composite Average. The Dow Jones Industrial Average, consisting of the thirty industrial stocks, is more often reported than the Composite Average.

5. **(c)** The Federal Reserve Board, established in 1913, distributes currency to banks and oversees the sales and purchases of government securities. All national banks and certain state banks belong to the Federal Reserve System, which is regulated by the Board; many of these banks are "banker's banks," acting for banks as smaller banks do for individuals.

6. **(d)** In Roman numerals, M = 1000, D = 500, C = 100, L = 50, X = 10, V = 5, and I = 1. Certain numbers are more complicated to write; 9, for example, is written IX, and 19 is XIX.

7. **(a)** A market does not have to have a physical entity; it is any context in which goods or services are bought and sold. For instance, telecommunications networks over which stocks are sold can be considered markets.

8. **(c)** Euclid, who lived about 300 B.C., developed the system of deductive proofs that is the basis of plane geometry. He wrote his theories in a series of thirteen books called the *Elements*. The other mathematicians mentioned are Archimedes, Descartes, and Hero.

9. **(b)** Thomas Malthus (1766–1834) was an English economist whose *Essay on the Principle of Population* stated that population increases in a geometric ratio while the means of subsistence increases arithmetically, leading to poverty. He claimed that disease, war, famine, and moral restraint act as checks on population growth.

10. **(d)** When a number is multiplied by itself, the result is the second power, or square, of the base number. A base number to the sixth power is multiplied by itself, and the result multiplied by the base, and so on three more times. $3^2 = 9$, $3^3 = 27$, $3^4 = 81$, $3^5 = 243$, and $3^6 = 729$.

11. **(b)** The gross national product is the flow of production over a given period of time, usually a year. You can measure the GNP in two ways: by measuring the money spent on the output of goods and services, called the flow-of-product method, or by measuring the money received for producing the goods and services, called the earnings or income method. The GNP aids economists in forecasting the movement of the economy.

12. **(c)** The measurement of angles was developed by the Babylonians, who divided circles into 360 parts and named the parts degrees. Therefore, a straight angle is 180°, a right angle is 90°, and an angle with half the measurement of a right angle would be 45°.

13. **(a)** When a person or business is insolvent, meaning that its liabilities exceed its assets and it cannot pay debts, bankruptcy may be declared. Bankruptcy can free the bankrupt's assets for equal distribution among creditors and often releases the bankrupt from liability.

14. **(b)** The phenomenon of increasing returns to scale is applied to mass production. When all inputs, such as labor and machinery, are increased by a certain amount, the amount of output will be increased still more. However, this phenomenon exists only when input is on a large scale—when organization is elaborate and the labor force is large.

15. **(d)** Pythagoras (c. 582–507 B.C.) was a Greek philosopher and mathematician whose followers considered him a god. They were among the first to postulate that the earth is a sphere; they believed that the essence of all things is numbers and that all concepts could be expressed numerically.

16. **(d)** The laws of supply and demand run the marketplace. Demand can be graphed in a downward slope: its law states that when the price of a good rises, less of it is demanded; or when a large quantity of a good is on the market, its price will fall. The law of supply, when graphed, slopes upward, and states that as the price of a good rises, suppliers will put more of it on the market. Where these two graphs intersect is the price and quantity of that good at which market equilibrium is reached.

17. **(b)** In classical economic theory, inflation is said to be either *demand-pull* (when the nation's aggregate demand for goods and services outruns supply) or *cost-push* (when prices rise due to higher labor costs, producer cartels, or other factors). In addition, the *monetarist* school of economists blames inflation on increases in the nation's supply of money. For recent bouts of inflation, such as the one in the mid-1970s, it is difficult to pinpoint a single cause.

18. **(c)** Before and during the Great Depression of the 1930s, banks failed regularly, losing depositors millions of dollars. In 1933 the FDIC (Federal Deposit Insurance Corporation) was formed to insure bank deposits up to a certain amount in the event of bank failure.

19. **(c)** A yard, equal to 0.9144 meter, is 3 feet, or 36 inches. Inches, feet, yards, and miles are English measurements of length. Much of the rest of the world uses metric measurement.

20. **(a)** Protectionism is the method of protecting national goods and services by placing tariffs or quotas on imports. The desire to lower trade deficits, provide revenues, raise wages, and equalize the costs of national and international production are some reasons given for tariffs, reasons many economists call fallacious. Tariffs can work in the short run to equalize prices and provide jobs, as well as to aid underdeveloped nations and help struggling businesses, but long-term or prohibitive tariffs draw resources away from their best use, diminish trade freedom, and lessen the chance for raising the standard of living.

21. **(a)** A mortgage is a contract between a lending association and a homeowner. Most home buyers must take out a loan to pay for a house. The mortgage is repaid on a monthly schedule that can be spread over as much as thirty years. For a fixed-rate mortgage, payments are level over the life of the mortgage, although in the first several years, these payments consist primarily of interest, not principal payments. If the homeowner does not keep up with the mortgage payments, the lender can foreclose or force a sale of the house to pay off the loan.

22. **(c)** When a corporation needs to raise large amounts of capital, common stock can be issued and sold in part to outside investors. The corporation can borrow short-term funds from a commercial bank or in the commercial paper market and can also issue bonds. Bonds are long-term securities that promise a certain amount in interest until the time they

mature, when the bond's principal is paid off. Most bonds carry credit ratings from national rating agencies. Preferred stock can be sold, too; this is less risky for buyers than common stock but riskier than bonds.

23. **(b)** Proportional income taxes take the same percentage of income from each taxpayer. Progressive income taxes take a larger percentage from those who earn more. Regressive income taxes take a smaller percentage from those who earn more. Although recent tax reforms move our system closer to the proportional, and loopholes tend to move it closer to the regressive, the personal income tax system is still progressive.

24. **(c)** The federal deficit is the difference between the amount the government receives in revenues and the amount it spends. For 1993 the deficit was expected to be about $401 billion, more than double the deficit in 1988, and the interest continues to soar. The trade deficit, another national problem, is calculated by finding the difference between the money value of imports and the money value of exports, when imports are greater.

25. **(c)** A bullish market is one in which stock averages are rising because of heavy investment and positive economic expectations for the future. A bearish market occurs when the market lacks conviction, stock prices are falling, and a recession threatens.

26. **(a)** When one person's money is used by another, the first usually calculates a percentage of the amount of money borrowed and charges the borrower accordingly. The interest rate is that percentage. It can either be fixed for the life of the loan or floating. A prime rate is the floating-rate percentage banks charge their best customers. The prime rate in the United States soared above 20 percent in 1981, but it has not reached that level since.

27. **(a)** John Maynard Keynes (1883–1946) redefined equilibrium in the economy by showing that capitalists would provide jobs in proportion to their anticipated sales, so unemployed workers could not necessarily accept lower wages and thus become employed. In other words, because sales depend on the income of buyers, more sales cannot be anticipated by capitalists who are paying lower wages; therefore, they will not tend to hire additional workers, even at those lower wages. Adjustments,

Keynes felt, were only possible through a long-range plan on the part of a government. Keynes supported public-works programs as means for providing income and stimulating buying. The other ideas mentioned are from theories attributed to John Stuart Mill, Thomas Malthus, and Adam Smith.

28. (d) In the United States 1 billion is represented as 1 followed by nine zeros. This makes it equivalent to $1,000 \times 1,000,000$, or one thousand million. In Great Britain 1 billion is 1 followed by twelve zeros, or a million million.

29. (d) An economic resource is considered to be anything that goes into the production of goods and services. This includes natural resources such as land and minerals; human resources such as labor; buildings; and real capital—machinery and tools that aid in production. Money capital is not considered an economic resource because it is not directly productive.

30. (c) The average of a set of values equals the sum of the values divided by the number of values. The average height of three people whose heights are 67 inches, 69 inches, and 74 inches

$$= \frac{67 + 69 + 74}{3} = \frac{210}{3} = 70 \text{ inches}$$

31. (b) An index is a figure that shows a change in value compared to a base value. The consumer price index figures the change in cost over time of a set of goods and services considered essential for an urban American family. The index shows change due to inflation and is used to determine the cost of living, which in turn is used to determine wages and social security benefits.

32. (c) An export is merchandise sold abroad; an import is merchandise received from abroad. A country whose imports exceed its exports is buying more from other nations than it is selling to them. Such a discrepency over a period of time is called an "unfavorable balance of trade."

33. (b) Pi is a Greek letter used to represent a number equal to about 3.14. The number is the ratio of the circumference, or distance around, any circle to that circle's diameter, or longest possible distance across:

$$\pi = \frac{C}{d}.$$

Pi is an irrational number; that is, it is expressed as an infinite decimal with no repetition of sets of digits. Computers have enabled mathematicians to calculate the value of pi to thousands of decimal places.

34. (d) The aim of the monopoly and the competitive business is the same: to maximize profits. If a business is a monopoly, it controls the supply of a product, thereby controlling the rate of its release. Most large businesses in the world today are not monopolies; government regulations see to that. They are, however, oligopolies; that is, a very few businesses control most of the release of a given product. Although a hundred businesses may create a given product, a mere two or three may control as much as 75 percent of the market.

35. (d) A line graph is often used to show how data change over time. This particular graph shows the population of New York State according to ten-year censuses from 1900 to 1980. The population increased through 1970, whereupon it started to decline.

36. (b) A recession is a mild depression. Both situations involve low prices, high unemployment, and a slowdown in business activity. Both are major parts of the business cycle, a sequence that moves from prosperity to decline to recovery. Recession occurs more commonly today because of government controls and supports that keep many economies afloat despite conditions that would normally lead to depression.

37. (c) Karl Marx (1818–1883) delineated a theory of class struggle that showed the irreconcilable tension between exploiter (who might be feudal baron or a factory owner) and exploited (who might be a serf or a mechanic). Despite the overthrow of the feudal system, workers are still used by employers to produce what Marx referred to as "surplus vaue." That is, a worker does not work merely for the value of his or her own subsistence; the worker produces enough to pay for his or her needs in a fraction of the working day. The rest of the day is spent producing for the benefit of the employer. Surplus value (or profit) can be produced only by the worker, and only an uprising by the workers en masse can alter the imbalance.

38. (a) Credit is a promise of future payment to be made for a present purchase or loan. An individual may charge an item on a credit card, or a nation may borrow from another nation; both involve credit. Some people believe that the business cycle depends on the control of bank credit; that easy credit causes inflation, and tight credit causes deflation.

39. (c) Tariffs may be imposed to protect domestic industry or to raise money for a government. Tariffs may discriminate against a given country; if country A charges country B twice as much as country C for the same goods, it has imposed a discriminatory tariff. They may be retaliatory; if country A objects to country B's tariffs or trade restrictions, it may charge country B a huge tariff on any goods country B ships over.

40. (b) It was clear to Adam Smith (1723–1790) that self-interest motivates society. According to Smith, the greed of individuals was controlled through the market system of competition. No one who demands more money for labor or goods and services than the going rate will succeed. As demand increases, supply will increase to meet it; as demand decreases, supply decreases. Thus, individual greed is thwarted by the public will. Smith's belief that the market would regulate itself as if by an "invisible hand" led to the policy of laissez-faire economics—economic systems without government interference or control. Two hundred years and one Industrial Revolution later, this is still the policy of choice for many conservative economists.

41. (c) The Industrial Workers of the World was an amalgam of forty-three small labor unions joined in 1905 in Chicago under the leadership of Eugene V. Debs, Daniel De Leon, and Big Bill Haywood (1869–1928). The new union advocated direct confrontation as opposed to arbitration. Like many European unions at the time, the IWW considered the union itself the basic social unit and favored the control of the means of production by an organized working class. It reached its peak of power just before World War I. With the outbreak of war, the union leaders were jailed and accused of sedition, and the union was essentially broken. The American Federation of Labor was formed in 1886 with Samuel Gompers (1850–1924) as president. A central conflict emerged between factions who preferred to organize around industrial units (steelworkers, autoworkers, etc.) and those who favored organization by skill (mechanics, painters, etc.). This led to a split in the federation in 1935, with John L. Lewis (1880–1969) leading the industrial faction and forming the Congress of Industrial Organizations. Lewis later pulled his United Mine Workers out of the CIO. In 1955 the CIO merged again with the AFL, forming an international amalgam now known as the AFL-CIO.

42. (d) A meter is the basic unit of length in the metric system. One meter is approximately equal to 3.28 feet. Two meters, therefore, is about 6.56 feet.

43. **(d)** Pure capitalism is an economic system in which private ownership and individual profit are the mainstays. The state plays a very small role in the economic system; it protects the rights of the individual by maintaining order and preventing abuses. Capitalism is also known as free enterprise, since everyone is theoretically free to compete in the market. Many things keep pure capitalism from being realized: Antitrust laws regulate growth, labor laws affect profit, corporate power minimizes the ability of smaller corporations to compete, and the evolution of a world economy that assigns corporations and nations the rights of individuals redefines many of the terms that make up the capitalist credo.

44. **(a)** A heptagon has seven sides. In order from three sides to ten, the names of the shapes are triangle, quadrilateral, pentagon, hexagon, heptagon, octagon, nonagon, decagon. The first two are from the Latin; *triangle* means "three angles," and *quadrilateral* means "four sides." *Gon* is a Greek root meaning "angles."

45. **(c)** The Federal Trade Commission was created in 1914 to prevent illegal price-fixing agreements and other monopolistic behavior on the part of businesses. It also has a mandate to seek out and eliminate unfair or deceptive advertising and to issue cease-and-desist orders to businesses that conspire to restrain interstate trade. The other duties listed belong to the Federal Savings and Loan Insurance Corporation, the Small Business Administration, and the Social Security Administration.

46. **(a)** A subsidy may be paid in money or in property to assist a business that is considered essential to the public welfare. It may also be paid to a manufacturer or producer (such as farmers in the United States) to keep prices from being raised.

47. **(b)** A baseball team with a 4-to-1 win-loss ratio may have played five games, but it may just as easily have played ten. A ratio is a way of comparing two numbers. The team in question won four games for every one that it lost. There is no telling from the information given how many games it played. If it played five games, it won four and lost one. If it played ten games, it won eight and lost two. If it played twenty games, it won sixteen and lost four. Ratios may be expressed in many ways. This one may be written

$$4:1, \text{ 4 to 1, or } \frac{4}{1}.$$

48. **(b)** A standard of living is generally based on per capita income and gross national product. It states the minimum level of consumption of goods and services to which a group aspires or is accustomed, and it may involve such things as educational opportunities and luxury items. The cost of living is the cost of maintaining that standard. In the United States the cost-of-living index has been used to determine wages, pensions, and social security benefits.

49. **(a)** A line has no endpoints; it continues infinitely. Two lines in the same plane that do not intersect are parallel. Two lines that intersect to form right angles are perpendicular.

50. **(c)** Many countries have some form of social security; in 1888 Germany was the first European country to establish a system of health insurance for workers. Some systems provide benefits from a fund paid into by workers; socialist countries require no such direct contribution. In the United States the Social Security Administration administers old-age, survivor's, and disability insurance, Medicare, Medicaid, and Supplemental Security Income for the disabled. Since retired people live on the money contributed by working people, as the population ages, the system faces serious deficits. The other programs mentioned are part of the Fair Labor Standards Act, the U.S. Employment Service, and the Office of Economic Opportunity.

Here and Now: Current Events

> *I have seen the future, and it works.*
> —LINCOLN STEFFENS, *after visiting two-year-old Soviet Russia in 1919*

Well—maybe not. The exciting thing about living in the present is that it's forever nullifying the past. When *Test Your Cultural Literacy* was first published in 1988, who would have thought that only a few years later we'd need to correct all references to "East Germany" or "Leningrad"? Or that an allusion to riots in Los Angeles would suddenly evoke images of Rodney King rather than Watts in 1965? The pace of events in these past few years has convinced us of the shifting, elusive nature of "cultural literacy" and the impossibility of establishing a permanent, immutable canon.

As to this chapter, which we call "Current Events," who knows which of the things we've chosen to list will stand the test of time? Some of these people, places, and events have very recently appeared in the news but strike us as significant; others have been around for awhile but seem now to have settled into our collective consciousness. In another five years, perhaps we'll know which items were no more than coffee-table chat and which were truly important; from this vantage point, we have no more predictive ability than poor Mr. Steffens, starstruck by the revolution and looking toward a future concealed behind a curtain.

1. What is the world's largest living organism, and where is it found?

   a. the blue whale; all oceans

   b. the *Armillaria ostoyae* fungus; Washington State

   c. the sequoia tree; California

   d. the African elephant; Africa

2. Which of these republics have *not* seceded from Yugoslavia?

   a. Slovenia and Croatia

   b. Bosnia and Herzegovina

   c. Macedonia and Croatia

   d. Serbia and Montenegro

3. Why was the economic situation in the United States in the early 1990s termed a recession?

   a. Consumer spending was down, unemployment was up, and growth was slow.

   b. Interest rates and inflation rose sharply.

   c. The stock market plunged dramatically.

   d. Income taxes increased, profits rose slowly, and the deficit soared.

4. Which of these writers is the author of the plays *Fences* and *The Piano Lesson*?

   a. August Wilson

   b. Charles Fuller

   c. Jay McInerney

   d. David Rabe

5. Where did "Operation Just Cause" take place?

   a. Iraq

   b. Panama

   c. Grenada

   d. Los Angeles

6. Why was the writer Salman Rushdie forced into hiding?

   a. He was discovered to be a Nazi war criminal.

   b. He was wanted by the FBI as a spy and a traitor.

   c. He wrote a book that was deemed blasphemic by certain members of a religious group.

   d. He testified in court against mob boss John Gotti.

7. What results are expected from the depletion of ozone in the atmosphere?

   a. an increase in skin cancer and cataracts and a reduction in crop yields

   b. an increase in lung and heart disease

   c. melting of the polar ice caps and flooding of low-lying regions

   d. an increase in acid rain and a depletion of forested areas

8. Which of these judges were appointed to the Supreme Court under President George Bush?

   a. William Rehnquist and Harry Blackmun

   b. Robert Bork and Sandra Day O'Connor

   c. David Souter and Clarence Thomas

   d. Thurgood Marshall and Antonin Scalia

9. What major political change occurred in South Africa in 1991?

   a. Apartheid was outlawed.

   b. Nelson Mandela was released from prison.

   c. Whites passed a referendum to share political power with blacks.

   d. all of the above

10. How does a CD work?

   a. Sound is transferred from a tape to a disc.

b. Audio frequencies are digitally encoded on a disc.

c. Audio frequencies are pressed onto a disc by computer.

d. Sound is recorded live, stored in a computer, and transferred onto a computer disc by laser.

11. If you "drop science" to someone, what are you doing?
    a. giving away money
    b. explaining something
    c. performing a scientific experiment on that person
    d. cheating on a test

12. Which of the following was supposed to happen in 1992 in Europe?
    a. All nuclear weapons were to have been banned.
    b. An open immigration policy was to have been tried.
    c. A single economic community was to be formed.
    d. NATO was to have been disbanded.

13. Which of these novels is by writer Toni Morrison?
    a. *Beloved*
    b. *Jazz*
    c. *The Bluest Eye*
    d. all of the above

14. What were the immediate economic effects of German unification on what had been East Germany?
    a. a rise in employment and an influx of workers from western Germany
    b. a rapid increase in consumer spending and in real estate prices
    c. price reductions and business expansion
    d. price increases, business closings, and unemployment

15. What happened at the Ukrainian (then Soviet) town of Chernobyl in 1986?

   a. A POW camp containing World War II soldiers was discovered.

   b. The remains of the so-called missing link were found.

   c. An asteroid collided with Earth.

   d. A nuclear reactor melted down.

16. What is scheduled to happen to the British crown colony of Hong Kong in 1997?

   a. It will become independent.

   b. It will become an administrative region of China.

   c. It will assume control of the nearby Portuguese territory of Macao.

   d. It will become an overseas province of Taiwan.

17. What were the "thousand points of light" praised by George Bush in his 1988 presidential campaign?

   a. the great works of literature produced by America's writers

   b. the brilliant cultural institutions of America's large cities

   c. the thousands of private charity and community service groups operating across America

   d. the stars that will be explored by future American space probes

18. Why was Canada hesitant to join in the North American Free Trade Agreement?

   a. Canadians feared losing jobs to low-paid Mexican workers.

   b. Canadians were afraid U.S. companies would become too powerful.

   c. Canadians were hoping to join the European Economic Community instead.

   d. all of the above

19. What problem are "twelve-step" programs designed to help?

    a. depression

    b. addiction

    c. phobias

    d. learning disabilities

20. What does the Chaos Theory posit?

    a. The universe was formed randomly.

    b. There is no order in life.

    c. Random behaviors can in fact be analyzed.

    d. Global warming can change the predictability of nature and plunge the world into chaos.

21. What event or events resulted in the scandal called Irangate?

    a. The CIA made secret deals with Iran's Ayatollah Khomeini to obtain the release of U.S. hostages held in Tehran.

    b. U.S. officials sold arms to Iran and funneled the profits to Nicaraguan *contra* guerrillas.

    c. President Ronald Reagan authorized a break-in at Democratic Party National Headquarters.

    d. U.S. forces attempted to rescue hostages in Iran but failed.

22. Which of the following African countries are located in the so-called AIDS belt?

    a. South Africa and Namibia

    b. Zimbabwe and Lesotho

    c. Rwanda, Burundi, and Uganda

    d. Algeria and Tunisia

Questions 23–25 refer to the following map of central and eastern Europe.

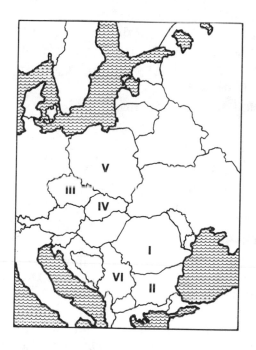

23. What happened in the countries labeled III and IV in 1992?

a. They went to war against each other.

b. They split from a single country to form two countries.

c. They joined into a single country, linking their economies.

d. They both defaulted on loans from the West, in effect declaring bankruptcy.

24. Which country was the first to oust its Communist regime?

a. I   **c.** IV

b. II   **d.** V

25. In which country was the Communist leader executed following a sudden popular uprising?

    a. I   **c.** III

    b. II   **d.** VI

26. A likely application of virtual reality might be in the areas of

    a. medicine and surgery

    b. design and manufacturing

    c. education and entertainment

    d. all of the above

27. Which one of these statements is true?

    a. The United States gave Iraqi leader Saddam Hussein financial and military aid until just weeks before the Gulf War began.

    b. Before its invasion by Iraq, Kuwait was a democracy.

    c. On the eve of the Gulf War, more than 50 percent of Americans polled supported entering into a war with Iraq.

    d. When the January 15, 1990, deadline for Iraq's withdrawal from Kuwait had passed, the Bush administration decided to strike militarily.

28. The opening of the Berlin Wall followed

    a. a West German rally calling for reunification

    b. the sudden death of East German leader Erich Honecker

    c. mass protests and an exodus of East Germans to the West

    d. the breakup of the Soviet Union

29. "Buckyballs" have revolutionized the field of

    a. sports medicine

    b. chemistry

    c. food science

    d. market research

30. How does a fax machine work?

    a. Printed material is scanned and converted into electronic signals, which are reconverted and printed.

    b. It sends out sound impulses, which bounce off a satellite that converts them to light waves.

    c. A computer translates an image into modified Morse Code, and a second computer converts the code to print.

    d. A lens refracts an image, and a laser-light pen copies the refracted image.

31. What causes the "greenhouse effect"?

    a. Clouds of pollution reflect the sun's rays.

    b. A hole in the ozone layer allows infrared light to enter.

    c. Gases keep infrared radiation from escaping into space.

    d. No one yet knows.

32. Raymond Carver is known as a(n)

    a. lyrical poet

    b. minimalist short-story writer

    c. stream-of-consciousness novelist

    d. absurdist playwright

33. Which man was *not* charged with date rape?

    a. William Kennedy Smith

    b. Mike Tyson

    c. Jim Brown

    d. Yusef Salaam

34. What is the goal of the Human Genome Project?

    a. to feed the world by the year 2000

    b. to identify cancer-causing agents in the environment

    c. to determine the DNA sequence of humans

    d. to make all buildings accessible to the handicapped

35. How did a change in venue affect the Rodney King trial?

    a. An all-white jury found King guilty as charged.

    b. The suburban jury supported the white police.

    c. Moving the trial led to riots in Simi Valley.

    d. Only the black defendants were found guilty.

36. The best definition of *perestroika* is

    a. "openness"

    b. "solidarity"

    c. "economic reform"

    d. "reconstruction"

37. Tiananmen Square on June 4, 1989, was reminiscent of

    a. Prague, Czechoslovakia, on August 20, 1968

    b. Paris, France, on July 13, 1789

    c. Dien Bien Phu, Vietnam, on May 5, 1954

    d. Petrograd, Russia, on October 24, 1917

38. As of January 1992, the estimated cost of bailing out failed savings and loan institutions was around

    a. $50 million

    b. $450 million

    c. $50 billion

    d. $450 billion

39. The best descriptor for CD-ROM might be

    a. auditory

    b. multimedia

    c. visual

    d. olfactory

Questions 40–42 refer to the following map of the western portion of the former Soviet Union.

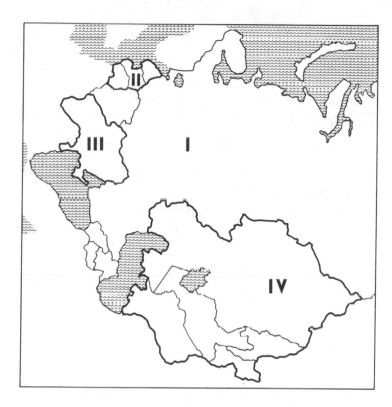

40. What is the name of the area labeled I?

   a. Siberia   **c.** Ukraine

   b. Russia   **d.** Soviet Union

41. The area labeled IV is home to a high concentration of

   a. Kurds   **c.** Muslims

   b. Russians   **d.** Armenians

42. The area known as the Baltic States is labeled

   a. I   **c.** III

   b. II   **d.** IV

43. Which of these was *not* a United States weapon used against Iraq?

   a. the Patriot   **c.** the Scud

   b. the Stealth   **d.** the Tomahawk

44. The primary cause of species extinction today is

   a. destruction of habitat

   b. acid rain

   c. predation

   d. worldwide temperature fluctuations

45. An exhibition of photographs by Robert Mapplethorpe in a Cincinnati museum led to

   a. Mapplethorpe's being refused an NEA grant

   b. a new Supreme Court ruling on what constitutes art

   c. the museum director's arrest

   d. riots in a suburban Ohio town

46. "People Power" was the slogan of a political movement in

   a. Yugoslavia   **c.** Korea

   b. Czechoslovakia   **d.** the Philippines

47. Howard Beach, Crown Heights, and Bensonhurst were sites of famous

   a. sporting events   **c.** hate crimes

   b. concerts   **d.** political rallies

48. MIDI is an important development in the field of

   a. music   **c.** psychology

   b. astronomy   **d.** genetics

49. Around 5,000 sea otters have died since 1989 due to

   a. radiation from undersea nuclear testing

   b. infestations of zebra mussels

    c. new "dolphin safe" fishing nets

    d. petroleum poisoning from the Exxon *Valdez*

50. The term "politically correct" has come to mean

    a. repressive and reactionary

    b. unusually sensitive to racism and sexism

    c. belonging to the party in power

    d. defiantly left-wing

Test 15: Explanatory Answers

1. **(b)** In April 1992 scientists reported the discovery of a giant *Armillaria ostoyae* fungus in Michigan. However, in May another was found, this time in southwestern Washington. The Washington fungus is forty times larger than the Michigan organism and covers 1500 acres. Because it possesses a uniform genetic composition, scientists consider it a single entity. It grows mainly underground and feeds on the roots of trees.

2. **(d)** In 1918 the country of Yugoslavia was formed out of what had been Serbia, Montenegro, and parts of the defunct Austro-Hungarian Empire. After World War II, following expulsion of the German armies by partisans led by General Tito, a Communist regime was established. Yugoslavia was proclaimed a Socialist Federal Republic with six constituent republics: Slovenia, Croatia, Bosnia and Herzegovina, Serbia, Macedonia, and Montenegro. Tito later clashed with Soviet dictator Joseph Stalin, and after 1948 the country pursued an independent course in foreign affairs. Internal stability was maintained until the 1980s, but conflicts then intensified among the country's ethnic groups, and the economy became shaky. In 1991 four republics—Slovenia, Croatia, Bosnia and Herzegovina, and Macedonia—seceded, leaving only Serbia and Montenegro. In parts of Bosnia, members of the Serb minority launched violent attacks on Catholic and Muslim Croats in an effort to create "ethnically pure" Serb enclaves. By mid-1992 hundreds of people—including many civilians—had been killed, thousands more had been driven from their homes, and the city of Sarajevo was under siege by Serb forces.

3. (a) Economists usually define a recession as two quarters of declining growth, but the National Bureau of Economic Research, which officially declares recessions, often disagrees with this definition. The NBER looks at unemployment, housing, consumer spending, and other factors. Slow growth in the early 1990s, linked with rising unemployment, less spending, a drop in profits, and meager business investments led many experts to declare a recession.

4. (a) August Wilson was born in Pittsburgh in 1945. He quit school in the ninth grade but went on to become a poet and well-known playwright. He is the winner of two Pulitzer Prizes, for *Fences* (1987) and *The Piano Lesson* (1990). His plays, including *Two Trains Running* (1992), deal with the African-American experience.

5. (b) Operation Just Cause was the military code name for the 1989 invasion of Panama by U.S. forces. The aim of the operation was to capture General Manuel Noriega, the Panamanian dictator, whom a U.S. court had convicted of drug running and money laundering. However, in the initial attack the general was not captured, 23 U.S. soldiers were killed, and 200 were wounded. About 50 Panamanian soldiers and over 200 civilians died, according to official U.S. reports, but by some accounts the number of civilian deaths was over 3000. The invasion was condemned by the UN General Assembly in December 1989. Noriega took shelter in the Vatican mission, but in January 1990 he surrendered to U.S. forces. He was tried in the United States, and in July 1992 he was sentenced to 40 years in prison.

6. (c) In 1989, Salman Rushdie's fourth novel, *The Satanic Verses*, was published. A fantastical exploration of the Islamic faith, the book was declared blasphemic by the Ayatollah Khomeini of Iran, who put a bounty of $1 million on Rushdie ($2.6 million if the author were killed by an Iranian). Rushdie then went into hiding in England. His marriage fell apart, his freedom was curtailed, and he was forced to move from safe house to safe house. However, his situation did not prevent him from publishing; his novel *Haroun and the Sea of Stories* was published in 1991 to generally positive reviews.

7. (a) Ozone is a gas that absorbs the sun's ultraviolet radiation, protecting Earth from its damaging effects. In 1985 a hole in the ozone layer was discovered above Antarctica; another hole was later found over the northern United States, Canada,

Europe, and Russia. The results expected from this ozone depletion include increases in skin cancers and cataracts, decreases in crop production and in production of oceanic phytoplankton and krill, and possibly a change in humans' immune response to disease.

8. (c) By appointing Anthony Kennedy, Antonin Scalia, and Sandra Day O'Connor to replace the retiring Potter Stewart, Warren Burger, and Lewis Powell, President Ronald Reagan was able to increase conservative representation on the Supreme Court. President George Bush continued this process when William Brennan retired, appointing David Souter to replace him. When Thurgood Marshall retired in 1990, Bush nominated Clarence Thomas, the onetime chairman of the Equal Employment Opportunity Commission. However, during the confirmation hearing charges of sexual harassment were brought against Thomas by a university law professor and former colleague named Anita Hill. Thomas was eventually confirmed; the acrimonious hearings resulted in an increased awareness of the problem of sexual harassment in the workplace.

9. (d) In 1989, F. W. de Klerk was elected president of South Africa on a platform of reform in apartheid laws. In 1991 he announced plans to legalize black political opposition and lift the ban on the African National Congress, the principal black opposition party. Shortly afterward, Nelson Mandela, the leader of the ANC, was released after 28 years in prison, and the Population Registration Act, which required registration of all South Africans on the basis of color, was repealed. A referendum reforming apartheid laws and allowing political power to be shared with blacks was passed by white-only voters. Nevertheless, actual change was slow to come to South Africa, and bloody conflicts arose between black factions, particularly the two largest, the Inkatha Freedom Party and the ANC.

10. (b) In the late 1970s electronics companies began developing the compact disc, on which audio frequencies are digitally encoded and stored for scanning by laser. This technique produced better sound quality than records or tapes, and CDs were found to be harder to bootleg. In 1978, Sony and Phillips jointly decided on a 4.72-inch (12-cm) disc. The new product was introduced in 1983, and in just a few years it was obvious that CDs would soon take the place of LPs and cassettes in the market. While in 1983 over 295 million LPs were shipped, by 1991 only 4.8 million were produced, as compared to 333 million CDs.

11. **(b)** Rap and hip-hop, two musical genres that became popular in the late 1980s and early 1990s, spawned a form of street slang that amounted to a language. Popularized by hip-hop movies such as *House Party* and gritty movies of street life such as *Boyz 'n the Hood*, hip-hop terms (*homeboy, fly, fresh*, and so on) have entered the mainstream of American English. Other terms are less known and may disappear before becoming widely used: *outbox* ("from the beginning"), *poot-butt* (a lazy person), and *wax* (to have sex) are examples.

12. **(c)** In 1992, the European Economic Community planned to erase all limitations on free trade between member states. The Treaty of Maastricht, outlining this plan, proposed a single currency and a frontier-free common market, a common foreign policy, and a common European army. The treaty was 250 pages long and included 282 measures to do away with internal barriers. However, in early 1992, Denmark held a referendum on the treaty and it was defeated. Even though it was subsequently approved in a referendum in France, its ultimate implementation remains uncertain.

13. **(d)** Toni Morrison was born Chloe Anthony Wofford in 1931. Her first novel, *The Bluest Eye*, was published in 1969 to wide acclaim, and later novels, especially *Beloved* (1988), for which she won the Pulitzer Prize, have won her a large following. Morrison's novels, including her 1992 book *Jazz*, often treat the topic of racism and deal with the myths and realities of African-American life.

14. **(d)** When the East German currency was replaced by the deutsche mark, prices in what had been East Germany rose, businesses closed, and East Germans flocked to western Germany in search of jobs. At the same time, interest rates rose and economic growth—even in what had been prosperous West Germany—slowed. By 1992, unemployment in eastern Germany had reached nearly 40 percent. The German government, faced with this economic emergency, was forced to curtail social programs, but even so, a deficit of $280 billion was deemed possible by 1995.

15. **(d)** On April 28, 1986, Scandinavian scientists detected high levels of radiation in the air over much of Scandinavia. Gradually, over the next several weeks, the Soviet Union

revealed that there had been a major accident at the nuclear reactor at Chernobyl, in Ukraine. The cooling system had malfunctioned, causing the uranium fuel to melt. Hydrogen gas was emitted and ignited, causing an explosion; the reactor cone was exposed, and large amounts of radiation were released. Five years later, radiation levels were still considered highly unsafe within a 60-kilometer radius of the site, and there was a dramatic rise in thyroid disease, anemia, cancer, and immunity problems in the local population.

16. **(b)** Hong Kong, a British colony since 1842, has developed into one of Asia's leading commercial and financial centers. In 1984, Britain agreed to transfer sovereignty over the colony to China in 1997 in return for assurances that Hong Kong's social freedoms and capitalist economy would be preserved for at least 50 years. Under this "one country, two systems" arrangement, Hong Kong is to be a special administrative region of China with its own laws, currency, tax system, and free-port status. Whether the Chinese government allows continuing political freedom, or honors its other promises, remains to be seen.

17. **(c)** George Bush used the phrase "a thousand points of light" in his speech accepting the 1988 Republican nomination for the presidency. The speech was written by professional speechwriter Peggy Noonan, and the context in which the phrase appeared was as follows: "This is America: the Knights of Columbus, the Grange, Hadassah, the Disabled American Veterans, the Order of Anepa, the Business and Professional Women of America, the union hall, the Bible study group, LULAC, Holy Name—a brilliant diversity spread like stars, like a thousand points of light in a broad and peaceful sky." Critics charged that Bush's emphasis on private charitable organizations masked his administration's funding cutbacks for government social programs.

18. **(a)** The North American Free Trade Agreement, which in mid-1992 still had not been ratified by Congress, is a treaty among the United States, Canada, and Mexico allowing free trade among the three countries and setting certain standards for foreign imports. For example, automobiles and computers imported into any one of the three countries must be at least 60 percent financed or manufactured by North American interests. The agreement would create an economic bloc with an annual output of $6 trillion, larger than that of the European

Community. U.S. exports could climb by as much as $10 billion. Canada initially hesitated to join in the agreement, mainly because Canadians worried that employers would shift manufacturing jobs away from Canada to Mexico to take advantage of low Mexican wage rates. In 1992, however, Canada agreed to join in the new economic union.

19. **(b)** The first twelve-step program was originally a part of the Alcoholics Anonymous strategy to battle alcohol addiction. However, by 1990 twelve-step programs were adopted by groups battling addictions of all sorts, from Debtors Anonymous to Sex Addicts Anonymous. The program's steps are:

1. Admit powerlessness over your addiction.
2. Believe in a Power greater than yourself to return your self to sanity.
3. Decide to turn your will and life over to God.
4. Make a searching moral inventory.
5. Admit to God, yourself, and another human your wrongs.
6. Become ready to have God remove your defects.
7. Humbly ask God to remove your defects.
8. Make a list of persons you've harmed; be willing to make amends.
9. Make amends.
10. Continue to take personal inventory and admit wrongs.
11. Seek prayer and meditation to improve your contact with God.
12. Having had a spiritual awakening, carry the message to others and practice the principles.

20. **(c)** The idea behind the Chaos Theory, which is still hotly debated by scientists, was first introduced in the nineteenth century by Henri Poincare, who wondered if the solar system was truly stable. He calculated that when a third body is added to the Newtonian orbitary equations of two bodies, orbits can become chaotic—that is, irregular or random. The Chaos Theory helps us understand that complex random behaviors can in fact be analyzed. Specialists have found applications of the theory in astronomy, chemistry (when certain chemicals react chaotically), meteorology (meteorologists feel that atmospheric chaos makes long-term predictions impossible), politics, economics, and physiology.

21. **(b)** In 1979 the leftist Sandinista National Liberation Front took power in Nicaragua. Right-wing leaders soon organized the so-called *contra* guerrillas to fight the Sandinistas, often

from base camps in neighboring countries. The U.S. Congress forbade the administration of President Ronald Reagan from providing the *contras* with U.S. government funding, but administration officials sought to circumvent the ban by raising money from private sources. Oliver North, a Marine colonel, was put in charge of the secret project. Meanwhile, in a seemingly unrelated development, officials of the U.S. National Security Council began selling arms clandestinely (in opposition to stated U.S. policy) to Iran in the hope that Iran would pressure guerrillas in Lebanon to release U.S. hostages. These secret sales produced profits, which North and others began funneling to the *contra* leaders. Late in 1986, news stories about these arrangements began to surface. In November, for the first time, congressional leaders were briefed about the arms sale. In December, President Reagan agreed to appoint an independent counsel to investigate the entire affair. A 23-count indictment was brought against North and other officials. North was eventually convicted, but his conviction was overturned on appeal. Indictments and trials of other officials continued into the early 1990s.

22. (c) Rwanda, Burundi, and Uganda, clustered around Lake Victoria in east Africa, form the heart of the so-called AIDS belt—the African area hit earliest and hardest by the AIDS epidemic. In this region heterosexual contact is the main vehicle for AIDS transmission. Some specialists speculate that populations in this area will actually decline because of the spread of the disease. As of 1992, six million men, women, and children in Africa were infected with the virus; by the end of the decade, more than two million African children are expected to be orphaned by AIDS.

23. (b) Until 1992 the Czech and Slovak republics formed the single state of Czechoslovakia. Their breakup followed the relatively peaceful "Velvet Revolution" of 1989, in which the Czechoslovak Communist regime was ousted in favor of a democratic government headed by the playwright Vaclav Havel. During 1990 and 1991 political and economic tensions grew between the wealthier, more industrialized Czech regions and the poorer, more rural Slovak area. In 1992, Czech and Slovak leaders agreed to split Czechoslovakia into two sovereign states, and Havel resigned the presidency.

24. (c) In Poland in 1980, widespread wildcat strikes forced the Communist regime to concede the right to form independent labor unions, and workers in Gdansk established the democratic trade union Solidarity. In 1981, however, martial law was declared, Solidarity was banned, and many of its leaders were jailed. Nevertheless, the union continued to operate clandestinely and to enjoy widespread support. Meanwhile, the Polish economy deteriorated dramatically, and in April 1989 the government agreed to re-legalize Solidarity, to permit the formation of opposition political parties, and to hold elections. Two months later, when legislative elections were held, Solidarity took control of parliament, and for the first time in decades, a non-Communist prime minister was selected.

25. **(a)** The Communist government of Rumania, led by the dictator Nicolae Ceauşescu, was considered one of the most oppressive regimes in Eastern Europe. However, following the overthrow of Communist governments in neighboring countries in 1989, anti-Communist protests erupted in Rumania as well. In December government forces fired on protesters in the city of Timisoara, killing hundreds. The protests then spread to Bucharest, the capital. When his military leaders abandoned him, Ceauşescu tried to flee, but he and his wife were captured and executed by firing squad.

26. **(d)** Virtual reality is a computer-generated display that imitates reality and allows the user to interact using the senses of sight, hearing, and touch as if with the real world. For example, the user may put on a headset, which projects slightly different images onto two screens, as the images would appear naturally to the user's two eyes. This makes the images seem three-dimensional. Turning the head shifts the images, which reorient to correspond to the angle of the head. A special glove is worn on one hand and acts much like a PC mouse in manipulating the display. Potential uses range from constructing molecules to practicing surgical techniques, from designing safer airplanes to assembling car bodies, from providing travel fantasies for armchair tourists to teaching the principles of physics.

27. **(a)** The United States supported Saddam Hussein in the Iran-Iraq War, and only withdrew financial and advisory support completely when Iraq invaded Kuwait. Supporting Kuwait might have been embarrassing had anyone in the United States paid attention to that nation's anti-democratic policies, which culminated in the arrests of many pro-democracy leaders only weeks before the Iraqi invasion. In fact, fewer than 50 percent of Americans supported the war; most hoped to see a Mideast Peace Conference that would end the hostilities before the United States became involved. Even the Senate was deeply divided over the issue. This changed only when it became clear that the United States would win decisively. After a brief experiment with sanctions, the United States urged the United Nations to support setting a deadline for Iraq's withdrawal from Kuwait. The choice of Martin Luther King's birthday for this deadline incensed many African-Americans, who would prove to be the staunchest supporters of the peace movement. George Bush revealed months after the war, however, that he had decided to strike militarily and had, in fact, approved a timetable for such action much earlier, in October 1990.

28. (c) The division of Germany into East and West was a pivotal symbol of the Cold War. The Wall was built across Berlin in 1961 to prevent East Germans from escaping to the West. In August 1989, Hungary removed its barbed wire border with Austria, and suddenly East Germans, who before could only travel as far as another Communist state, could move to the West through Hungary. A huge exodus began. Then, in October, Soviet leader Mikhail Gorbachev arrived for an anniversary ceremony marking 40 years of the East German state. Tens of thousands of Germans took to the streets of East Germany's main cities, embarrassing party chief Erich Honecker, who was forced to resign. On November 4, East Germany agreed to allow its citizens to leave for the West via Czechoslovakia. In effect, this decision rendered the Wall irrelevant. On November 7, the East German cabinet resigned, and on November 9, the new party chief, Egon Krenz, officially opened the borders, and the Wall came down.

29. (b) "Buckyball" is the pet name for "Buckminsterfullerene," a newly discovered form of pure carbon whose molecular structure resembles Buckminster Fuller's geodesic dome. Buckyballs were discovered serendipitously when researchers aimed an arc welder at some soot. The carbon is stable at extremely high temperatures, and its neat structure allows other molecules to be sealed inside it. Applications in the areas of cancer treatments, agriculture, and energy production are currently being studied. The other two forms of pure carbon are graphite and diamonds.

30. (a) Fax technology has been around since the nineteenth century. By 1910, a photoelectric scanning system developed by a German inventor named Korn allowed the transmission of photographs between Berlin and other European cities, and the first transatlantic transmission took place in 1922. Early uses of the system included the transmission of news photos, weather maps, and telegrams. When direct-dial telephones achieved widespread use in the 1960s, nationwide faxing became possible. Today, fax machines use a digital scanning process to encode information in terms of the density of each dot on the page of text, convert that information into electronic impulses, send the impulses over phone lines, and reconvert the signals at the other end.

31. **(c)** The greenhouse gases include water vapor, CO_2, methane, nitrous oxide, and ozone. Ordinarily, these gases trap and hold a certain amount of infrared—if they did not, our planet would be frigid at all times. Human pollution is causing the gases to build up faster than before, and new gases, such as chlorofluorocarbons, have been added to the mixture. This increase in production has unbalanced the chemistry of the atmosphere, escalating the greenhouse effect and causing many scientists to predict a global warming. Figures from the Natural Resources Defense Council and *Science* magazine indicate that the 1980s were significantly hotter worldwide than any previous decade in recorded history. Predicted effects include the erosion of shorelines and disappearance of islands as global sea levels rise, and the extermination of temperature-sensitive species.

32. **(b)** Raymond Carver (1938–1988) studied at the University of Iowa Writers' Workshop and with novelist John Gardner. He wrote poems but is best known for his short stories, which are available in several collections: *Will You Please Be Quiet, Please* (1976); *What We Talk About When We Talk About Love* (1981); *Cathedral* (1983); and *Where I'm Calling From* (1988), which contains some stories from the other collections. Carver's distinctive, minimalist style and his focus on the lives of blue-collar workers have inspired a generation of imitators.

33. **(d)** Yusef Salaam was accused and convicted of rape in the "Central Park Jogger" case, but since he did not know his victim, this was not a case of date, or acquaintance, rape. Date rape has always been common, but only recently has it been acknowledged as a crime that can be prosecuted. William Kennedy Smith was charged with the crime stemming from an incident in Palm Beach, Florida; he was acquitted. Former football star Jim Brown was accused of date rape in 1985; the

charges were dismissed. In 1992 in Indiana, Mike Tyson, former heavyweight champion, was tried and sentenced to six years in prison for raping a beauty pageant contestant.

34. **(c)** The worldwide project, begun in 1990, will last 15 years and cost billions of dollars. One goal is to map, or locate, the genes on the chromosomes, but the big challenge is to sequence the more than 3 billion nucleotide pairs of DNA that make up the human genome. Here is an example of the value of this project: Human chromosome 7 contains the gene for cystic fibrosis. Having identified and located that gene, scientists may use it to diagnose the disease prenatally, or they may find ways to manipulate the gene to eliminate the disease.

35. **(b)** On March 3, 1991, African-American motorist Rodney King was stopped by Los Angeles police and beaten senseless, allegedly for resisting arrest, an event that was captured on amateur videotape and played endlessly on American television. Four white policemen were subsequently charged in the assault. Because of pretrial publicity he deemed harmful to a fair trial, a judge granted the defense's motion for a change of venue from Los Angeles County to mostly white Ventura County. The jury of ten whites, one Asian, and one Hispanic acquitted on all counts but one, on which they deadlocked. This verdict, surprising in light of the video evidence, led to riots across the country. Nearly 4,000 fires were set in Los Angeles alone, mostly targeting successful businesses (many Korean) in the poorest sections of the city. Dozens of people were killed, and over 7,000 were arrested, the majority of them Hispanic.

36. **(d)** *Perestroika* and *glasnost* ("openness") were the watchwords of the Soviet Union under Mikhail Gorbachev. With the introduction of perestroika in 1985, reforms in the vast Kremlin bureaucracy were begun. A three-day failed coup attempt in August 1991 proved that at least some of the Soviet leadership did not approve of the reconstruction. Russian leader Boris Yeltsin announced that the Communist Party had been the organizing force behind the coup. On August 24, Gorbachev disbanded the party leadership, in effect removing the Communists from power. He also recognized the independence of Estonia and Latvia, paving the way for the dissolution of the Soviet Union.

37. **(a)** Inspired by democratic reforms in Poland, the Philippines, and the Soviet Union, students throughout China began meeting in small groups to discuss reform. The sudden death of Hu Yaobang, former Party chief and onetime heir apparent to Deng Xiaoping, led to large-scale demonstrations by students who respected Hu's tolerance for intellectuals and for change. On April 19, 1989, nearly 10,000 students took over Tiananmen Square in Beijing. The number grew tenfold in two days' time and became embarrassing to the government, which alternated between threats and promises. On May 13, a group of students began a hunger strike. During a visit by Mikhail Gorbachev a few days later, over 1 million citizens of Beijing marched in the streets, calling for Deng's resignation and for democratic reforms. Martial law was declared on May 20, and Deng ousted his protégé, Zhao Ziyang, for his attempts at a peaceful solution. From that point, the finale was assured. On June 4, trucks and tanks filled with People's Liberation Army soldiers stormed the city, randomly shooting citizens and firing into the crowd in Tiananmen Square. As many as 5,000 people were killed, and leaders of the movement were arrested or forced into exile. China's steadily improving relations with the rest of the world were thrown into turmoil by the brutal crackdown. Although it was bloodier, this abrupt ending to a democratic crusade was similar to the sudden end of the Prague Spring, as Warsaw Pact tanks rolled in to quash that budding reform movement. The other dates refer to *successful* revolutions: the formation of the Paris Commune, the battle that marked the end of French rule in Vietnam, and the October Revolution, in which the Bolsheviks seized power.

38. **(d)** This alarming figure appeared in the *Congressional Quarterly Weekly Report* for January 18, 1992. Plagued by bad investments and criminal mishandling of funds, savings and loan corporations began to show losses toward the end of the 1980s but often were allowed to continue in business by a government loath to take action. Federally guaranteed deposit insurance, designed to prevent a recurrence of the losses of the Great Depression, meant that the burden of loss fell on the taxpayer rather than on bank stockholders. One of the most scandalous failures was that of the Lincoln Savings and Loan, owned by Charles Keating, Jr. Federal regulators, attempting to audit Lincoln's books, were stonewalled. In an unprecedented meeting with regulators, five senators—Cranston, DeConcini, Glenn, McCain, and Riegle—tried to plead Lincoln's case. It turned out that Lincoln had repeatedly granted loans using federally insured deposits without even getting credit reports on the borrowers. Its accounting and legal firms had covered up losses for years. In the end, the senators were brought up before Congress, Charles Keating was tried and sentenced to ten years in jail for securities fraud, and his law firm was sued by the government for misleading regulators, eventually settling the case for $41 million.

39. **(b)** CD-ROM technology gives computers audio and video capability, making them multimedia machines with interactive potential. Examples of uses include the new electronic books, which allow a user with a handheld Sony Data Discman to skim a bestseller on-screen while a narrator reads aloud; Ecodisc, which gives users a visual and auditory walk through the woods, allowing them to choose the path and see the landscape from any angle they choose; and language dictionaries that include oral pronunciation. A single 3.14-inch CD-ROM disc can hold 100,000 pages of text, about one-third that many pages of graphics, or six hours of sound.

40. **(b)** Siberia is only one part of the vast republic of Russia, which contains three-fourths of the territory of the former Soviet Union, one-half of its population, and two of its major cities—Moscow and St. Petersburg. President Boris Yeltsin is faced with a crumbling infrastructure and economic stagnation, despite Russia's potential as a cornucopia of natural resources. Ukraine (a) is the area labeled III. It is bounded on the west by Moldava, now contemplating reunification with Rumania, and on the north by Belarus, still a Communist stronghold.

41. **(c)** Clockwise from the north, these republics are Kazakhstan, Kyrgyzstan, Tajikistan, Uzbekistan, and Turkmenistan. Together with Azerbaijan, directly to the west of the Caspian Sea, these nations house over 50 million Muslims. These republics now must decide whether to choose a Western, democratic form of government or to follow an Islamic model such as that in Iran. The republics that abut Azerbaijan are predominantly Christian: Armenia to the west and Georgia to the northwest.

42. **(b)** From west to east, these republics are Lithuania, Latvia, and Estonia. The Baltics were independent between the World Wars but were overrun once more by the Soviet Union in 1940. Lithuania declared its independence again in 1990, but it took over a year for the three states to be recognized by the

rest of the world. Although their pattern of domination and independence is similar, the republics have very different populations and histories. Lithuania was a powerful state in the Middle Ages and united with Poland in 1569 to try to avoid Russian takeover. Latvia was controlled at various times by Poland and Sweden before being taken over by Russia. Estonia was run by the Danes, the Teutonic Knights, and the Swedes before passing to Russia.

43. **(c)** Scud missiles were Iraqi weapons of war. Among America's high-tech weapons were the Patriot missiles, at first thought to be 90 percent accurate, a figure now assessed by the Army at about 40–70 percent; the F-117A Stealth bomber, hailed as being 90 percent accurate, a figure now revised to around 60 percent; and the Tomahawk missile, called 85 percent accurate in the heat of battle, but now estimated to have been on target about 50 percent of the time. Critics of the weapons systems believe even these revised figures are inflated. Tomahawks have an internal computer, which is programmed with maps and topographic information that enable the missile to locate its target. Patriots rely on radar, both internal and on the ground, to sense and destroy incoming missiles. Despite the Army's having been forced to revise its figures downward following revelations of many civilians killed and nonmilitary sites destroyed, these so-called smart bombs of the Gulf War apparently were the most precise missiles ever launched.

44. **(a)** Around 20 years ago, the Earth lost about one species a day, out of the perhaps 100 million species existing (only 1.4 million of which are recognized and classified). Now the figure is closer to one species per hour—nearly 10,000 per year—of *known species.* Biodiversity studies examine the variety of species on the planet with an eye toward conserving that diversity, which is necessary for the functioning of ecosystems on Earth. The major reason for the increase in extinction rates is human expansion into the habitats of other species. Only a little over 3 percent of the Earth's landmass is protected land. Deforestation, flood control dams, inorganic fertilizers— nearly every human product meant to control land and water has an adverse effect on flora and fauna. Scientists disagree about biodiversity policy, but most agree that human population and consumption must be controlled if extinction rates of other species are to be slowed.

45. **(c)** Robert Mapplethorpe (1946–1989) had already died of AIDS-related illness when the exhibition opened at Cincinnati's

Contemporary Arts Center. Cincinnati has some of the most restrictive antipornography laws in the United States, and a very vocal group of protestors immediately took action to see the exhibit closed and the museum and its director Dennis Barrie charged with pandering obscenity and illegal use of minors. The seven photographs singled out for prosecution involved homosexual activity and nude children. Basing their argument on *Miller v. California*'s 1973 definition of obscenity as "lacking serious . . . artistic value," defense lawyers convinced the jury that just because something was not lovely did not mean it was not art. Barrie and his museum were acquitted.

46. **(d)** On September 23, 1973, President Ferdinand Marcos of the Philippines declared martial law and had many opponents arrested, including Senator Benigno Aquino. In 1980, Aquino was allowed to travel to the United States for surgery, where he remained until 1983. On his return to the Philippines, Aquino was murdered on the airport tarmac in front of reporters and well-wishers. For the first time, Philippine opposition leaders were able to rally the people in mass demonstrations, which continued weekly following Aquino's funeral. Following the acquittal of Aquino's assassins, his wife, Corazon Aquino, announced her candidacy for President. The National Citizen's Movement for Free Elections (NAMFREL) showed her winning by a large margin on election day, February 7, 1986, but Marcos's commission declared him the winner. As the Catholic Bishops' Conference and the United States Senate condemned the election results as fraudulent, Corazon Aquino called for mass civil disobedience to force Marcos's resignation. The defection of Marcos's generals and minister of defense, a human blockade that prevented troops from attacking, and the takeover of television and radio services by reformist soldiers led to Marcos's retreat to Hawaii, where he died in 1989. Plagued by Communist insurgencies and a succession of coup attempts, Corazon Aquino served as President until 1992.

47. **(c)** In Howard Beach, Queens, in 1986, three African-American men were attacked by a group of white men. Michael Griffith was chased into traffic and killed. The white teenagers were convicted of manslaughter. In Bensonhurst, Brooklyn, in 1989, Yusuf Hawkins was beaten to death by a crowd, apparently in a case of mistaken identity. Joseph Fama and Keith Mondello were given maximum sentences for that racially motivated murder. In 1991, an auto accident involving a rabbi that killed a seven-year-old African-American boy apparently prompted the murder of a visiting Hasidic Jew, Yankel Rosenbaum, by a group of young African-American men. The accident and murder took place in Crown Heights, Brooklyn, the scene of much racial violence over the past few decades. As reported hate crimes increase, in what some are calling a new age of racism, penalties in most states have become more severe.

48. **(a)** Musical Instrument Digital Interface allows composers and musicians to connect computers to MIDI instruments—synthesizers, keyboards, and rhythm machines—in order to compose, arrange, edit, record, overdub, print out, and play back music. The system has transformed the world of musical composition.

49. **(d)** On March 24, 1989, the oil tanker *Valdez* ran aground in Prince William Sound, Alaska, fracturing its hull and sending over 10 million gallons of crude oil into the sound. The massive clean-up that followed, which cost Exxon more than $2.5 billion, indicated how far our resources for cleaning up environmental catastrophes lag behind our abilities to manufacture those catastrophes. Thousands of birds died, and nesting sites and migration patterns were damaged, perhaps permanently. Sea otters, river otters, killer whales, salmon, puffins, clams, crabs—hundreds of species were affected by the spill. Even now, oil is turning up in shellfish, which are eaten by other animals. The major long-term effect will probably be in the breeding cycles of fish and birds and thus in the cycle of life itself in that part of Alaska. Litigation related to the spill will apparently drag on for years.

50. **(b)** Supposedly, it is "politically correct" to show sensitivity toward issues of "isms"—racism, sexism, ageism, and so on. Its detractors ignorantly call "political correctness" McCarthyism; its more rabid proponents have gone so far as to remove classic nudes from campus walls and classic books from libraries. In their attempts to be inclusive, "PC" advocates exclude anyone who is not "PC." The issue directly affects what we call "cultural literacy." How should we deal with traditionally significant matters that offend our modern sensibilities? How should we recognize the significance of matters previously ignored by the dominant members of our society? Very few rational proposals for change have been offered.

Bibliography

This bibliography lists reference books that can help expand your general knowledge in each of the fifteen categories tested. It is not intended as a complete compendium of available books on the subject but instead offers a basic collection of introductory volumes that are available in most public libraries and bookstores.

TEST 1: AMERICAN HISTORY

Adler, Mortimer, ed. *The Annals of America*. Chicago: Encyclopaedia Britannica, Inc., 1986. A nineteen-volume history of the United States from 1492 to 1986.

Andrews, Charles M. *The Colonial Period of American History*. New Haven: Yale University Press, 1964. A four-volume Pulitzer Prize-winning history of colonial America.

Foner, Philip. *The History of Black Americans*. Westport, CT: Greenwood Press, 1975. A history of the roles of blacks in America from their roots in Africa to the Civil War.

Garraty, John, ed. *Encyclopedia of American Biography*. New York: Harper & Row, 1974. Biographies of famous and not-so-famous Americans.

Handlin, Oscar, ed. *Readings in American History*. New York: Alfred A. Knopf, 1966. Original sources from colonial days through the cold war.

Leitch, Barbara, ed. *A Concise Dictionary of Indian Tribes of North America*. Algonac, MI: Reference Publications, 1979. Descriptions of Indian tribes from the Inuit in the North to the Tonkawa in the South.

Morris, Richard, ed. *Encyclopedia of American History*. New York: Harper & Row, 1982. Alphabetized entries on the history of the United States.

Peirce, Neal R., and Hagstrom, Jerry. *The Book of America*. New York: W. W. Norton, 1983. Descriptions of states' characters and histories.

TEST 2: WORLD HISTORY

Alpher, Joseph, ed. *Encyclopedia of Jewish History.* New York: Facts on File, 1986. Jewish history from biblical times to the present.

The Cambridge Ancient History. Cambridge, England: Cambridge University Press, 1973. A twelve-volume history of the ancient world from prehistory to the Roman Empire.

Cary, M., ed. *The Oxford Classical Dictionary.* London: Oxford University Press, 1968. A dictionary of classical names, places, and terms.

Dunan, Marcel, ed. *The Larousse Encyclopedia of Modern History.* New York: Harper & Row, 1964. A history of the world from 1500 to the twentieth century.

Durant, Will, and Durant, Ariel. *The Story of Civilization.* New York: Simon & Schuster, 1975. A history of the world from Egyptian civilization to the age of Napoleon.

Fossier, Robert, ed. *The Cambridge Illustrated History of the Middle Ages.* Cambridge, England: Cambridge University Press, 1986. A three-volume, lavishly illustrated history of Western Europe and Byzantium from 350 to 1520.

Gron, Bernard. *The Timetables of History.* New York: Simon & Schuster, 1979. Includes time lines that link people and events through history.

Holt, P. M., ed. *The Cambridge History of Islam.* Cambridge, England: Cambridge University Press, 1978. A two-volume history of the Islamic world.

Mowatt, C. L., ed. *The New Cambridge Modern History.* New York: Cambridge University Press, 1964. A fourteen-volume history of the modern world from the Renaissance through World War II.

Tuchman, Barbara. *The March of Folly.* New York: Alfred A. Knopf, 1984. Records the pursuits of governments that have been contrary to their own best interests.

TEST 3: CIVICS

Cook, Chris, and Paxton, John. *European Political Facts.* New York: Facts on File, 1978. A reference work of information on European politics from 1848 to 1973; two volumes.

Corwin, Edward S. *The Constitution and What It Means Today.* Princeton, NJ: Princeton University Press, 1978. An explanation of Constitutional imperatives and cases that challenge and define the Constitution.

De Conde, Alexander, ed. *Encyclopedia of American Foreign Policy.* New York: Charles Scribner's Sons, 1978. Essays exploring themes and doctrines of American foreign policy.

Elliott, Stephen, ed. *A Reference Guide to the United States Supreme Court.* New York: Facts on File. 1986. A concise description of the role of the Supreme Court.

Greene, Jack P., ed. *Encyclopedia of American Political History.* New York: Charles Scribner's Sons, 1984. A three-volume encyclopedia of movements and ideals in American politics.

Ross, Martha. *Rulers and Governments of the World.* London: R. R. Bowker Publishing Co., 1978. A three-volume, country-by-country guide from prehistory to 1975.

Safire, William. *Safire's Political Dictionary.* New York: Random House, 1978. A dictionary of political terms.

Schlesinger, Arthur M., Jr., ed. *History of American Presidential Elections, 1789–1984.* New York: Chelsea House Publications, 1986. Descriptions of and speeches from presidential elections to Reagan's second term.

Stineman, Esther. *American Political Women.* Littleton, CO: Libraries Unlimited, 1980. Biographical sketches of women in politics, including Bella Abzug, Barbara Jordan, and Geraldine Ferraro.

TEST 4: GEOGRAPHY

The International Geographic Encyclopedia and Atlas. Boston: Houghton Mifflin, 1979. Entries on locations from Aachen to Zyradow, plus maps and charts.

Kurian, George. *Encyclopedia of the Third World.* New York: Facts on File, 1987. Maps, facts, and figures on third world countries.

Paxton, John. *The Statesman's Year-Book World Gazetteer.* New York: St. Martins Press, 1986. Details on places of world importance as well as definitions of geographic terms.

Rand McNally *Quick Reference World Atlas.* Chicago: Rand McNally, 1988. Includes city and country maps of the world.

TEST 5: ART AND ARCHITECTURE

Berenson, Bernard. *Italian Painters of the Renaissance.* London: The Phaidon Press, 1967. Illustrated volume of biographical information on painters from Cimabue to Tiepolo.

Brown, Milton. *American Art.* New York: Harry N. Abrams, Inc., 1979. Description and reproductions of American art.

Encyclopedia of World Art. New York: McGraw-Hill, 1965. Sixteen-volume compendium of art of the world.

Gardner, Louise. *Art through the Ages.* New York: Harcourt Brace Jovanovich, 1980. An informative survey of art from prehistory through the present.

Newhall, Beaumont. *The History of Photography.* New York: Museum of Modern Art, 1982. Illustrated volume of the works of photographers.

Roud, Richard, ed. *Cinema: A Critical Dictionary.* New York: The Viking Press, 1980. A two-volume book of articles on the great filmmakers, illustrated with stills from movies.

Trachenberg, Marvin, and Hyman, Isabelle. *Architecture from Prehistory to Post-Modernism.* New York: Harry N. Abrams, 1986. A study of architecture with over 1,000 illustrations.

TEST 6: MUSIC

Abraham, Gerald, ed. *The New Oxford History of Music.* Oxford: Oxford University Press, 1974. A ten-volume history of world music from ancient to modern times.

Ammer, Christine. *The Harper Dictionary of Music.* New York: Harper & Row, 1987. Entries on terms, composers, works, and instruments.

Arnold, Denis, ed. *The New Oxford Companion to Music.* Oxford: Oxford University Press, 1983. A two-volume reference guide of 6,600 articles on composers, works, instruments, history, and terms.

Kinkle, Roger. *The Complete Encyclopedia of Popular Music and Jazz.* New Rochelle, NY: Arlington House, 1974. A four-volume guide to musicals, songs, performers, recordings, and broadcasts from 1900 to the 1970s.

May, Elizabeth, ed. *Musics of Many Cultures.* Berkeley, CA: University of California Press, 1980. Descriptions of music from

China, India, Japan, Bali, Australia, Africa, South America, and other places.

Osborne, Charles. *The Dictionary of the Opera.* New York: Simon & Schuster, 1983. Includes over 2,000 entries on composers, singers, conductors, and librettists.

Schonberg, Harold C. *Lives of the Great Composers.* New York: W. W. Norton, 1981. Biographical details of composers from Monteverdi to Schoenberg.

TEST 7: MYTH AND RELIGION

Achtemeier, Paul J., ed. *Harper's Bible Dictionary.* San Francisco: Harper & Row, 1985. Entries on all important names, places, and subjects in the Bible.

Bulfinch, Thomas. *Bulfinch's Mythology.* New York: Thomas Y. Crowell, 1970. The texts of well-known myths and legends by a nineteenth-century expert.

Burland, Cottie. *Mythology of the Americas.* London: The Hamlyn Publishing Group, 1970. The myths of North American Indians; Eskimos; Mexican, Central American, and South American Indians.

Graves, Robert. *The Greek Myths.* Harmondsworth, England: Penguin Books, 1960. A two-volume collection of myths from the creation through Odysseus' homecoming.

Livingstone, Elizabeth, ed. *Concise Oxford Dictionary of the Christian Church.* Oxford: Oxford University Press, 1977. Emphasis on the Bible and the history of the Christian church.

Werblowsky, R. J. Zwei, ed. *The Encyclopedia of the Jewish Religion.* New York: Adama Books, 1986. A comprehensive volume on all aspects of the Jewish tradition.

TEST 8: QUOTES, PHRASES, AND APHORISMS

Auden, W. H. *The Viking Book of Aphorisms.* New York: Penguin Books, 1985. Pithy quotes and sayings covering many topics.

Bartlett, John. *Bartlett's Familiar Quotations.* Boston: Little, Brown, 1980. The well-known book of world quotations.

Grosse, Lloyd T., ed. *1500 Literary References Everyone Should Know.* New York: Arco Books, 1983. Alphabetical list of quotations and references from Aaron's Rod to Zion.

Mieder, Wolfgang, ed. *The Prentice-Hall Encyclopedia of World Proverbs.* Englewood Cliffs, NJ: Prentice-Hall, 1986. The sources of proverbs from many languages and cultures.

The Oxford Dictionary of Quotations. Oxford: Oxford University Press, 1979. Quotes from around the world and their sources.

TEST 9: AMERICAN LITERATURE

Barksdale, Richard. *Black Writers of America.* New York: Macmillan, 1972. An anthology of black literature from the eighteenth century to the present.

Baym, Nina, ed. *The Norton Anthology of American Literature.* New York: W. W. Norton, 1985. A two-volume collection of works by American writers such as Walt Whitman, Henry Thoreau, Mark Twain, Henry James, William Faulkner, and others.

Bloom, Harold, ed. *American Fiction, 1914–1945.* New York: Chelsea House Publishers, 1987. Essays by scholars on writers from World War I to World War II.

Bordman, Gerald. *The Oxford Companion to American Theatre.* New York: Oxford University Press, 1984. Includes 3,000 entries on productions, playwrights, trends, and movements in American theater.

Elliott, Emory, ed. *The Columbia Literary History of the United States.* New York: Columbia University Press, 1988. A one-volume survey of American literary history by eminent critics.

Ellman, Richard, ed. *The New Oxford Book of American Verse.* New York: Oxford University Press, 1976. A collection of 300 years of American poetry.

Faust, Langdon L. *American Women Writers.* New York: Frederick Ungar, 1983. A two-volume reference work of biographies and criticism of works from colonial times to the present.

Hart, James, ed. *The Concise Oxford Companion to American Literature.* Oxford: Oxford University Press, 1986. A compact volume of 2,000 entries on authors, works, and movements.

Herzberg, Max J., ed. *Readers Encyclopedia of American Literature*. New York: Thomas Y. Crowell, 1962. A comprehensive reference book with information on authors, titles, characters, and literary movements.

TEST 10: WORLD LITERATURE

Abrams, M. H., ed. *The Norton Anthology of English Literature*. New York: W. W. Norton, 1986. Works by Chaucer, John Milton, D. H. Lawrence, William Butler Yeats, Dylan Thomas, and others.

Allison, Alexander W., ed. *The Norton Anthology of Poetry*. New York: W. W. Norton, 1983. An anthology of poetry in the English language, from Chaucer to the present.

Bain, Carl E., ed. *The Norton Introduction to Literature*. New York: W. W. Norton, 1986. Uses literature to discuss plot, character, genre, theme, tone, figurative language, and more.

Benét, William Rose. *The Reader's Encyclopedia*. New York: Harper & Row, 1987. Includes articles on authors, characters, places, works, and movements.

Cudden, J. A. *A Dictionary of Literary Terms*. Garden City, NY: Doubleday, 1977. Definitions of literary terms from *ab ovo* to *zeugma*.

Drabble, Margaret, ed. *The Oxford Companion to English Literature*. Oxford: Oxford University Press, 1985. Information on English-language authors and their works.

Garland, Henry, and Garland, Mary. *The Oxford Companion to German Literature*. Oxford: Oxford University Press, 1986. Discusses German literature by authors such as Goethe, Kleist, and Mann.

Gilbert, Sandra M., ed. *The Norton Anthology of Literature by Women*. New York: W. W. Norton, 1985. Includes works by Mary Wollstonecraft, Jane Austen, the Brontës, Emily Dickinson, Flannery O'Connor, and others.

Harvey, Sir Paul, ed. *The Oxford Companion to Classical Literature*. Oxford: Clarendon Press, 1974. Information on Greek and Roman literature.

Harvey, Paul, and Heseltine, Janet. *The Oxford Companion to French Literature*. Oxford: Oxford University Press, 1959. Information on authors such as Flaubert, Voltaire, and Hugo.

Lang, D. M., and Dudley, D. R., eds. *The Penguin Companion to Classical, Oriental, and African Literature.* New York: McGraw-Hill, 1969. Information on literature from Greece, Rome, Byzantium, Japan, China, Africa, and other places.

Russell, Bertrand. *A History of Western Philosophy.* New York: Simon & Schuster, 1960. An overview of philosophers from Plato through Rousseau and Locke to the moderns.

TEST 11: LIFE SCIENCE

Gamlin, Linda, ed. *The Evolution of Life.* Oxford: Oxford University Press, 1987. Clear text on how life evolved, including photographs and diagrams.

Grzimek, Bernhard. *Grzimek's Encyclopedia of Ethnology.* New York: Van Nostrand Reinhold, 1977. An in-depth explanation of animal behavior.

Holmes, Sandra. *Henderson's Dictionary of Biological Terms.* New York: Van Nostrand Reinhold, 1979. Definitions of terms used in botany, biology, anatomy, physiology, and more.

McFarland, David, ed. *The Oxford Companion to Animal Behavior.* Oxford: Oxford University Press, 1982. An explanation of animal behavior, arranged alphabetically.

Sax, N. Irving, and Lewis, Richard J. *Hawley's Condensed Chemical Dictionary.* New York: Van Nostrand Reinhold, 1987. An up-to-date dictionary of industrial chemicals, terms, processes and reactions.

Whitfield, Philip, ed. *Macmillan Illustrated Animal Encyclopedia.* New York: Macmillan, 1984. An illustrated encyclopedia of thousands of animals and their conservation status, habits, and habitats.

TEST 12: PHYSICAL SCIENCE

Asimov, Isaac. *Asimov's Biographical Encyclopedia of Science and Technology.* Garden City, NY: Doubleday, 1982. 1,510 biographies of scientists from ancient times to the present, arranged chronologically.

Kerrod, Robin. *The Concise Dictionary of Science.* New York: Arco, 1985. Alphabetical definitions of substances, processes, laws, and terms.

Longman Illustrated Dictionary of Astronomy and Astronautics. Beirut: York Press, 1987. Basic principles of astronomy and astronautics are defined.

Menzel, Donald H. *A Field Guide to the Stars and Planets.* Boston: Houghton Mifflin, 1983. Includes maps, charts, and descriptions of the stars and planets.

Parkinson, Claire. *Breakthroughs: A Chronology of Great Achievements in Science and Mathematics.* Boston: G. K. Hall, 1985. A description of discoveries and theories from 1200 to 1930.

Rickard, Terry. *Barnes & Noble Thesaurus of Physics.* New York: Harper & Row, 1984. Discusses concepts of atomic physics, mechanics, and energy.

Rinsberger, Boyce. *How the World Works.* New York: William Morrow, 1986. Alphabetical listings of terms, concepts, and scientists.

Whitten, D. G. A. *The Penguin Dictionary of Geology.* Harmondsworth, England: Penguin Books, 1986. Definitions of geological terms.

TEST 13: TECHNOLOGY

Bisacre, Michael, ed. *Illustrated Encyclopedia of Technology.* New York: Exeter Books, 1984. Includes consumer, building, transport, military, and space technology.

Desmond, Kevin. *A Timetable of Inventions and Discoveries.* New York: M. Evans, 1986. A chronological list of inventions with over 4,000 entries.

Douglas-Young, John. *Illustrated Encyclopedic Dictionary of Electronics.* Englewood Cliffs, NJ: Prentice-Hall, 1987. Illustrated dictionary with charts, tables, and information on how things work.

Godman, Arthur, ed. *Barnes & Noble Thesaurus of Science and Technology.* New York: Harper & Row, 1985. Entries on physical science, technology, and biological science.

Rand McNally Encyclopedia of Transportation. Chicago: Rand McNally, 1976. Covers all aspects of land, sea, and air transport.

The Way Things Work. New York: Simon & Schuster, 1971. A two-volume encyclopedia of technology with over 300 explanations of how things work.

Williams, Trevor T. *The History of Invention*. New York: Facts on File, 1987. History of invention from the beginnings of civilization to the future.

TEST 14: MATHEMATICS AND ECONOMICS

Clough, Shepard B. *European Economic History*. New York: McGraw-Hill, 1975. Economic history from the ancient world to the present.

Currier, Chet. *The Investor's Encyclopedia*. New York: Franklin Watts, 1987. Reviews 66 savings and investment vehicles.

Downes, John, and Goodman, Jordan Elliot. *Barron's Finance and Investment Handbook*. New York: Barrons, 1987. An explanation of terms, annual reports, tax laws, and stock listings.

Gellert, W., ed. *The VNR Concise Encyclopedia of Mathematics*. New York: Van Nostrand Reinhold, 1977. From traditional elementary math to contemporary mathematics, using examples.

Nelson, Charles R. *The Investor's Guide to Economic Indicators*. New York: John Wiley & Sons, 1987. Explanation of leading indicators, consumer price index, GNP, and other terms and their impacts.

Pearce, David W., ed. *The MIT Dictionary of Modern Economics*. Cambridge, MA: The MIT Press, 1986. 2,650 entries on economic theory, practice, concepts, and economists.

Rachlin, Harvey, ed. *The Money Encyclopedia*. New York: Harper & Row, 1984. A description of terms and concepts concerning money.

Rosenberg, Jerry M. *Dictionary of Banking and Finance*. New York: John Wiley & Sons, 1982. 10,000 terms defined.

Silk, Leonard. *Economics in Plain English*. New York: Simon & Schuster, 1986. An easy-to-follow guide to the basic concepts of economics.

West, Beverly. *The Prentice-Hall Encyclopedia of Mathematics*. Englewood Cliffs, NJ: Prentice-Hall, 1982. Information from algebra to zero, with puzzles, formulas, and tables.

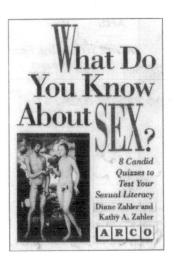

Handy, pocket-size references from
Webster's New World™

Available at fine bookstores everywhere

Webster's New World™
Compact Dictionary
of American English

Webster's New World™
Pocket Dictionary

Webster's New World™
Vest Pocket Dictionary

Webster's New World™
Misspeller's Dictionary

PRENTICE HALL